THE LORD'S PRAYER

OUR Father, who art in heaven; Hallowed be Thy name. Thy kingdom come. Thy will be done; On earth as it is in heaven. Give us this day our daily bread. And forgive us our debts; As we forgive our debtors. And lead us not into temptation; But deliver us from evil; For Thine is the kingdom, and the power, and the glory, for ever. Amen.

THE APOSTLES' CREED

I BELIEVE in God the Father Almighty, Maker of heaven and earth;

And in Jesus Christ His only Son our Lord; Who was conceived by the Holy Ghost; Born of the Virgin Mary; Suffered under Pontius Pilate; Was crucified, dead, and buried; He descended into hell; The third day He rose again from the dead; He ascended into heaven; And sitteth on the right hand of God the Father Almighty; From thence He shall come to judge the quick and the dead.

I believe in the Holy Ghost; The Holy Catholic Church; The Communion of Saints; The Forgiveness of sins; The Resurrection of the body; And the Life everlasting. Amen.

THE BOOK OF
COMMON WORSHIP

Approved by the General Assembly
of the Presbyterian Church
in the United States of America

PHILADELPHIA

PUBLISHED FOR THE
OFFICE OF THE GENERAL ASSEMBLY
BY THE
GENERAL DIVISION OF PUBLICATION OF
THE BOARD OF CHRISTIAN EDUCATION
OF THE UNITED PRESBYTERIAN CHURCH
IN THE UNITED STATES
OF AMERICA

PREFACE

THE General Assembly of 1941 designated *The Book of Common Worship* as an official publication of the Presbyterian Church in the United States of America and lodged its supervision in the Office of the General Assembly. At the same time it authorized the appointment of a Committee to act in collaboration with the Stated Clerk, requesting this Committee to bring to the General Assembly at stated intervals suggested changes deemed advisable. The first Chairman of the Committee was the late William Chalmers Covert. The Committee is composed of the following ministers: Jesse Halsey; Park Hays Miller, Editor; J. V. Moldenhawer; Morgan P. Noyes; Eliot Porter; J. Shackelford Dauerty, Secretary; Hugh Thomson Kerr, Chairman; William B. Pugh, Stated Clerk.

The reports of the Committee to successive assemblies have been approved and the Committee from time to time has been enlarged. The Assembly of 1944 approved the work of the Committee and empowered it, in collaboration with the Stated Clerk, to prepare the book for publication. The Committee began its work with the purpose of making slight revisions in *The Book of Common Worship* and *The Book of Common Worship* (Revised), both editions having been prepared under the competent chairmanship of Dr. Henry van Dyke. As the work progressed many changes seemed desirable and as now published it expresses more adequately the Standards of our Presbyterian Church.

The Committee has been influenced in its work by movements within the Church which have taken place since *The Book of Common Worship* was first issued and later revised. We have been passing through a period when the forms and orders of worship of the Reformed Churches have received sympathetic and critical study on the part of interested scholars. The customs and teachings concerning worship prevailing under the leadership of the Reformers, together with the direction given by the Westminster Divines, have been rediscovered, and are profoundly influencing discussions now going on. Your Committee has carefully followed this movement and those who know intimately the worship and doctrines of the Reformed faith will find that the forms and orders in this book express faithfully the Standards of our Church.

A second movement that has influenced the Committee is the revival of interest in Christian worship. This revival is common to all the Churches. Our Presbyterian Church has always emphasized its liberty and has left its ministers free as to the form and order of worship. This freedom, however, has often resulted in worship as formal and as fixed as a prepared liturgy. The movement within the Church looking to the improvement of worship seeks therefore not only to provide the minister with the treasures in thought and expression that are the inheritance of the Church, but to encourage Christian congregations to more active participation in Christian worship, which was the custom in the Early Church and is the heritage of the Protestant Reformation. The Committee has been aided in its work by the publication of helpful treatises on worship and prayer. Within the Reformed Churches there have been important publications which have supplied the Committee with suggestions, forms of expression, and prayers. Among these publications we mention *The Book of Common Order* of the Church of Scotland, which bears the same name as John Knox's *Book of Common Order*, a book which was in use in Scotland for nearly one hundred years. With the approval of the Church of Scotland the Committee has taken freely from this excellent book, and to the Mother Church, which has given us permission to make such use of it as desired, we express our grateful thanks. We have found in *The Book of Common Prayer*, in the *Service Book and Ordinal* of the Presbyterian Church of South Africa, in *The Book of Common Order* of the United Church of Canada, in the *Book of Worship* of the Evangelical and Reformed Church, and in other publications, much that has helped.

The Committee has thought best to omit from the book The Psalter, together with the Ancient Hymns and Canticles. Since this material appears in *The Hymnal*, it seems unnecessary to reproduce it, thus making the new book of more convenient size.

A complete Lectionary or order of Scripture readings for every Sunday of the year covering two years and for special occasions, taken from *The Book of Common Order* of the Church of Scotland, has been added. The Committee feels that more careful consideration should be given to the reading of Holy Scripture in public worship, and guidance is given in this Lectionary.

There has been provided a form and order for

morning worship and one for evening worship.
Four additional complete services for morning and
for evening worship have been included. These
forms and orders are so prepared that they include
all the elements belonging in a true service of public
worship and give such variety and inclusiveness as
will make the worship services helpful and inspiring to both minister and people. It is the hope
of the Committee, therefore, that this book will
be in the hands of every worshiper.

Three orders are provided for Holy Communion:
The order for the Celebration of the Lord's Supper
found in *The Book of Common Worship* (Revised)
has been retained without change. Another order
is given which conforms closely to that used by
the Reformers, giving a complete and unified Communion Service. An order for the Administration
of Holy Communion to the Sick is also included.
There have been some slight but important changes
in the orders for the Administration of the Sacrament of Baptism to Infants and to Adults. The
Committee has sought in these services to express
the sacramental doctrine of the Church. The
closing part of the service for the Administration
of Baptism to Adults and the closing part of the
service for the Confirmation of Baptismal Vows
are the same, thus making possible when required
a combined, unified service.

The section providing prayers for the Christian
and for the Civil Year, and for personal and family
devotions, has been enlarged. Without departing
from time-honored language and inherited forms
of expression the Committee has endeavored to include the needs of contemporary life. The Committee has sought to retain everything possible that

has approved itself in the former books of Common Worship and, while faithfully adhering to the Standards of our own Church, it has endeavored to recognize our part in the Holy Catholic or Universal Church. It has sought to bring forth from the Christian heritage of the past the treasures that have enriched the worship of the Church in all ages.

The Ordinal containing forms and orders of Church ordinances has been given careful thought and has been in a large measure revised. An order for the Recognition of Candidates for the Holy Ministry has been prepared. The order for Ordination has been dignified and a Charge to the Minister added. In the order 'for Installation a Charge to the Pastor and a Charge to the People are provided. The Committee has sought to add dignity and beauty to each form and order, and if this Ordinal is faithfully used the services of the Church and of the courts of the Church will be enhanced.

The members of the Committee wish to express to the Church their gratitude for the privilege of being associated in the task of preparing this *Book of Common Worship*. It has not been an easy task. It has required laborious research and painstaking exactitude, but it has brought its own reward. It is the prayer of the Committee that this book may truly express the Common Worship of the people of God.

THE COMMITTEE

January, 1946.

ACKNOWLEDGMENTS

MANY prayers and other liturgic materials have long been in use and appear in different publications in various forms, but the Committee has endeavored to secure permission and give proper credit to the owners of copyrights for materials in this book.

We wish to express our indebtedness to the following: The Committee on Public Worship and Aids to Devotion of the Church of Scotland, for material from *The Book of Common Order, One Hundred Scottish Prayers, Ordinal and Service Book, Prayers for Divine Service,* and *Prayers for the Christian Year;* Dr. John Wallace Suter, for material from *The Book of Common Prayer* of the Protestant Episcopal Church, of which he is Custodian, and for material from *The Book of English Collects* (Harper & Brothers) and from *Prayers of the Spirit* (Harper & Brothers); The United Church Publishing House, for material from *The Book of Common Order* of the United Church of Canada; The United Lutheran Publication House, for material from *Common Service Book;* E. P. Dutton & Co., Inc., for material from *A Chain of Prayer Across the Ages,* by Selina Fitzherbert Fox, and *Devotional Services,* by John Hunter; Oxford University Press, for material from *Order of Divine Service, Grey Book,* and *Westminster Prayers;* The Provincial Elders' Conference of the Moravian Church in America, for material from *Liturgy of the Moravian Church;* The Presbyterian Church of South Africa, for material from the *Service Book and Ordinal;* Charles Scribner's Sons, for material from *Prayers for Services,* by Morgan Phelps Noyes; Harper & Brothers, for material from *Prayers for Private Devotions in War-Time,* by Dean Willard L. Sperry; the late William Temple, for a prayer on his installation as Archbishop of Canterbury; Mrs. Rauschenbusch and The Pilgrim Press, for material from *Prayers of the Social Awakening,* by Walter Rauschenbusch; the Prayer Book Copyright Committee of the Central Board of Finance of the Church of England, for extracts adapted and reprinted from the *Prayer Book* as proposed in 1928.

CONTENTS

xiii

CONTENTS

I. PREPARATION
FOR WORSHIP

PREPARATION FOR WORSHIP

THE PEOPLE'S PREPARATION

O ALMIGHTY God, from whom every good prayer cometh, who pourest out on all who desire it the spirit of grace and of supplication: Deliver us, when we draw nigh to Thee, from coldness of heart and wanderings of mind, that with steadfast thoughts and kindled affections we may worship Thee in spirit and in truth; through Jesus Christ our Lord. Amen.

O GOD, who makest Thyself known in the stillness: Make me to know Thy presence in this sacred place; make me to be of the company of brave saints who have worshiped here in spirit and in truth; through the voices of men and the instruments of praise lift my heart to Thee; and so, O Lord, purify my life that, going forth into the world, I may go in Thy strength and in Thy love; through Jesus Christ our Lord. Amen.

ALMIGHTY God, as we pray for the Church Universal, we pray for God's blessing on the Church in this place. Here may the faithful find salvation, and the careless be awakened; may the doubting find faith and the anxious be encouraged; may the tempted find help and the sorrowful comfort; may the weary find rest and the strong be renewed; may the aged find consolation and the young be inspired; through Jesus Christ our Lord. Amen.

THE MINISTER'S PREPARATION

Before Divine Worship

O LORD God Almighty, who didst endue Thine apostles with the gifts of the Holy Spirit, so that they proclaimed Thy Word with power: Grant unto me, who am set to minister and teach in Thy holy name, the same spirit of wisdom and love and power; that the truth Thou givest me to declare may search the conscience, convince the mind, and win the heart of those who hear it, and the glory of Thy kingdom be advanced; through Jesus Christ my Lord. Amen.

Before Holy Communion

ALMIGHTY God, Father of mercies, who hast called us this day to the Communion of Thy blessed Son, our Lord: Make Thy grace sufficient for me, I humbly beseech Thee, that I may acceptably celebrate Thy most high worship, and worthily minister before Thee; and grant such faith unto all Thy people, that in the holy Sacrament they may behold Thy love which passeth knowledge, and be made partakers of Thy heavenly grace; through Jesus Christ our Lord. Amen.

PRAYER WITH THE SESSION

ALMIGHTY God, who hast built Thy Church upon the foundation of the apostles and prophets, Jesus Christ Himself being the head cornerstone: Grant us to be joined together by their doctrine that we may be made a holy temple acceptable unto Thee.

Send, we beseech Thee, Thy Holy Spirit upon us, whom Thou hast ordained to guard the fullness of Thy Church, that we, guided by Thy Word, strengthened and confirmed by Thy sacraments, and serving Thee in purity of life, may devise and do those things which shall be for the good of Thy Church and the glory of Thy name; through Jesus Christ our Lord. *Amen.*

PRAYERS WITH THE CHOIR

1.

O LORD, open Thou our lips:

And our mouth shall show forth Thy praise.

O GOD, who hast given us minds to know Thee, hearts to love Thee, and voices to show forth Thy praise: Give us grace, we beseech Thee, to dedicate ourselves freely to Thy service, that we may reverently fulfill the worship of Thy sanctuary, and beautify the praises of Thy house; through Jesus Christ our Lord. *Amen.*

2.

PRAISE ye the Lord:

The Lord's name be praised.

O LORD our God, who art worthy to be praised and to be had in reverence of all those who are about Thee: Grant unto us, as we lead the worship of Thy house, the gift of Thy Holy Spirit, that being cleansed and sanctified we may serve Thee with gladness and find our joy in singing to Thy glory; through Jesus Christ our Lord. *Amen.*

3.

SERVE the Lord with gladness:
Come before His presence with singing.

O GOD, whose glory the countless hosts of heaven do ceaselessly proclaim: Graciously aid us, we beseech Thee, as we seek worthily to fulfill our ministry and service in Thy house, that in psalms and hymns and spiritual songs we may sing and make melody unto Thee with our whole heart; through Jesus Christ our Lord. *Amen.*

4.

O MAGNIFY the Lord with me:
And let us exalt His name together.

ALMIGHTY God, who dwellest with the humble and contrite, and seekest such to worship Thee: Cleanse us now from all sin and keep us undefiled, that the songs we sing in Thy house may arise unto Thee from hearts that are holy and lips that are pure; and that all our worship, begun in Thee, may in Thee be ended, to the honor and glory of Thy holy name; through Jesus Christ our Lord. *Amen.*

5.

PRAISE ye the Lord. Praise God in the sanctuary:
We will be glad and rejoice in Thee.

HOLY Father, who callest us to serve Thee in the worship of Thy house: Grant us so to praise Thee with our hearts as with our voices that the souls of all assembled with us may be uplifted, purified, and strengthened, and that they and we together may be confirmed in faith and love to Thee; through Jesus Christ our Lord. *Amen.*

II. THE ORDER
OF PUBLIC WORSHIP

FIRST ORDER
OF MORNING WORSHIP

Let the Minister say:

Let us worship God.

Then may be sung a Hymn, setting forth the power, the goodness, and the grace of God, all the People standing, and then the Minister may read the Call to Worship. Or the service may begin with the Call to Worship.

Call to Worship

OUR help is in the name of the Lord, who made heaven and earth.

O come, let us worship and bow down: let us kneel before the Lord our Maker. For He is our God; and we are the people of His pasture, and the sheep of His hand.

Then, the People kneeling or bowing down, the Minister shall say:

Let us pray.

Adoration

O GOD, who art infinite, eternal, and unchangeable, glorious in holiness, full of love and compassion, abundant in grace and truth: All Thy works praise Thee in all places of Thy dominion, and Thy glory is revealed in Jesus Christ Thy Son. Wherefore we praise Thee, Father, Son, and Holy Spirit, one God, blessed for ever.
Amen.

Confession

Then the Minister shall say:

Let us humbly confess our sins unto Almighty God.

To be said by the Minister and People.

MOST holy and merciful Father; We acknowledge and confess before Thee; Our sinful nature prone to evil and slothful in good; And all our shortcomings and offenses. Thou alone knowest how often we have sinned; In wandering from Thy ways; In wasting Thy gifts; In forgetting Thy love. But Thou, O Lord, have mercy upon us; Who are ashamed and sorry for all wherein we have displeased Thee. Teach us to hate our errors; Cleanse us from our secret faults; And forgive our sins; For the sake of Thy dear Son. And O most holy and loving Father; Help us, we beseech Thee; To live in Thy light and walk in Thy ways; According to the commandments of Jesus Christ our Lord. Amen.

Assurance of Pardon

To be said by the Minister.

ALMIGHTY God, who doth freely pardon all who repent and turn to Him, now fulfill in every contrite heart the promise of redeeming grace; remitting all our sins, and cleansing us from an evil conscience; through the perfect sacrifice of Christ Jesus our Lord. *Amen.*

Psalter

Then let a portion of the Psalter be chanted, or read responsively by the Minister and the People, all standing, and at the end may be said or sung:

Glory be to the Father, and to the Son, and to

the Holy Ghost; As it was in the beginning, is now, and ever shall be, world without end. Amen.

First Scripture Lesson

Before each Lesson shall be said:

Hear the Word of God, as it is written in . . . ., the . . . . chapter, at the . . . . verse.

At the end of each Lesson shall be said:

The Lord bless to us the reading of His holy Word, and to His name be glory and praise.

Hymn or Anthem

Second Scripture Lesson

The Creed

The Apostles' or Nicene Creed may be said by the Minister and People together, all standing:

I BELIEVE in God the Father Almighty, Maker of heaven and earth;

And in Jesus Christ His only Son our Lord; Who was conceived by the Holy Ghost; Born of the Virgin Mary; Suffered under Pontius Pilate; Was crucified, dead, and buried; He descended into hell; The third day He rose again from the dead; He ascended into heaven; And sitteth on the right hand of God the Father Almighty; From thence He shall come to judge the quick and the dead.

I believe in the Holy Ghost; The Holy Catholic Church; The Communion of Saints; The Forgiveness of sins; The Resurrection of the body; And the Life everlasting. Amen.

Or

I BELIEVE in one God the Father Almighty, Maker of heaven and earth, and of all things visible and invisible;

And in one Lord Jesus Christ, the only-begotten Son of God, begotten of His Father before all worlds; God of God; Light of Light; Very God of Very God; Begotten, not made; Being of one substance with the Father, by whom all things were made; Who for us men, and for our salvation, came down from heaven; And was incarnate by the Holy Ghost of the Virgin Mary, and was made man; And was crucified also for us under Pontius Pilate. He suffered and was buried; And the third day He rose again according to the Scriptures; And ascended into heaven; And sitteth on the right hand of the Father. And He shall come again with glory to judge both the quick and the dead; Whose kingdom shall have no end.

And I believe in the Holy Ghost; The Lord and Giver of Life; Who proceedeth from the Father and the Son; Who with the Father and the Son together is worshiped and glorified; Who spake by the prophets. And I believe one Holy Catholic and Apostolic Church. I acknowledge one Baptism for the remission of sins. And I look for the Resurrection of the dead; And the Life of the world to come. Amen.

Hymn or Anthem

Here or after the Sermon may be offered these or other prayers of Thanksgiving, Supplication, Intercession, and Communion of Saints, followed by the Lord's Prayer.

Thanksgiving

Then the Minister shall say:

> Let us give thanks unto Almighty God.

The Minister and People shall say:

ALMIGHTY and most merciful Father; From whom cometh every good and perfect gift; We give Thee praise and hearty thanks for all Thy mercies; For Thy goodness that hath created us; Thy bounty that hath sustained us; Thy Fatherly discipline that hath corrected us; Thy patience that hath borne with us; And Thy love that hath redeemed us.

Grant unto us with Thy gifts a heart to love Thee; And enable us to show our thankfulness for all Thy benefits; By giving up ourselves to Thy service; And delighting in all things to do Thy blessed will; Through Jesus Christ our Lord. Amen.

Supplication

Then the Minister shall say:

ALMIGHTY and merciful Father, restore our souls in Jesus Christ, that we may be merciful and kind, even as Thou art. Let Thy forgiveness make us willing to forgive all wrong which we have suffered, and to ask forgiveness for every wrong which we have done. Give us the spirit of Him who dwelt among men in great humility, and was meek and lowly of heart. Let the same mind be in us which was also in Him. Let our love and charity be abundant as our joy, that our hearts may be tender to all need, and our hands give freely for His sake. And grant that, being rooted and grounded in the mystery of the Word made flesh, we may receive power to overcome the world and gain the life eternal; through the same Jesus Christ our Lord. *Amen.*

Intercession

O THOU who hast founded the Church, and hast promised to dwell in it for ever: Enlighten and sanctify it, we beseech Thee, by Thy Word and Spirit; endue all pastors and ministers with Thy grace, that with joy and assurance they may guard and feed Thy sheep, looking to the great Shepherd and Bishop of souls. Bless all who serve Thee in the rule of the Church, in the care of the poor, in the ministry of praise, and in the teaching of Thy people. Strengthen them in their labors; give them courage to witness a good confession; and cause Thy Church to increase more and more, that every knee may bow before Thee, and every tongue confess that Jesus Christ is Lord.

O Lord God of our fathers, who rulest the nations of the earth: Give the spirit of wisdom and godly fear to the President of the United States, the Governor of this state, and to all in authority, that our land may be strengthened in righteousness, enriched with liberty and order, and preserved in unity and peace; through Jesus Christ our Lord.

O God, who hast made of one blood all nations of men for to dwell on the face of the whole earth, and didst send Thy blessed Son to preach peace to them that are far off and to them that are nigh: Grant that all men everywhere may seek after Thee and find Thee. Bring the nations into Thy fold, pour out Thy Spirit upon all flesh, and hasten Thy kingdom; through the same Thy Son Jesus Christ our Lord.

O God of all the families of the earth, we pray that purity, love, and honor may dwell in our homes, and duty and affection be the bond of family life; help us to train our children in the ways of reverence and truth; and keep those absent from us under the shield of Thy care; through Jesus Christ our Lord.

God of all comfort, we commend unto Thee all in any wise afflicted, all persons oppressed with poverty, sickness, or other trouble of body or sorrow of mind, and all such as we name in our hearts . . . . Grant them the consolations of which they have need, and overrule their present sufferings to their eternal good; through Jesus Christ our Lord. *Amen.*

Communion of Saints

O LORD Most High, we give Thee thanks for all Thy saints, martyrs, and confessors; for all the faithful who in every age have witnessed a good confession, and have been the chosen vessels of Thy grace and the lights of the world, in their several generations. Grant us grace so to follow them as they followed Christ; and bring us, with them, to those things that eye hath not seen, nor ear heard, which Thou hast prepared for those who love Thee; through Jesus Christ our Lord, to whom with Thee the Father and the Holy Spirit be all honor and glory, world without end. Amen.

And now, as our Saviour Christ hath taught us, we humbly pray:

Our Father, who art in heaven; Hallowed be

Thy name. Thy kingdom come. Thy will be
done; On earth as it is in heaven. Give us this
day our daily bread. And forgive us our debts;
As we forgive our debtors. And lead us not into
temptation; But deliver us from evil; For Thine
is the kingdom, and the power, and the glory,
for ever. Amen.

*Here, or after the Sermon, the Offering may be received.
The Minister, having made such Announcements as are
needful, shall say:*

Let us make our offering unto Almighty God.

REMEMBER the words of the Lord Jesus,
how He said, It is more blessed to give than
to receive.

Offering

After the Offering there may follow:

Doxology, Response, or this Prayer of Dedication

O LORD, our God, send down upon us Thy
Holy Spirit, we beseech Thee, to cleanse
our hearts, to hallow our gifts, and to perfect
the offering of ourselves to Thee; through Jesus
Christ our Lord. *Amen.*

Additional Prayers of Dedication will be found on page 345.

Hymn or Anthem

Before the Sermon the Minister may say:

LET the words of our mouth, and the meditation of our heart, be acceptable in Thy
sight, O Lord, our Strength and our Redeemer.
Amen.

Sermon

After the Sermon this Ascription may be said:

NOW unto Him that is able to do exceeding abundantly above all that we ask or think, according to the power that worketh in us; unto Him be glory in the Church by Christ Jesus, throughout all ages, world without end. *Amen.*

Hymn

Benediction

THE grace of the Lord Jesus Christ, and the love of God, and the communion of the Holy Spirit, be with you all. *Amen.*

SECOND ORDER
OF MORNING WORSHIP

Let the Minister say:

Let us worship God.

Then may be sung a Hymn, setting forth the power, the goodness, and the grace of God, all the People standing, and then the Minister may read the Call to Worship. Or the service may begin with the Call to Worship.

Call to Worship

OUR help is in the name of the Lord, who made heaven and earth.

Thus saith the high and lofty One who inhabiteth eternity, whose name is holy: I dwell in the high and holy place, with him also that is of a contrite and humble spirit, to revive the spirit of the humble, and to revive the heart of the contrite.

If thou shalt seek the Lord thy God, thou shalt find Him, if thou seek Him with all thy heart, and with all thy soul.

Adoration   *Minister*

ALMIGHTY God, Maker and Preserver of all things visible and invisible: We adore Thee in Thine infinite majesty, and bless Thee for Thy wondrous love revealed in Jesus Christ Thy Son, our Saviour; to whom with Thee, O Father, and the Holy Spirit, be all honor and glory, world without end. *Amen.*

Confession   *Minister and People*

ALMIGHTY and most merciful Father; We
have erred and strayed from Thy ways like
lost sheep. We have followed too much the devices and desires of our own hearts. We have
offended against Thy holy laws. We have left
undone those things which we ought to have done;
And we have done those things which we ought
not to have done; And there is no health in us.
But Thou, O Lord, have mercy upon us, miser-
able offenders. Spare Thou those, O God, who
confess their faults. Restore Thou those who are
penitent; According to Thy promises declared unto
mankind in Christ Jesus our Lord. And grant, O
most merciful Father, for His sake; That we may
hereafter live a godly, righteous, and sober life;
To the glory of Thy holy name. Amen.

Assurance of Pardon   *Minister*

ALMIGHTY God, who doth freely pardon all
who repent and turn to Him, now fulfill in
every contrite heart the promise of redeeming
grace; remitting all our sins, and cleansing us from
an evil conscience; through the perfect sacrifice of
Christ Jesus our Lord. *Amen.*

Psalter

First Scripture Lesson

Hymn or Anthem

Second Scripture Lesson

The Creed

Hymn or Anthem

Thanksgiving   *Minister and People*

ALMIGHTY God, Father of all mercies; We Thine unworthy servants; Do give Thee most humble and hearty thanks; For all Thy goodness and loving-kindness to us and to all men. We bless Thee for our creation, preservation, and all the blessings of this life; But above all for Thine inestimable love in the redemption of the world by our Lord Jesus Christ; For the means of grace, and for the hope of glory. And, we beseech Thee, give us that due sense of all Thy mercies; That our hearts may be unfeignedly thankful; And that we show forth Thy praise, not only with our lips, but in our lives; By giving up ourselves to Thy service; And by walking before Thee in holiness and righteousness all our days; Through Jesus Christ our Lord; To whom, with Thee and the Holy Spirit, be all honor and glory; World without end.   Amen.

Supplication   *Minister*

ALMIGHTY God, who hast given us grace at this time with one accord to make our common supplications unto Thee; and dost promise that when two or three are gathered together in Thy name Thou wilt grant their requests: Fulfill now, O Lord, the desires and petitions of Thy servants, as may be most expedient for them; granting us in this world knowledge of Thy truth, and in the world to come life everlasting.   *Amen.*

Intercession   *Minister*

O ALMIGHTY God, who hast built Thy Church upon the foundation of the apostles and prophets, Jesus Christ Himself being the head cornerstone: Grant, we beseech Thee, that being gathered together in unity by Thy Holy Spirit, Thy Church may manifest Thy power among all peoples to the glory of Thy name; through Jesus Christ our Lord, who liveth and reigneth with Thee and the same Spirit, one God, world without end.

O Lord, our Governor, whose glory is in all the world: We commend this nation to Thy merciful care, that, being guided by Thy providence, we may dwell secure in Thy peace. Grant to the President of the United States, and to all in authority, wisdom and strength to know and to do Thy will. Fill them with the love of truth and righteousness, and make them ever mindful of their calling to serve this people in Thy fear; through Jesus Christ our Lord, who liveth and reigneth with Thee and the Holy Spirit, one God, world without end.

Almighty God, we beseech Thee with Thy gracious favor to behold our universities, colleges, and schools, that knowledge may be increased among us, and all good learning flourish and abound. Bless all who teach and all who learn, and grant that in humility of heart they may ever look unto Thee, who art the Fountain of all wisdom; through Jesus Christ our Lord.

O God, the Creator and Preserver of all mankind: We humbly beseech Thee for all sorts and conditions of men; that Thou wouldst be pleased to make Thy ways known unto them, Thy saving health unto all nations. More especially, we pray for Thy holy Church Universal; that it may be so guided and governed by Thy good Spirit that all who profess and call themselves Christians may be led into the way of truth, and hold the faith in unity of spirit, in the bond of peace, and in righteousness of life. Finally, we commend to Thy Fatherly goodness all those who are any ways afflicted or distressed in mind, body, or estate (especially those whom we remember before Thee); that it may please Thee to comfort and relieve them according to their several necessities, giving them patience under their sufferings, and a happy issue out of all their afflictions. And this we beg for Jesus Christ's sake. *Amen.*

Communion of Saints   *Minister*

O LORD of all worlds, before whom stand the spirits of the living and the dead: We bless Thy holy name for all Thy servants who have finished their course and kept the faith, and who are now at rest with Thee. Grant us grace to follow their good example, that we with them may finally be partakers of Thy heavenly kingdom. Take now the veil from every heart, and unite us in one communion with all the saints on earth and the saints in heaven; through Jesus Christ our Lord, to whom with Thee and the Holy Spirit we ascribe glory in the Church throughout all ages, world without end. *Amen.*

And now, as our Saviour Christ hath taught us, we humbly pray:
Our Father, . . .

Offertory Sentence   *Minister*

ALL things whatsoever ye would that men should do to you, do ye even so to them.

Offering

Doxology, Response, or Dedication of Offering

Hymn or Anthem

Sermon

Ascription   Minister

NOW unto Him that is able to keep you from falling, and to present you faultless before the presence of His glory with exceeding joy; to the only wise God our Saviour, be glory and majesty, dominion and power, both now and ever.   *Amen.*

Hymn

Benediction   Minister

THE peace of God, which passeth all understanding, keep your hearts and minds in the knowledge and love of God, and of His Son Jesus Christ our Lord; and the blessing of God Almighty, the Father, the Son, and the Holy Spirit, be upon you, and remain with you always.   *Amen.*

THIRD ORDER
OF MORNING WORSHIP

Let the Minister say:

Let us worship God.

Then may be sung a Hymn, setting forth the power, the goodness, and the grace of God, all the People standing, and then the Minister may read the Call to Worship. Or the service may begin with the Call to Worship.

Call to Worship

OUR help is in the name of the Lord, who made heaven and earth.

The hour cometh, and now is, when the true worshipers shall worship the Father in spirit and in truth: for the Father seeketh such to worship Him. God is a Spirit: and they that worship Him must worship Him in spirit and in truth.

Adoration   *Minister*

ETERNAL and ever-blessed God, Lord of heaven and earth: We praise Thy glorious majesty. Thy wisdom is seen in all Thy works; Thy grace and truth are revealed in Jesus Christ Thy Son; Thy power and presence are vouchsafed to us through Thy Holy Spirit; wherefore we adore Thy holy name, O blessed Trinity, for ever and ever. *Amen.*

Confession   *Minister and People*

O MOST merciful God, Father of our Lord Jesus Christ; Who pardonest all such as truly repent and turn to Thee; We humbly confess our

sins and implore Thy mercy. We have not loved
Thee with a pure heart fervently; Neither have
we loved our neighbor as ourselves. We have not
done justly, nor loved mercy, nor walked humbly
with Thee, our God.

Have mercy upon us, O Lord, according to Thy
loving-kindness; According to the multitude of
Thy tender mercies, blot out our iniquity. Create
in us a clean heart, O God; And renew a right
spirit within us. Cast us not away from Thy
presence; And take not Thy Holy Spirit from us.
Restore unto us the joy of Thy salvation; And
uphold us with Thy free Spirit. Amen.

Assurance of Pardon   *Minister*

ALMIGHTY God, who doth freely pardon all
who repent and turn to Him, now fulfill in
every contrite heart the promise of redeeming
grace; remitting all our sins, and cleansing us from
an evil conscience; through the perfect sacrifice of
Christ Jesus our Lord. *Amen.*

Psalter

First Scripture Lesson

Hymn or Anthem

Second Scripture Lesson

The Creed

Hymn or Anthem

Thanksgiving   *Minister and People*

MOST merciful Father, from whom come all
the blessings of the light; And who in
darkness still art near; All praise and thanks be

unto Thee for all Thy dealings with us which manifest Thy goodness; And for those also in which Thy love is hidden from our eyes. We thank Thee for Thy holy Word delivered to Thy Church; For the faith which it has conveyed to men from one generation to another; And for the mercies by which it has enlarged and comforted our souls. For these and all Thine other benefits, we give Thee thanks, O Father; Through Jesus Christ our Lord. Amen.

Supplication   *Minister*

ALMIGHTY and everlasting God, in whom we live and move and have our being, who hast made us for Thyself, so that our hearts are restless till they rest in Thee: Grant us purity of heart and strength of purpose, that no selfish passion may hinder us from knowing Thy will, no weakness from doing it; that in Thy light we may see light clearly, and in Thy service find perfect freedom.

O God of Mercy, have mercy upon us.
O God of Wisdom, illumine our minds.
O God of Light, shine into our hearts.
O Thou Eternal Goodness, deliver us from evil.
O God of Power, be Thou our refuge and our strength.

Let Thy blessing rest, O Lord, upon our common life, that our spirit be disciplined and earnest. Grant that our homes be holy, our work honorable, and our pleasures and enjoyments pure. Guard and save us from every selfish use of the liberty in which we stand. Bless our just and lawful undertakings, and grant that in time of prosperity we may not forget Thee, nor in time of adversity think ourselves forgotten of Thee.

Grant us, with all our heart and soul and strength and mind, evermore to love and obey Thee; and finally, in Thy great mercy, present us before the presence of His glory with exceeding joy; through Jesus Christ our Lord. *Amen.*

Intercession   *Minister*

MOST gracious God, who hast promised to reveal Thy glory among all nations: Hear us as we pray for Thy Holy Catholic Church. Bless the ministers of Thy Word and sacraments; unite all Christians in the bonds of a holy faith; and so replenish them with the grace of Thy Holy Spirit that they may bring forth abundantly the fruits of peace and good works. Grant that the Sun of Righteousness may arise and shine upon all lands; that the darkness of ignorance, error, and sin may be dispelled; and that the earth may be filled with Thy glory; through Jesus Christ our Lord.

O God, who didst send the Holy Spirit upon the apostles, to teach them and lead them into all truth, that they might go into all the world and preach the Gospel to every creature: Bless with the mighty aid of the Holy Spirit those who now work to the glory of Thy name in distant lands. Give them faithfulness and courage, and take out of their way all hindrances. Hasten the time, O Lord, for the coming of Thy kingdom, and for the gathering in of all nations unto Thee; through Thine only Son our Saviour Jesus Christ.

Lord God of our fathers, be favorable unto our

land.   Give us peaceful times and fruitful seasons; prosper our industries, and defend us from all enemies.   Grant to the President of the United States, and to all in authority, wisdom and strength to know and to do Thy will.   Fill them with the love of truth and righteousness; and make them ever mindful of their calling to serve this people in Thy fear.   Enrich our land with liberty and order, unity and peace, to the glory of Thy name.   O God, who hast revealed Thy purpose for all mankind in Him who is the King of Righteousness and Prince of Peace: Inspire the hearts of all men to follow after justice, and hasten the time when nation shall not lift sword against nation, neither shall they learn war any more; through Jesus Christ our Lord.

Most merciful Father, we pray for all who are distressed with poverty . . . , sickness . . . , bereavement . . . , or who are afflicted in body or mind, especially for all such known to us, whom we name in our hearts before Thee . . . that it may please Thee to comfort and relieve them according to their several necessities; giving them patience under their sufferings and a happy issue out of all their afflictions.   And this we beg for Jesus Christ's sake.   *Amen.*

Communion of Saints   *Minister*

O LORD God, the Light of the faithful, the Strength of those who labor, and the Repose of the blessed dead: We give Thee thanks for all Thy saints who have witnessed in their lives a good confession, for all the faithful departed, and for those dear to our hearts who have entered into rest. . . . Grant us grace so to follow their good example, that we may be one with them in spirit, and, at the last, together with them, be made partakers of Thine eternal kingdom; through Jesus Christ our Lord, to whom with Thee and the Holy Spirit be all honor and glory, world without end. *Amen.*

And now, as our Saviour Christ hath taught us, we humbly pray:
Our Father, . . .

Offertory Sentence   *Minister*

GIVE unto the Most High according as He hath enriched thee, and, as thou hast gotten, give with a generous hand.

Offering

Doxology, Response, or Dedication of Offering

Hymn or Anthem

Sermon

Ascription   *Minister*

UNTO Him that loved us, and washed us from our sins in His own blood, and hath made us kings and priests unto God and His Father; to Him be glory and dominion for ever and ever. *Amen.*

Hymn

Benediction   *Minister*

THE grace of the Lord Jesus Christ, and the love of God, and the communion of the Holy Spirit, be with you all. *Amen.*

FOURTH ORDER
OF MORNING WORSHIP

Let the Minister say:

Let us worship God.

Then may be sung a Hymn, setting forth the power, the goodness, and the grace of God, all the People standing, and then the Minister may read the Call to Worship. Or the service may begin with the Call to Worship.

Call to Worship

OUR help is in the name of the Lord, who made heaven and earth.

Seek ye the Lord while He may be found, call ye upon Him while He is near; let the wicked forsake his way, and the unrighteous man his thoughts; and let him return unto the Lord, and He will have mercy upon him; and to our God, for He will abundantly pardon.

Adoration   Minister

GLORY be to Thee, O Father everlasting, who didst send Thine only-begotten Son into the world, that we might live through Him. Glory be to Thee, O Lord Jesus Christ, who hast brought life and immortality to light through the Gospel. Glory be to Thee, O Holy Spirit, who dost quicken us together with Christ, and dost shed abroad His love in our hearts. Blessed be Thou, Father, Son, and Holy Spirit, one God; and blessed be Thy glorious name for ever. *Amen.*

Confession   Minister and People

ALMIGHTY God, who art rich in mercy to
all those who call upon Thee; Hear us as
we come to Thee humbly confessing our sins and
transgressions, and imploring Thy mercy and forgiveness. We have broken Thy holy laws by our
deeds and by our words, and by the sinful affections of our hearts. We confess before Thee our
disobedience and ingratitude, our pride and willfullness; And all our failures and shortcomings
toward Thee and toward our fellow men. Have
mercy upon us, most merciful Father; And of Thy
great goodness grant that we may hereafter serve
and please Thee in newness of life; Through the
merit and mediation of Jesus Christ our Lord.
Amen.

Assurance of Pardon   Minister

ALMIGHTY God, who doth freely pardon all
who repent and turn to Him, now fulfill in
every contrite heart the promise of redeeming
grace; remitting all our sins, and cleansing us from
an evil conscience; through the perfect sacrifice of
Christ Jesus our Lord *Amen.*

Psalter

First Scripture Lesson

Hymn or Anthem

Second Scripture Lesson

The Creed

Hymn or Anthem

Thanksgiving   Minister and People

O LORD our God, the Author and Giver of all good things; We thank Thee for all Thy mercies, and for Thy loving care over all Thy creatures. We bless Thee for the gift of life; For Thy protection round about us; For Thy guiding hand upon us; And for all the tokens of Thy love. We thank Thee for friendship and duty; For good hopes and precious memories; For the joys that cheer us; And the trials that teach us to trust in Thee. Most of all we thank Thee for the saving knowledge of Thy Son our Saviour; For the living presence of Thy Spirit, the Comforter; For Thy Church, the Body of Christ; For the ministry of Word and sacrament; For all the means of grace; And for the hope of glory.

In all these things, O Heavenly Father, make us wise unto a right use of Thy benefits; That we may render an acceptable thanksgiving unto Thee all the days of our life; Through Jesus Christ our Lord. Amen.

Supplication   Minister

O THOU who art strong and mighty, we beseech Thee to make us strong in Thee. Give us strength of body, that we may do our work well and cheerfully, and bear the burdens of others. Give us strength of mind, that we may fearlessly accept Thy truth and faithfully hold to it. Give us strength of heart, that we may love Thee with all our powers, and love our neighbor as ourselves. Increase our faith, that we may trust in Thy promises, and may ever keep

fast our hold on Jesus Christ our Saviour. And
give us patience, that we may with our Lord and
Master be made perfect through suffering, knowing that all things work together for good to them
that love Thee. Grant this, we beseech Thee;
through Jesus Christ our Lord. *Amen.*

Intercession   Minister

O GOD, who didst send the Holy Spirit upon
the apostles, to teach them and lead them
into all truth, that they might go into all the
world and preach the Gospel to every creature:
Pour out, we beseech Thee, the same Holy Spirit
upon Thy Church, that it may send forth the good
tidings of great joy unto all people. Revive Thy
work, O Lord; raise up laborers, and strengthen
their hands, that they may tell of salvation unto
the ends of the earth. Bless with the mighty aid
of the Holy Spirit those who now work to the
glory of Thy name in distant lands. Give them
faithfulness and courage, and take out of their way
all hindrances. Hasten the time, O Lord, for the
coming of Thy kingdom, and for the gathering
in of all nations unto Thee. And while we pray
for the outward growth of Thy kingdom in the
world, we pray also for its inward growth in
the hearts of men; and especially for our own
Church and country, that true religion may
abound unto all righteousness and peace; through
Thine only Son our Saviour Jesus Christ.

Almighty God, our Heavenly Father, guide,
we beseech Thee, the nations of the world into
the way of justice and truth, and establish among
them that peace which is the fruit of righteous-

ness, that so they may become the kingdom of
our Lord and His Christ.

Almighty God, who hast given us this good
land for our heritage: We beseech Thee that we
may always prove ourselves a people mindful of
Thy favor and glad to do Thy will. Bless our
land with honorable industry, sound learning, and
pure manners. Save us from violence, discord,
and confusion; from pride and arrogancy; and
from every evil way. Defend our liberties, and
fashion into one happy people the multitudes
brought hither out of many kindreds and tongues.
Endue with the spirit of wisdom those to whom
in Thy name we entrust the authority of government, that there may be justice and peace at home,
and that, through obedience to Thy law, we may
show forth Thy praise among the nations of the
earth; through Jesus Christ our Lord.

Father of mercies and God of all comfort, we
commend unto Thee all those who are in any kind
of trouble or affliction; those who are in danger
by land, sea, or air; all oppressed with sorrow
. . . , need . . . , sickness of body or mind . . . ,
or any other adversity. Hear us for all whom
in silence we remember before Thee . . . ; grant
them Thy peace, and show them Thy salvation;
through Jesus Christ our Lord. *Amen.*

Communion of Saints   Minister

O GOD, before whose face the generations rise
and pass away, the Strength of those who
labor, and the Repose of the blessed dead: We
rejoice in the communion of saints. We remem-

ber all who have faithfully lived; all who have peacefully died; and especially those most dear to us. Lift us into Thy light and love; and give us at last our portion with those who have trusted in Thee and striven in all things to do Thy holy will. And unto Thy name, with the Church on earth and the Church in heaven, we ascribe all honor and glory, world without end. *Amen.*

And now, as our Saviour Christ hath taught us, we humbly pray:
Our Father, . . .

Offertory Sentence   Minister

LET every man give according as he hath purposed in his heart, not grudgingly or of necessity; for God loveth a cheerful giver.

Offering

Doxology, Response, or Dedication of Offering

Hymn or Anthem

Sermon

Ascription   Minister

UNTO the Father, and unto the Son, and unto the Holy Spirit, be ascribed in the Church all honor and glory, might, majesty, dominion, and blessing, now, henceforth, and for ever. *Amen.*

Hymn

Benediction   *Minister*

THE peace of God, which passeth all understanding, keep your hearts and minds in the
knowledge and love of God, and of His Son
Jesus Christ our Lord; and the blessing of God
Almighty, the Father, the Son, and the Holy Spirit,
be upon you, and remain with you always.   *Amen.*

FIFTH ORDER
OF MORNING WORSHIP

Let the Minister say:

Let us worship God.

Then may be sung a Hymn, setting forth the power, the goodness, and the grace of God, all the People standing, and then the Minister may read the Call to Worship. Or the service may begin with the Call to Worship.

Call to Worship

OUR help is in the name of the Lord, who made heaven and earth.

Seeing that we have a great high priest, that is passed into the heavens, Jesus the Son of God, let us therefore come boldly unto the throne of grace, that we may obtain mercy, and find grace to help in time of need.

Adoration *Minister*

WE PRAISE Thee, O God, the Father Almighty. We praise Thee, O God, Thou adorable, true, and only Son. We praise Thee, O God, the Holy Spirit, the Comforter, the Lord and Giver of Life. We praise Thee, O God, Father, Son, and Holy Spirit, one God; and blessed be Thy glorious name for ever and ever.
Amen.

Confession *Minister and People*

ALMIGHTY and most merciful God; We acknowledge and confess that we have sinned against Thee in thought, word, and deed; That we have not loved Thee with all our heart and

soul, with all our mind and strength; And that
we have not loved our neighbor as ourselves.
We beseech Thee, O God, to forgive what we
have been, to help us to amend what we are, and
of Thy mercy to direct what we shall be; So that
we may henceforth walk in the way of Thy
commandments, and do those things which are
pleasing in Thy sight; Through Jesus Christ our
Lord. Amen.

Assurance of Pardon   *Minister*

ALMIGHTY God, who doth freely pardon all
who repent and turn to Him, now fulfill in
every contrite heart the promise of redeeming
grace; remitting all our sins, and cleansing us from
an evil conscience; through the perfect sacrifice of
Christ Jesus our Lord. *Amen.*

Psalter

First Scripture Lesson

Hymn or Anthem

Second Scripture Lesson

The Creed

Hymn or Anthem

Thanksgiving   *Minister and People*

O GOD, by whose hand all living things were
made, and by whose blessing they are nourished and sustained; We give Thee hearty thanks
for all the bounties of Thy providence, wherewith
Thou hast enriched our life. Enjoying Thy gifts

in contentment, may we be enabled by Thy grace
to use them to Thy praise. Especially we thank
Thee for Thy great love; In sending Thy Son to
be the Saviour of the world and in calling us into
fellowship with Him; And we beseech Thee to
grant us always Thy Holy Spirit; Through whom
we may grow continually in thankfulness toward
Thee; And also into the likeness of Thy Son
Jesus Christ our Lord. Amen.

Supplication   *Minister*

O GOD, who hast prepared for those who love
Thee such good things as pass man's understanding: Pour into our hearts such love toward
Thee that we, loving Thee above all things, may
obtain Thy promises, which exceed all that we
can desire; through Jesus Christ our Lord, to
whom, with Thee and the Holy Spirit, be all
honor and glory, world without end. *Amen.*

Intercession   *Minister and People Responsively*

ALMIGHTY God, who hast committed unto
Thy people the ministry of intercession:
Hear us as we pray for others, and grant that
our hearts may be filled with all peace and charity;
through Jesus Christ our Lord.

For Thy holy Church throughout all the world,
that Thou wouldst bestow upon the ministers of
Thy Word and sacraments the abundance of Thy
grace and truth, and confirm Thy people in the
faith of the Gospel, that Christ may be exalted
over all:

We beseech Thee to hear us, good Lord.

For Thy people here and everywhere, that
Thou wouldst inspire them with love for Thy
house, zeal for Thy service, and joy in the advancement of Thy kingdom:

We beseech Thee to hear us, good Lord.

For the fulfillment of Thy promise to pour out
Thy Spirit upon all flesh, that all who are in the
bondage of sin and error may be brought to the
liberty and joy of the Gospel:

We beseech Thee to hear us, good Lord.

For all the nations, that Thou wouldst grant
them the spirit of peace and understanding; and
for those who take counsel for the peoples of the
earth, that Thou wouldst inspire them with a true
desire for justice and a love of concord:

We beseech Thee to hear us, good Lord.

For the President of the United States, and for
all others in authority, that it may please Thee so
to rule their hearts that they may rightly use the
trust committed to them for the good of all people:

We beseech Thee to hear us, good Lord.

For all schools, colleges, and universities, that
through them knowledge may be increased among
us, and good learning flourish and abound; and
for all who teach in them and all who learn, that
in humility of heart they may ever look unto
Thee, the Fountain of all wisdom:

We beseech Thee to hear us, good Lord.

For all those who at home or abroad, by land,
by sea, or in the air, are serving their country,

that they, being armed with Thy defense, may be preserved evermore in all perils; and being filled with wisdom and girded with strength, may do their duty to Thy honor and glory:

We beseech Thee to hear us, good Lord.

For all who are in trouble . . . , sorrow . . . , need . . . , sickness . . . , or any other adversity . . . , that Thou in Thy mercy wouldst comfort and sustain them:

We beseech Thee to hear us, good Lord.

Communion of Saints   Minister

WE GIVE Thee thanks, O God, for all who have fought the good fight and finished their course and kept the faith, and for those dear to us who are at rest with Thee. . . . And we beseech Thee that we may follow them as they have followed Christ, that we, redeemed and cleansed, may stand with them before Thy throne; through Jesus Christ our Lord, to whom, with Thee and the Holy Spirit, we ascribe all honor and glory, world without end. *Amen.*

And now, as our Saviour Christ hath taught us, we humbly pray:
Our Father, . . .

Offertory Sentence   Minister

TO DO good and to communicate forget not: for with such sacrifices God is well pleased.

Offering

Doxology, Response, or Dedication of Offering

Hymn or Anthem

Sermon

Ascription   *Minister*

UNTO the Father, and unto the Son, and unto the Holy Spirit, be ascribed in the Church all honor and glory, might, majesty, dominion, and blessing, now, henceforth, and for ever. *Amen.*

Hymn

Benediction   *Minister*

THE grace of the Lord Jesus Christ, and the love of God, and the communion of the Holy Spirit, be with you all. *Amen.*

SPECIAL ORDER
OF WORSHIP

*This Order may be used for Morning or Evening Worship,
or by a Company of Christians gathered on land or sea
where there are no regular Church Ordinances. The
service may be led by a Minister or a Layman.*

*The service may begin with a Hymn or with the reading
of one or more of the following Sentences.*

Sentences

Morning

OUR help is in the name of the Lord, who
made heaven and earth.

The Lord is nigh unto all them that call upon
Him, to all that call upon Him in truth. He
will fulfill the desire of them that fear Him; He
also will hear their cry, and will save them.

Where two or three are gathered together in
My name, saith the Lord Jesus, there am I in
the midst of them.

This is the confidence that we have in Him,
that, if we ask anything according to His will, He
heareth us.

Having these promises, let us draw near to the
throne of grace with true hearts, in full assurance
of faith.

My voice shalt Thou hear in the morning, O
Lord; in the morning will I direct my prayer
unto Thee, and will look up.

Evening

He that dwelleth in the secret place of the
Most High shall abide under the shadow of the
Almighty.

Lord, I cry unto Thee: make haste unto me; give ear unto my voice, when I cry unto Thee.

Let my prayer be set forth before Thee as incense; and the lifting up of my hands as the evening sacrifice.

I will say of the Lord, He is my Refuge, and my Fortress: my God; in Him will I trust.

Return unto thy rest, O my soul; for the Lord hath dealt bountifully with thee.

Abide with us: for it is toward evening, and the day is far spent.

Then shall be said:

Let us pray.

Let all the Company bow down, following the Prayer in their hearts, and, if they so desire, joining audibly in the Confession of Sins and the Lord's Prayer.

Invocation

ALMIGHTY God, unto whom all hearts are open, all desires known, and from whom no secrets are hid: Cleanse the thoughts of our hearts by the inspiration of Thy Holy Spirit, that we may perfectly love Thee, and worthily magnify Thy holy name; through Christ our Lord. *Amen.*

Confession

MOST holy and merciful Father; We acknowledge and confess before Thee; Our sinful nature prone to evil and slothful in good; And all our shortcomings and offenses. Thou alone knowest how often we have sinned; In wandering from Thy ways; In wasting Thy gifts; In forgetting Thy love. But Thou, O Lord, have mercy upon us; Who are ashamed and sorry for all wherein

we have displeased Thee. Teach us to hate our
errors; Cleanse us from our secret faults; And
forgive our sins; For the sake of Thy dear Son.
And O most holy and loving Father; Help us, we
beseech Thee; To live in Thy light and walk in
Thy ways; According to the commandments of
Jesus Christ our Lord. Amen.

Our Father, who art in heaven; Hallowed be
Thy name. Thy kingdom come. Thy will be
done; On earth as it is in heaven. Give us this
day our daily bread. And forgive us our debts;
As we forgive our debtors. And lead us not into
temptation; But deliver us from evil; For Thine
is the kingdom, and the power, and the glory.
for ever. Amen.

Psalter

*A Psalm or Responsive Selection may then be read, closing
with this Ascription:*

Glory be to the Father, and to the Son, and to
the Holy Ghost; As it was in the beginning, is now,
and ever shall be, world without end. Amen.

Let all the Company, standing, repeat together

The Apostles' Creed

I BELIEVE in God the Father Almighty, Maker
of heaven and earth;

And in Jesus Christ His only Son our Lord; Who
was conceived by the Holy Ghost; Born of the
Virgin Mary; Suffered under Pontius Pilate; Was
crucified, dead, and buried; He descended into
hell; The third day He rose again from the dead;
He ascended into heaven; And sitteth on the right
hand of God the Father Almighty; From thence

He shall come to judge the quick and the dead.

I believe in the Holy Ghost; The Holy Catholic Church; The Communion of Saints; The Forgiveness of sins; The Resurrection of the body; And the Life everlasting. Amen.

The Reading of the Holy Scriptures

An appropriate Lesson or Lessons from Holy Scripture shall be read. Before reading, these words may be said:

Hear the Word of God, as it is written in . . . . , the . . . . chapter, at the . . . . verse.

And after the reading may be said,

The Lord bless to us the reading of His holy Word, and to His name be glory and praise.

Then may be sung a Hymn, followed by a Sermon, an Address, or the reading of an appropriate selection of Devotional Literature, and afterward a Hymn may be sung. Then Prayers shall be offered, the Leader using, if desired, any of the following Prayers. All present kneeling or bowing down, the Minister or Layman shall say:

Let us pray.

Thanksgiving

O GOD, by whose hand all living things were made, and by whose blessing they are nourished and sustained: We give Thee hearty thanks for all the bounties of Thy providence, wherewith Thou hast enriched our life; and we humbly pray that, enjoying Thy gifts in contentment, we may be enabled by Thy grace to use them to Thy praise. Especially we thank Thee for Thy great love in sending Thy Son to be the Saviour of the world and in calling us out of our sins into fellowship with Him; and we beseech Thee to grant us always Thy Holy Spirit, through whom we may grow continually in thankfulness toward Thee, as also into the likeness of Thy Son Jesus Christ our Lord. *Amen.*

Supplication

O God, most holy, wise, and powerful Preserver and Governor of all Thy creatures and all their actions: Keep us this day in health of body and soundness of mind, in purity of heart and cheerfulness of spirit, in contentment with our lot and charity with our neighbor; and further all our lawful undertakings with Thy blessing. In our labor strengthen us; in our pleasure purify us; in our difficulties direct us; in our perils defend us; in our troubles comfort us: and supply all our needs, according to the riches of Thy grace in Christ Jesus our Lord. *Amen.*

A Travelers' Prayer

Lord God omnipotent, who reignest in the heavens and on the earth: We implore Thy guidance and protection for all our journeyings. Against all perils be Thou our strong Defense, and in far regions be Thou our faithful Friend; keep us in health and heart; prosper the ends of our adventure, and make the way of our going and of our returning both safe and happy; and so direct the steps of all Thy pilgrims through this world that we shall finally arrive in the better country, even the heavenly, with Jesus Christ our Lord. *Amen.*

A Prayer at Sea

O eternal Lord God, who alone spreadest out the heavens, and rulest the raging sea: We commend ourselves to Thine almighty protection on the great deep. Guard us, we beseech Thee, from the dangers of the sea, from sickness, from the violence of enemies, from every evil; and conduct us in safety to our desired haven, with a grateful sense of Thy mercies; through Jesus Christ our Lord. *Amen.*

A General Intercession

O God, the Creator and Preserver of all mankind: We humbly beseech Thee for all sorts and conditions of men; that Thou wouldst be pleased to make Thy ways known unto them, Thy saving health unto all nations. More especially we pray for Thy holy Church Universal; that it may be so guided and governed by Thy good Spirit that all who profess and call themselves Christians may be led into the way of truth, and hold the faith in unity of spirit, in the bond of peace, and in righteousness of life. Finally, we commend to Thy Fatherly goodness all those who are any ways afflicted, or distressed in mind, body, or estate; that it may please Thee to comfort and relieve them, according to their several necessities; giving them patience under their sufferings, and a happy issue out of all their afflictions. And this we beg for Jesus Christ's sake. *Amen.*

A General Prayer in the Morning

Almighty God, our Father and Preserver: We give Thee thanks that of Thy goodness Thou hast watched over us the past night, and brought us to a new day; and we beseech Thee to strengthen and guard us by Thy Spirit, that we may spend it wholly in Thy service and to Thy glory, looking for all prosperity to Thy blessing, and seeking only those things which are well-pleasing in Thy sight. Enable us, O Lord, while we labor for the life that now is, ever to have regard unto that heavenly life which Thou hast promised Thy children. Defend us in soul and body from all harm. And seeing it is a small thing to have begun well except we also persevere, take us, O Lord, into Thy good keeping this day and all our days; continue and increase Thy grace within us, until we shall be perfectly united in the glory of Thy Son. Show Thy loving-kindness unto all men and women and little children, according to the need of every living soul, especially unto those whom we love, and those who are in any kind of trouble or distress, whom we now remember silently before Thee (*here let there be a moment of prayer in silence*). Protect our country and prosper Thy Church. Bless all who do good in the world, and restrain and convert all who do evil. And finally, be pleased to cast out of Thy remembrance all our past offenses, forgiving them in Thy boundless mercy and purifying our hearts that we may lead a better life; through Jesus Christ our Lord. *Amen.*

A General Prayer in the Evening

O God, who hast appointed the day for labor and the night for rest: Grant, we beseech Thee, that we may so rest in peace and quietness during the coming night that afterward we may go forth to our appointed labors. Take us into Thy holy keeping, so that no evil may befall us nor any ill come nigh our dwelling. And when at length our days are ended and our work is finished in this world, grant that we may depart in Thy peace and in the sure hope of that glorious kingdom where there is day without night, and light without darkness, and life without the shadow of death for ever; through Jesus Christ our Lord. *Amen.*

A Prayer of Saint Chrysostom

Almighty God, who hast given us grace at this time with one accord to make our common supplications unto Thee; and dost promise that when two or three are gathered together in Thy name Thou wilt grant their requests: Fulfill now, O Lord, the desires and petitions of Thy servants, as may be most expedient for them; granting us in this world knowledge of Thy truth, and in the world to come life everlasting. *Amen.*

All the People still bowing down, the service may end with this:

Ascription

NOW unto Him that is able to keep us from falling, and to present us faultless before the presence of His glory with exceeding joy; to the only wise God our Saviour, be glory and majesty, dominion and power, both now and ever. *Amen.*

FIRST ORDER
OF EVENING WORSHIP

Let the Minister say:

Let us worship God.

Hymn of Praise, Introit, or Antiphon

Call to Worship

GRACE be unto you, and peace, from God our Father, and from the Lord Jesus Christ.

He that dwelleth in the secret place of the Most High shall abide under the shadow of the Almighty.

Rest in the Lord, and wait patiently for Him.

Let us pray.

Invocation and Confession

To be said by the Minister and People.

ETERNAL God, in whom we live and move and have our being; Whose face is hidden from us by our sins; And whose mercy we forget in the blindness of our hearts; Cleanse us, we beseech Thee, from all our offenses; And deliver us from proud thoughts and vain desires; That with lowliness and meekness we may draw near to Thee; Confessing our faults, confiding in Thy grace, and finding in Thee our refuge and our strength; Through Jesus Christ Thy Son. Amen.

Hymn or Anthem

Scripture Lesson

53

Before the Lesson shall be said:

Hear the Word of God, as it is written in
. . . ., the . . . . chapter, at
the . . . . verse.

At the end of the Lesson shall be said:

The Lord bless to us the reading of His holy
Word, and to His name be glory and praise.

Canticle

Venite, Exultemus Domino

O come let us sing unto the Lord: let us heartily
rejoice in the strength of our salvation.

Let us come before His presence with thanksgiving: and show ourselves glad in Him with
psalms.

For the Lord is a great God: and a great King
above all gods.

In His hand are all the corners of the earth:
and the strength of the hills is His also.

The sea is His, and He made it: and His hands
prepared the dry land.

O come let us worship and fall down: and kneel
before the Lord our Maker.

For He is the Lord our God: and we are the
people of His pasture, and the sheep of His hand.

O worship the Lord in the beauty of holiness:
let the whole earth stand in awe of Him.

For He cometh, for He cometh to judge the
earth: and with righteousness to judge the world,
and the peoples with His truth.

Glory be to the Father, and to the Son, and to the Holy Ghost;

As it was in the beginning, is now, and ever shall be, world without end.   Amen.

Evening Prayer

Let the Minister say:

Let us pray.

O GOD who art eternal Love, and whose tender mercies are over all Thy works:

Our hope and our salvation are in Thee.

O God who didst so love the world that Thou gavest Thine only-begotten Son, that whosoever believeth in Him should not perish but have everlasting life:

Our hope and our salvation are in Thee.

Thy love is long-suffering and patient; Thou bearest with the ignorant and the froward; Thou art full of compassion for sinners who know not what they do:

Increase our love, we pray Thee.

Thou hast taught us in Christ not to seek vengeance, but to love our enemies, and to pray for them that despitefully use us:

Increase our love, we pray Thee.

O Thou of whom the whole family in heaven and earth is named, we give thanks for all Thy Fatherly gifts, for the bonds of kindred and friendship, for those whom we love and for those who love us:

Increase our love, we pray Thee.

Most heartily we beseech Thee to look with favor upon Thy servants, the President of the United States, the Governor of this state, and all others in authority. Endue them with the spirit of wisdom, goodness, and truth; and so rule their hearts that law and order, justice and peace, may everywhere prevail:

Hear us and help us, we beseech Thee.

Teach us how to promote peace on earth by good will and fair dealing among the nations, and make our land a strong pillar of that kingdom which is righteousness and peace and joy in the Holy Spirit:

Hear us and help us, we beseech Thee.

For all who dwell in darkness and distress, for all who are needy and in pain, for all who are lonely and cast down:

Hear us, we beseech Thee.

By the pure example of Jesus who went about doing good; by the perfect life of Jesus who obeyed Thy will in all things; by the holy sacrifice of Jesus who died for us men and for our salvation:

Forgive us and help us, O Lord.

As Thy love was incarnate for us, so may Thy love dwell in us and rule over us evermore in Christ:

Hear us and help us, O Lord.

Now unto Him that loved us and gave Himself for us, be all glory and praise and blessing, for ever and ever. *Amen.*

And now, as our Saviour Christ hath taught us, we humbly pray:
Our Father, . . .

The Minister, having made such Announcements as are needful, may say:

Let us make our offering unto Almighty God.

REMEMBER the words of the Lord Jesus, how He said, It is more blessed to give than to receive.

Offering

Dedication of Offering

O GOD, of whose bounty we have all received: Accept this offering of Thy people; and so follow it with Thy blessing that it may promote peace and good will among men, and advance the kingdom of our Lord and Saviour Jesus Christ.
Amen.

Hymn or Anthem

Before the Sermon the Minister may say:

Let Thy Gospel, O Lord, come unto us, not in word only, but also in power, and in the Holy Spirit, and in much assurance; through Jesus Christ our Lord. *Amen.*

Sermon

After the Sermon this Ascription and Prayer may be said:

UNTO the Father, and unto the Son, and unto the Holy Spirit, be ascribed in the Church all honor and glory, might, majesty, dominion, and blessing, now, henceforth, and for ever. *Amen.*

Let us pray.

O God, from whom all holy desires, all good counsels, and all just works do proceed: Give unto Thy servants that peace which the world cannot give; that our hearts may be set to obey Thy commandments, and also that by Thee, we, being defended from the fear of our enemies, may pass our time in rest and quietness; through the merits of Jesus Christ our Saviour. *Amen.*

Hymn or Canticle

Nunc Dimittis

Lord, now lettest Thou Thy servant depart in peace: according to Thy word.

For mine eyes have seen: Thy salvation,

Which Thou hast prepared: before the face of all people;

To be a light to lighten the Gentiles: and to be the glory of Thy people Israel.

Glory be to the Father, and to the Son, and to the Holy Ghost;

As it was in the beginning, is now, and ever shall be, world without end. Amen.

Benediction

THE Lord bless you, and keep you: the Lord make His face to shine upon you, and be gracious unto you: the Lord lift up His countenance upon you, and give you peace; through Jesus Christ our Lord. *Amen.*

SECOND ORDER
OF EVENING WORSHIP

Let the Minister say:

Let us worship God.

Hymn of Praise, Introit, or Antiphon

Call to Worship

GRACE be unto you, and peace, from God our Father, and from the Lord Jesus Christ.

The day goeth away, for the shadows of the evening are stretched out.

This is the message which we have heard of Him, and declare unto you, that God is light, and in Him is no darkness at all. If we walk in the light, as He is in the light, we have fellowship one with another, and the blood of Jesus Christ His Son cleanseth us from all sin.

Invocation and Confession   *Minister and People*

ETERNAL God our Father, who art from everlasting; Thou hast made us and not we ourselves. Thou hast set us but a handbreadth from Thee, that we, Thy children, may learn the ways of freedom and choose Thee with all our hearts. Grant us now Thy Holy Spirit; That confident in prayer, we may worship Thee with gladness and become as little children before Thee; Through Jesus Christ our Lord. Amen.

Hymn or Anthem

Scripture Lesson

Canticle

Te Deum Laudamus

We praise Thee, O God: we acknowledge Thee to be the Lord.

All the earth doth worship Thee: the Father everlasting.

To Thee all angels cry aloud: the Heavens, and all the Powers therein;

To Thee Cherubim and Seraphim: continually do cry,

Holy, Holy, Holy: Lord God of Sabaoth;

Heaven and earth are full of the Majesty: of Thy glory.

The glorious company of the Apostles: praise Thee.

The goodly fellowship of the Prophets: praise Thee.

The noble army of Martyrs: praise Thee.

The holy Church throughout all the world: doth acknowledge Thee;

The Father of an infinite Majesty;

Thine adorable, true: and only Son;

Also the Holy Ghost: the Comforter.

Thou art the King of Glory: O Christ.

Thou art the everlasting Son: of the Father.

When Thou tookest upon Thee to deliver man: Thou didst humble Thyself to be born of a Virgin.

When Thou hadst overcome the sharpness of death: Thou didst open the Kingdom of Heaven to all believers.

Thou sittest at the right hand of God: in the glory of the Father.

We believe that Thou shalt come: to be our Judge.

We therefore pray Thee, help Thy servants: whom Thou hast redeemed with Thy precious blood.

Make them to be numbered with Thy Saints: in glory everlasting.

O Lord, save Thy people: and bless Thine heritage.

Govern them: and lift them up for ever.

Day by day: we magnify Thee;

And we worship Thy name: ever, world without end.

Vouchsafe, O Lord: to keep us this day without sin.

O Lord, have mercy upon us: have mercy upon us.

O Lord, let Thy mercy be upon us: as our trust is in Thee.

O Lord, in Thee have I trusted: let me never be confounded.

Evening Prayer

The Minister shall say:

Let us pray.

ALMIGHTY God, who art from everlasting to everlasting, whose kingdom is righteousness, joy, and peace: Grant us, amid the conflicts of this passing world, the comfort of a perfect trust in Thee:

Save us and help us, O Lord.

From pride, selfishness, greed, and anger; from passions that beget strife in the soul and war

among brethren; from avarice, vainglory, and re-
vengefulness:

Save us and help us, O Lord.

As Thou hast given to our country liberty and
power, so guide Thy servant the President, and
all others in authority. Lead all our people and
all other nations into the ways that make for peace
on earth and good will among men. Give peace
in our time, O Lord:

Save us and help us, O Lord.

We beseech Thee to allay all enmity and strife,
that the rich may not scorn the poor nor the
poor hate the rich, that all unfairness may be re-
dressed and all inequities abolished, and the
peaceful labor of all promote the good of the
commonwealth:

Save us and help us, O Lord.

Especially for Thy holy Church Universal we
implore Thy blessing; that all who love the Lord
Jesus in sincerity and truth may learn to love and
help one another in His service; that all unhappy
divisions among the disciples of Christ may be
done away; and that the many folds of faith may
be embraced in one flock, following one Shepherd,
even Jesus Christ our Lord:

Save us and help us, O Lord.

For all who are disquieted and afflicted by war
within themselves, by the conflict of flesh and
spirit, by the invasions of doubt, the tumults of
a rebellious will, and the dark drivings of despair;
for all the solitary and the restless and the un-

happy, we implore Thy compassion and Thy very present help in time of trouble:

Save us and help us, O Lord.

By the example of Thy dear Son Jesus Christ our Saviour, who learned obedience by the things which He suffered; by His meekness, lowliness, and forgiving grace; by His courage, firmness, and constancy in Thy work; by His submission to Thy will and the giving of His life to take away the sin of the world, Lord have mercy upon us:

Christ have mercy upon us.

O God, who art the Author of peace and Lover of concord, in knowledge of whom standeth our eternal life, whose service is perfect freedom: Defend us, Thy humble servants, in all assaults of our enemies; that we, surely trusting in Thy defense, may not fear the power of any adversaries; through the might of Jesus Christ our Lord. *Amen.*

The Lord bless you, and keep you: the Lord make His face to shine upon you, and be gracious unto you: the Lord lift up His countenance upon you, and give you peace; through Jesus Christ our Lord. *Amen.*

And now, as our Saviour Christ hath taught us, we humbly pray:
Our Father, . . .

Offertory Sentence   Minister

FREELY ye have received, freely give.

Offering

Dedication of Offering

O GOD, the Fountain of all good: We bring to Thee our gifts, according as Thou hast prospered us. Enable us, with our earthly things, to give Thee the love of our hearts and the service of our lives. Let Thy favor, which is life, and Thy loving-kindness, which is better than life, be upon us now and always; through Jesus Christ our Lord. *Amen.*

Hymn or Anthem

Sermon

Ascription and Prayer

BLESSING, and honor, and glory, and power, be unto Him that sitteth upon the throne, and unto the Lamb, for ever and ever. *Amen.*

Let us pray.

Almighty God, who hast given us grace at this time with one accord to make our common supplications unto Thee; and dost promise that when two or three are gathered together in Thy name Thou wilt grant their requests: Fulfill now, O Lord, the desires and petitions of Thy servants, as may be most expedient for them; granting us in this world knowledge of Thy truth, and in the world to come life everlasting. *Amen.*

Hymn or Canticle

Benediction

THE grace of the Lord Jesus Christ, and the love of God, and the communion of the Holy Spirit, be with you all. *Amen.*

THIRD ORDER
OF EVENING WORSHIP

Let the Minister say:

Let us worship God.

Hymn of Praise, Introit, or Antiphon

Call to Worship

GRACE be unto you, and peace, from God our Father, and from the Lord Jesus Christ.

The Lord is in His holy temple: let all the earth keep silence before Him.

God is a Spirit: and they that worship Him must worship Him in spirit and in truth.

O come, let us worship and bow down: let us kneel before the Lord our Maker.

Invocation and Confession   *Minister and People*

O GOD, the Father of lights, with whom is no variableness nor shadow of turning; Look in mercy upon us, Thy sinful and wayward children; And so direct the eyes of our faith unto Thee; That we may receive a heavenly illumination through Thy Word and Spirit; And walk securely amid the shadows of this mortal life. Pardon our sins, and give us such a vision of the truth in Jesus; That darkness may be driven from our hearts; And we may render unto Thee songs of praise; Through Christ our Lord. Amen.

Hymn or Anthem

Scripture Lesson

Canticle

Gloria in Excelsis

Glory be to God on high: and on earth peace, good will toward men.

We praise Thee, we bless Thee, we worship Thee: we glorify Thee, we give thanks to Thee for Thy great glory.

O Lord God, Heavenly King: God the Father Almighty.

O Lord, the only-begotten Son, Jesus Christ: O Lord God, Lamb of God, Son of the Father,

That takest away the sins of the world: have mercy upon us.

Thou that takest away the sins of the world: receive our prayer.

Thou that sittest at the right hand of God the Father: have mercy upon us.

For Thou only art holy: Thou only art the Lord.

Thou only, O Christ, with the Holy Ghost: art most high in the glory of God the Father.   Amen.

Evening Prayer

The Minister shall say:

Let us pray.

MOST merciful and gracious God, whose earthly gifts foretell Thy heavenly favor: We bring our thank offering to Thee in this hour of evening sacrifice, and make mention of Thy loving-kindness in Thy house of prayer.

For the wonder and beauty of Thy world; for the light of day and the splendor of the starry night; for the wise order of Thy laws made known by science, and for things pure and lovely revealed by art; for the powers of our reason, the freedom of our will, and the joy of our pure affections: blessed be the Creator of all.

Thanks be unto Thee, O Lord.

For Thy words to us in Holy Scripture; for Thy living Word Jesus, sent to be the Saviour of the world; for the Church that He hath founded on earth, the company of all who love Him in sincerity and truth; for the privilege of prayer and praise and the grace of His sacraments; and for His abiding fellowship with all who seek and serve Thee: blessed be the God and Father of our Lord Jesus Christ.

Thanks be unto Thee, O Lord.

For our country and the liberty Thou hast given us; for the awakening sense of brotherhood; for the increasing readiness to serve and sacrifice; for the great brotherhood of man; for the deepening will to peace among the nations: blessed be the Father of mankind.

Thanks be unto Thee, O Lord.

For home and kindred; for our duties and our daily bread; for the joy of little children and the counsel of wise teachers; for the comfort of true comrades and the help of loyal friends; for life's labor, trial, and discipline; for rain and sunshine, the call to endure hardness as good soldiers and to rejoice in hope: blessed be the God whose hand leadeth us and by whose wisdom our way is ordered.

Thanks be unto Thee, O Lord.

Enable us, we pray Thee, to render thanks not in word only, but also in deed; and may the rest and worship of this holy day strengthen us to do Thy will on earth, after the example of Jesus Christ our Saviour.

Thanks be unto Thee, O Lord.

Minister: How excellent is Thy loving-kindness, O Lord!

People: Therefore the children of men put their trust under the shadow of Thy wings.

Minister: O continue Thy loving-kindness unto them that know Thee,

People: And Thy righteousness to the upright in heart.

Minister: The Lord bless us,

People: And keep us.

Minister: The Lord make His face to shine upon us,

People: And be gracious unto us.

Minister: The Lord lift up His countenance upon us,

People: And give us peace. Amen.

And now, as our Saviour Christ hath taught us, we humbly pray:
Our Father, . . .

Offertory Sentence   *Minister*

YE KNOW the grace of our Lord Jesus Christ, that though He was rich, yet for your sakes He became poor, that ye through His poverty might be rich.

Offering

Dedication of Offering

ALMIGHTY and ever-blessed God, who in the abundance of Thy goodness dost ever give us more than we desire or dare to ask: Pour forth upon us, we beseech Thee, a spirit of thankfulness, and increase in us that most blessed grace of charity, that we may ever be more willing to give than to receive; and so rule our hearts that all we have may be used for Thy service, and we ourselves be consecrated to Thee; through Jesus Christ our Lord. *Amen.*

Hymn or Anthem

Sermon

Ascription and Prayer

NOW unto the God of all grace, who hath called us unto His eternal glory by Christ Jesus, be glory and dominion for ever and ever.
Amen.

Let us pray.

Lighten our darkness, we beseech Thee, O Lord; and by Thy great mercy defend us from all perils and dangers of this night; for the love of Thine only Son our Saviour Jesus Christ. *Amen.*

Hymn or Canticle

Benediction

THE Lord bless you, and keep you: the Lord make His face to shine upon you, and be gracious unto you: the Lord lift up His countenance upon you, and give you peace; through Jesus Christ our Lord. *Amen.*

FOURTH ORDER
OF EVENING WORSHIP

Let the Minister say:

Let us worship God.

Hymn of Praise, Introit, or Antiphon

Call to Worship

GRACE be unto you, and peace, from God our Father, and from the Lord Jesus Christ.

Draw nigh to God, and He will draw nigh to you.

Enter into His gates with thanksgiving, and into His courts with praise.

Let our prayer be set forth before Thee as incense; and the lifting up of our hands as the evening sacrifice.

Invocation and Confession   *Minister and People*

O THOU whose chosen dwelling is the heart that longs for Thy presence and humbly seeks Thy face; We come to Thee as the day declines and the shadows of evening fall. Deepen within us the sense of shame and sorrow for the wrongs we have done, for the good we have left undone; And strengthen every desire to amend our lives according to Thy holy will. Restore unto us the joy of Thy salvation; Bind up that which is broken; Give light to our minds, strength to our wills, and rest to our souls; According to Thy loving-kindness in Jesus Christ our Lord. Amen.

Hymn or Anthem

Scripture Lesson

Canticle

Magnificat

My soul doth magnify the Lord, and my spirit hath rejoiced in God my Saviour.

For He hath regarded the lowliness of His handmaiden.

For behold from henceforth all generations shall call me blessed.

For He that is mighty hath magnified me; and holy is His name.

And His mercy is on them that fear Him throughout all generations.

He hath showed strength with His arm; He hath scattered the proud in the imagination of their hearts.

He hath put down the mighty from their seat, and hath exalted the humble and meek.

He hath filled the hungry with good things; and the rich He hath sent empty away.

He remembering His mercy hath holpen His servant Israel; as He promised to our forefather Abraham and his seed for ever.

Glory be to the Father, and to the Son, and to the Holy Ghost;

As it was in the beginning, is now, and ever shall be, world without end. Amen.

Evening Prayer

Then the Minister shall say:

Let us pray.

LORD GOD, Father in heaven:

Have mercy upon us.

Lord God, Son, Thou Saviour of the world:

Be gracious unto us.

Lord God, Holy Ghost:

Abide with us for ever.

From all sin,
From all error,
From all evil:

Preserve us, gracious Lord and God.

From pestilence and famine,
From calamity by fire or water, hail or tempest,
From war and bloodshed,
From the violence of wicked men:

Preserve us, gracious Lord and God.

From indifference to Thy merits and death,
From pride and self-complacency,
From needless perplexity,
From the unhappy desire of becoming great,
From hypocrisy and fanaticism,
From envy, hatred, and malice,
From the deceitfulness of sin,
From the influence of the spirit of this world:

. *Preserve us, gracious Lord and God.*

By all the merits of Thy life,
By Thy human birth,
By Thy obedience, diligence, and faithfulness,
By Thy humility, meekness, and patience,
By Thy extreme poverty,
By Thy baptism, fasting, and temptation,
By Thy griefs and sorrows,
By Thy prayers and tears,

By Thy having been despised and rejected:

Bless and comfort us, gracious Lord and God.

By Thy agony and bloody sweat,
By Thy bonds and scourging,
By Thy crown of thorns,
By Thy cross and Passion,
By Thy dying words,
By Thy atoning death,
By Thy glorious Resurrection and Ascension,
By Thy sitting at the right hand of God,
By Thy sending the Holy Spirit,
By Thy prevailing intercession,
By Thy holy sacraments,
By Thy divine presence,
By Thy coming again to Thy Church on earth,
or our being called home to Thee:

Bless and comfort us, gracious Lord and God.

And now, as our Saviour Christ hath taught us,
we humbly pray:
Our Father, . . .

Offertory Sentence   Minister

LET your light so shine before men that they
may see your good works, and glorify your
Father who is in heaven.

Offering

Dedication of Offering

O LORD our God, the Giver of all good: We
beseech Thee to behold in these our gifts
the earnest of our consecration to Thy service;
and grant that now and at all times our gratitude

to Thee may be as great as our need of Thy
mercy; through Jesus Christ our Lord. *Amen.*

Hymn or Anthem

Sermon

Ascription and Prayer

NOW unto the God of all grace, who hath
called us unto His eternal glory by Christ
Jesus, be glory and dominion for ever and ever.
Amen.

Let us pray.

O Lord, support us all the day long, until the
shadows lengthen and the evening comes, and
the busy world is hushed, and the fever of life
is over, and our work is done. Then in Thy
mercy grant us a safe lodging, and a holy rest,
and peace at the last; through Jesus Christ our
Lord. *Amen.*

Hymn or Canticle

Benediction

THE grace of the Lord Jesus Christ, and the
love of God, and the communion of the Holy
Spirit, be with you all. *Amen.*

FIFTH ORDER
OF EVENING WORSHIP

Let the Minister say:

Let us worship God.

Hymn of Praise, Introit, or Antiphon

Call to Worship

GRACE be unto you, and peace, from God our Father, and from the Lord Jesus Christ.

It is a good thing to give thanks unto the Lord, and to sing praises unto Thy name, O Most High:

To show forth Thy loving-kindness in the morning, and Thy faithfulness every night.

Delight thyself also in the Lord; and He shall give thee the desires of thine heart.

Invocation and Confession　　*Minister and People*

LORD of the evening hour, who hast often met with us at close of day; Be our Refuge now from the noise of the world and the care of our own spirits. Grant us Thy peace. Let not the darkness of our ignorance and folly, of our sorrow and sin, hide Thee from us. Draw near to us that we may be near to Thee. Speak to each of us the word that we need; And let Thy Word abide with us till it has wrought in us Thy holy will. Quicken and refresh our hearts, renew and increase our strength, so that we may grow into Thy likeness; And by our worship be enabled better to serve Thee in our daily life, in the Spirit of Jesus Christ our Lord. Amen.

Hymn or Anthem

Scripture Lesson

Canticle

Deus Misereatur

God be merciful unto us, and bless us: and show us the light of His countenance, and be merciful unto us;

That Thy way may be known upon earth: Thy saving health among all nations.

Let the people praise Thee, O God: yea, let all the people praise Thee.

O let the nations rejoice and be glad: for Thou shalt judge the folk righteously, and govern the nations upon earth.

Let the people praise Thee, O God: yea, let all the people praise Thee.

Then shall the earth bring forth her increase: and God, even our own God, shall give us His blessing.

God shall bless us: and all the ends of the world shall fear Him.

Glory be to the Father, and to the Son, and to the Holy Ghost;

As it was in the beginning, is now, and ever shall be, world without end.   Amen.

Evening Prayer

The Minister shall say:

Let us pray.

O GOD, the Father of heaven;
    O God, the Son, Redeemer of the world;
    O God, the Holy Ghost, the Sanctifier of Thy people:

   Hear us, we beseech Thee, O Lord.

In communion with all Thy saints in all ages, with patriarchs and prophets, with apostles and martyrs, with all who have passed from us into Thy presence, we adore Thee, and offer to Thee our praises, thanksgivings, and supplications:

Hear us, we beseech Thee, O Lord.

Give us a quick and tender conscience, that in all things we may be guided by Thine indwelling Spirit:

Hear us, we beseech Thee, O Lord.

We pray Thee to reveal to us the beauty of Thy perfect will, the gladness of Thy service, the power of Thy presence:

Hear us, we beseech Thee, O Lord.

May no perplexity create in us an impatient spirit, no temptation lead us into sin, no sorrow hide Thy loving will from us:

Hear us, we beseech Thee, O Lord.

Calm our passions, direct our affections, repress the waywardness of our wills; and lead us in the way everlasting:

Hear us, we beseech Thee, O Lord.

Help us to forgive as we would be forgiven, dwelling neither in speech nor in thought upon offenses committed against us, but loving one another as Thou lovest us:

Hear us, we beseech Thee, O Lord.

Help us with all diligence to keep our hearts,

and to conform ourselves to Thy will in things
both small and great:

Hear us, we beseech Thee, O Lord.

Gracious Father, who willest us to cast all our
care on Thee who carest for us: Preserve us from
all faithless fears and selfish anxieties, and grant
that no clouds of this mortal life may hide from
us the light of the love which is immortal and
which Thou hast manifested to us in Jesus Christ
our Lord:

Hear us, we beseech Thee, O Lord.

May the rich blessing of the Lord attend us,
and grant us all remission of our sins.

May the Lord graciously protect us from all
evil and mercifully preserve us in all good, and

May He who created and redeemed us preserve
us for Himself unspotted to the end. *Amen.*

And now, as our Saviour Christ hath taught us,
we humbly pray:

Our Father, . . .

Offertory Sentence   Minister

EVERY man according as he purposeth in his
heart, so let him give; not grudgingly, or
of necessity: for God loveth a cheerful giver.

Offering

Dedication of Offering

O GIVER of every good and perfect gift, we
acknowledge Thy bounty in these gifts,
which we now offer and dedicate unto Thee. We

pray Thee to accept them and multiply them for the work of Thy Church and the spread of Thy kingdom; through Jesus Christ our Lord. *Amen.*

Hymn or Anthem

Sermon

Ascription and Prayer

BLESSING, and glory, and wisdom, and thanksgiving, and honor, and power, and might, be unto our God for ever and ever. *Amen.*

Let us pray.

Almighty God, who hast sounded in our ears Thy saving truth: Enlighten our minds to the full understanding of what we have heard spoken, and deepen every serious impression, that we may be not only hearers of good words, but also doers of good deeds, striving ever to live blameless and faithful lives to the glory of Thy name. Bless all who worship Thee, from the rising of the sun unto the going down of the same. Of Thy goodness give us, with Thy love inspire us, by Thy Spirit guide us, by Thy power protect us, in Thy mercy receive us, now and always. *Amen.*

Hymn or Canticle

Benediction

THE Lord bless you, and keep you: the Lord make His face to shine upon you, and be gracious unto you: the Lord lift up His countenance upon you, and give you peace; through Jesus Christ our Lord. *Amen.*

FIRST
CHILDREN'S SERVICE

Let the Minister say:

Let us worship God.

Then may be sung a Hymn, setting forth the power, the goodness, and the grace of God, all the People standing, and then the Minister may read the Call to Worship. Or the service may begin with the Call to Worship.

Call to Worship

GRACE be unto you, and peace, from God our Father, and from the Lord Jesus Christ.

Give unto the Lord the glory due unto His name.

Worship the Lord in the beauty of holiness.

God is a Spirit: and they that worship Him must worship Him in spirit and in truth.

Adoration   *Minister*

OUR Heavenly Father, we worship and adore Thee. We are Thy children. We come to Thee. Thou art our Guide, our Saviour, and our Friend. May the grace of our Lord Jesus Christ and the love of God, be the joy of our salvation, now and always. *Amen.*

Confession   *Minister and People*

O GOD, our Father in heaven;
   We come to Thee in penitence, confessing
      our sins.
Create in us a clean heart, O God;
And renew a right spirit within us.
Restore unto us the joy of Thy salvation;
And uphold us with Thy free Spirit.

O Lord, open Thou our lips;
And our mouth shall show forth Thy praise.

Forgive us, O Lord;
For the wrong we have done;
For the unkind words we have said;
For our evil thoughts.

Forgive us, O Lord;
For forgetting Thee;
For our selfishness;
For our neglect of others.

Lord, hear our prayer;
Guide us and help us;
To do better and to be better;
For the sake of Jesus Christ our Lord.   Amen.

Assurance of Pardon   *Minister*

HEAR the gracious words of our Lord Jesus
Christ unto all that truly repent and turn to
Him: Come unto Me, all ye that labor and are
heavy-laden, and I will give you rest.   Him that
cometh to Me I will in no wise cast out.   The
grace of our Lord Jesus Christ be with you all.
Amen.

Psalter

First Scripture Lesson

Hymn or Anthem

Second Scripture Lesson

The Creed

Hymn or Anthem

Intercession and Thanksgiving   *Minister*

ALMIGHTY God, Thou hast taught us to
pray for ourselves, and for all people.
Hear us as, in the name of Jesus Christ our
Lord, we make our prayer to Thee.

We pray that we may be true and sincere
Christians;
Ready to serve Thee with pure hearts;
Ready to help others in all kindness and
gladness of heart.

We pray that we may hate everything that is
unworthy;
And love the things that are just and true
and of good report.

We pray for Christians everywhere,
That in the fellowship of Thy Church
They may find peace and joy.

We pray for our country, and for the President;
For all ministers of the Gospel;
For all teachers, and for our homes;
That we may be led in paths of righteousness
For Thy name's sake.

We thank Thee, O God,
For all Thy love to us and to all men;
For life and health, for Thy care;
For all who love us and whom we love.

We thank Thee
For our Lord and Saviour Jesus Christ;
For His example; His death on the cross;
His resurrection from the dead;
His presence with us now.   *Amen.*

THE Lord bless us, and keep us: the Lord make His face to shine upon us, and be gracious unto us: the Lord lift up His countenance upon us, and give us peace; for Jesus' sake.

Amen.

And now, as our Saviour Christ hath taught us, we humbly pray:

Our Father, . . .

Offertory Sentence

REMEMBER the words of the Lord Jesus, how He said, It is more blessed to give than to receive.

Offering

Doxology, Response, or Dedication of Offering

Hymn or Anthem

Sermon

Ascription

NOW unto Him that is able to keep you from falling, and to present you faultless before the presence of His glory with exceeding joy; to the only wise God our Saviour, be glory and majesty, dominion and power, both now and ever. *Amen.*

Hymn

Benediction

THE grace of the Lord Jesus Christ, and the love of God, and the communion of the Holy Spirit, be with you all. *Amen.*

SECOND
CHILDREN'S SERVICE

Let the Minister say:

Let us worship God.

Then may be sung a Hymn, setting forth the power, the goodness, and the grace of God, all the People standing, and then the Minister may read the Call to Worship. Or the service may begin with the Call to Worship.

Call to Worship

OUR help is in the name of the Lord, who made heaven and earth.

O come, let us worship and bow down: let us kneel before the Lord our Maker.

Let the words of our mouth, and the meditation of our heart, be acceptable in Thy sight, O Lord, our Strength, and our Redeemer.

Adoration *Minister*

HOLY, holy, holy is the Lord. We worship Thee. We adore Thee. We give thanks unto Thee, for Thou only art the Lord. To Thee we come in gladness of heart and humility of spirit. We commit ourselves to Thee and pray that Thou wilt receive us, protect us, guard and guide us, now and always. For the sake of Jesus Christ our Lord. *Amen.*

Confession *Minister and People*

THOU, O Lord, hast promised;
That if we will confess our sins Thou art faithful and just to forgive us our sins.

85

We come in penitence seeking Thy forgiveness;
  That we may know the joy of Thy presence;
  And the light of Thy face.

Thou alone knowest how often we have offended
    Thee;
  And hurt the lives of others.

Forgive us, O Lord;
  For every unkind thought;
  Every untrue word;
  Every wrong act.

Forgive us;
  For we have been selfish;
  And have not thought of the needs of others.

Forgive us;
  For our ingratitude;
  Our neglect of prayer;
  Our carelessness in the use of money;
  Our forgetfulness of our sacred vows.

O God, have mercy upon us.
  Create in us clean hearts;
  And renew a right spirit within us.
  For the sake of Jesus Christ our Lord. Amen.

Assurance of Pardon   *Minister*

O LORD JESUS CHRIST, who didst give Thy
  life for us that we might receive pardon and
peace: Mercifully cleanse us from all sin, and
evermore keep us in Thy favor and love, who
livest and reignest with the Father and the Holy
Spirit, ever one God, world without end. *Amen.*

Psalter

First Scripture Lesson

Hymn or Anthem

Second Scripture Lesson

The Creed

Hymn or Anthem

Intercession and Thanksgiving
Minister and People

O LORD, who hast taught us to pray: Hear our prayer not only for ourselves but for others:

Lord, hear our prayer.

For the Church of Christ in all lands; for all ministers, missionaries, and teachers, that all men may come to love our Saviour:

We beseech Thee to hear us, O Lord.

For our nation, for the President, for all judges, for all the people, that they may love the good and hate the evil:

We beseech Thee to hear us, O Lord.

For parents and friends, that they may be kept in health and happiness:

We beseech Thee to hear us, O Lord.

For any who suffer, for all who are in trouble, that Thou wouldst comfort them:

We beseech Thee to hear us, O Lord.

We give thanks unto Thee, O Lord:

For Thy mercy endureth for ever.

For the Gospel of our Lord Jesus Christ, for His lowly birth, His sinless life, His death on the cross, His rising again from the dead, His presence with us now:

We praise Thee, O Lord.

For all who have cared for us, protected us, and guided our feet in the way of truth:

We praise Thee, O Lord.

For everything that makes life fair and beautiful, the world about us, the love of little children, the kindness of friends, the helpfulness of good books and music; for all the goodness that is from Thee:

We praise Thee, O Lord.

God be merciful unto us and bless us:
Cause Thy face to shine upon us,
And give us Thy peace.

Through Jesus Christ our Lord. *Amen.*

And now, as our Saviour Christ hath taught us, we humbly pray:
Our Father, . . .

Offertory Sentence

FREELY ye have received, freely give.

Offering

Dedication of Offering

ALL things come of Thee, O Lord; and of Thine own have we given Thee. *Amen.*

Hymn or Anthem

Sermon

Ascription

NOW unto Him that is able to do exceeding abundantly above all that we ask or think, according to the power that worketh in us; unto Him be glory in the Church by Christ Jesus, throughout all ages, world without end. *Amen.*

Hymn

Dedication   Minister and People

O LORD our God, Thou art holy and we are sinful; Thou art strong and we are weak; Thou art ever in the light and we walk in darkness. Give us of Thy Spirit; That in penitence and trust we may grow in grace and in the knowledge of our Lord and Saviour. Enlighten our minds; Purify our hearts; Renew our wills; And may we give ourselves wholly to Thee; For the sake of Jesus Christ our Lord. Amen.

Benediction

THE grace of the Lord Jesus Christ, and the love of God, and the communion of the Holy Spirit, be with you all. *Amen.*

FIRST SERVICE
FOR YOUNG PEOPLE

Let the Minister say:

Let us worship God.

Then may be sung a Hymn, setting forth the power, the goodness, and the grace of God, all the People standing, and then the Minister may read the Call to Worship. Or the service may begin with the Call to Worship.

Call to Worship

SERVE the Lord with gladness; come before His presence with singing.

Enter into His gates with thanksgiving, and into His courts with praise; be thankful unto Him, and bless His name.

For the Lord is good; His mercy is everlasting, and His truth endureth to all generations.

Adoration   *Minister*

ALMIGHTY God, who dwellest in the high and holy place, and with him also that is of a contrite and humble spirit: Make us to be still and know that Thou art God. Lift up our hearts to Thee in love and adoration; then of Thy mercy send us forth into the world to do justly, to love mercy, and to walk humbly with Thee our God; through Jesus Christ our Lord. *Amen.*

Confession   *Minister and People*

WE CONFESS to Thee, O God, that we have sinned against heaven and in Thy sight; And are not worthy to be called Thy children. We have forgotten Thee; And have broken Thy holy laws; We have been wayward and disobedient; We have been selfish and unkind. For the sake of Thy dear Son our Saviour we beseech Thee to pardon our sins; To make clean our hearts within us; And to grant us Thy peace. Amen.

Assurance of Pardon   *Minister*

THE Lord is merciful and gracious, slow to anger, and plenteous in mercy. He hath not dealt with us after our sins, nor rewarded us according to our iniquities. As the heaven is high above the earth, so great is His mercy toward them that fear Him. As far as the east is from the west, so far hath He removed our transgressions from us. *Amen.*

Psalter

First Scripture Lesson

Hymn or Anthem

Second Scripture Lesson

The Creed

Hymn or Anthem

Thanksgiving   *Minister and People*

GLORY be to Thee, O God, for all Thy goodness to us and to all men. For the world in which Thou hast placed us, with all its wonder and beauty; For life and health, for food and clothing; For friends and homes; For Thy care that guards us always, and Thy faithfulness that never fails; Most of all for Jesus Christ Thine only Son our Saviour, who came into this world and died for us upon the cross; And who hath revealed to us the love that passeth knowledge; We praise Thee, O God; Father, Son, and Holy Spirit; world without end.   Amen.

Supplication   Minister

O THOU who art more ready to hear than we to pray, and who knowest our necessities before we ask and our ignorance in asking: Hear our prayer; answer us according to our need; and give us that peace which the world cannot give, nor take away.   Thou hast promised that where two or three are gathered together in Thy name Thou wilt be there in the midst of them.   Grant that we, each encouraged by the others' faith, may so seek that we may surely find Thee.   To the weary, grant Thy promised rest; to the injured, Thy comfort; to those who rejoice, Thy grace of gratitude; to those who have sinned, Thy forgiveness; and to all, Thy peace; through Jesus Christ our Lord.   *Amen.*

Intercession   Minister and People

O GOD and Father of our Lord Jesus Christ, we beseech Thee on behalf of all men, that Thou wouldst shed Thy light upon their darkness, and lead them into the way of truth.

For Thy holy Church, for her ministers and teachers, for all who serve Thee, that Thou wouldst bless and strengthen them:

We beseech Thee to hear us, O Lord.

For our President and country, and for others in authority, that Thou wouldst help them so to rule that Thy people may dwell together in peace:

We beseech Thee to hear us, O Lord.

For our homes, for companions and friends, that Thou wouldst keep them under the shelter of Thy care, and give them joy and gladness:

We beseech Thee to hear us, O Lord.

For all in trouble and distress, for the sick and the suffering, for all who have wandered from Thy way, grant Thy peace and Thy salvation:

We beseech Thee to hear us, O Lord.

O God, our Father, we present unto Thee our prayers and intercessions in the name and through the merits of Jesus Christ our Saviour. *Amen.*

And now, as our Saviour Christ hath taught us, we humbly pray:

Our Father, . . .

Offertory Sentence

FREELY ye have received, freely give.

Offering

Dedication of Offering

ALL things come of Thee, O Lord; and of Thine own have we given Thee. *Amen.*

Hymn or Anthem

Sermon

Hymn

Dedication   *Minister and People*

O GOD who art great and high and holy; Who hast loved us and freely given us all things; Here we humbly offer and present unto Thee; Ourselves, our souls and bodies; To be a reasonable, holy, and living sacrifice unto Thee; Whose service is perfect freedom; Through Jesus Christ our Lord; To whom, with Thee and the Holy Spirit, we give all glory for ever and ever.   Amen.

Benediction

THE grace of the Lord Jesus Christ, and the love of God, and the communion of the Holy Spirit, be with you all.   *Amen.*

SECOND SERVICE
FOR YOUNG PEOPLE

Let the Minister say:

Let us worship God.

Then may be sung a Hymn, setting forth the power, the goodness, and the grace of God, all the People standing, and then the Minister may read the Call to Worship. Or the service may begin with the Call to Worship.

Call to Worship

THUS saith the Lord: Ye shall seek Me, and find Me, when ye shall search for Me with all your heart.

Jesus said: Blessed are they that hunger and thirst after righteousness, for they shall be filled.

Adoration *Minister*

O GOD, our Heavenly Father, who hast made known Thy love in Jesus Christ, and Thy presence by Thy Holy Spirit: We praise Thee, we adore Thee, we worship Thee, ever world without end. *Amen.*

Confession *Minister and People*

ETERNAL God, in whom we live and move and have our being; Whose face is hidden from us by our sins; And whose mercy we forget in the blindness of our hearts; Cleanse us, we beseech Thee, from all our offenses; And deliver us from proud thoughts and vain desires; That with lowliness and meekness we may draw near to Thee; Confessing our sins, confiding in Thy grace, and finding in Thee our Refuge and our Strength; Through Jesus Christ Thy Son.   Amen.

Assurance of Pardon   *Minister*

HEAR the gracious words of our Lord Jesus Christ unto all that truly repent and turn to Him: Come unto Me, all ye that labor and are heavy-laden, and I will give you rest.   Him that cometh to Me I will in no wise cast out.   The grace of our Lord Jesus Christ be with you all.
Amen.

Psalter

First Scripture Lesson

Hymn or Anthem

Second Scripture Lesson

The Creed

Hymn or Anthem

Thanksgiving   *Minister and People*

O GOD, our Heavenly Father; We thank Thee for all things beautiful and good which Thou hast made.   We praise Thee for all the joy and happiness of our lives; For the land of our birth: For the homes in which we live; And for our companions and friends.   We praise Thee that Thou didst send to us the Lord Jesus Christ as a little child; That He gave us an example of how we ought to live; That He died for us upon the cross; That He rose again from the dead, and ever prays for us.   Help us to remember all that Thou hast given to us; And to love Thee with all our heart; For the sake of Jesus Christ our Lord; To whom, with Thee and the Holy Spirit, be the glory and the praise, for evermore. Amen.

Supplication   *Minister*

TEACH us, good Lord, to serve Thee as Thou deservest; to give and not to count the cost; to fight and not to heed the wounds; to toil and not to seek for rest; to labor and not to ask for any reward, save that of knowing that we do Thy will; through Jesus Christ our Lord. *Amen.*

Intercession   *Minister and People*

ALMIGHTY God, who hast taught us to pray not only for ourselves but for all men: Hear us as we pray for others, in the name of Jesus Christ our Lord.

For Thy holy Church upon earth; for her ministers and teachers, that all who love the Saviour may love Him more truly and serve Him more faithfully:

We beseech Thee to hear us, O Lord.

For all who do not know the Gospel of Thy love in Jesus Christ, that Thou wouldst gather them into Thy fold:

We beseech Thee to hear us, O Lord.

For Thy missionaries, especially those known to us, that they may cause Thy light to shine in the dark places of the earth:

We beseech Thee to hear us, O Lord.

For our beloved country, for our President and others in authority, that Thou wouldst guide them with Thy wisdom:

We beseech Thee to hear us, O Lord.

For those whom we love, our parents, our brothers and sisters, and our friends, that Thou wouldst bless them, and protect them from evil and danger:

We beseech Thee to hear us, O Lord.

For all who are in sickness, sorrow, and trouble, that Thou wouldst comfort and sustain them:

We beseech Thee to hear us, O Lord.

For the glorious company of apostles, prophets, and martyrs, and for the goodly fellowship of the faithful in all ages:

We praise Thee, O Lord.

Hear and accept us in these our prayers; through Jesus Christ our Lord and our Redeemer.   *Amen.*

And now, as our Saviour Christ hath taught us, we humbly pray:
Our Father, . . .

Offertory Sentence

REMEMBER the words of the Lord Jesus, how He said, It is more blessed to give than to receive.

Offering

Dedication of Offering

ALL things come of Thee, O Lord; and of Thine own have we given Thee.   *Amen.*

Hymn or Anthem

Sermon

Hymn

Dedication   *Minister and People*

ALMIGHTY God, who hast given us grace at
this time with one accord to make our common supplications unto Thee; And dost promise
that when two or three are gathered together in
Thy name Thou wilt grant their requests; Fulfill
now, O Lord, the desires and petitions of Thy
servants; As may be most expedient for them;
Granting us in this world knowledge of Thy truth;
And in the world to come life everlasting.   Amen.

Ascription

NOW unto Him that is able to keep you from
falling, and to present you faultless before
the presence of His glory with exceeding joy; to the
only wise God our Saviour, be glory and majesty,
dominion and power, both now and ever.   *Amen.*

Benediction

THE peace of God, which passeth all understanding, keep your hearts and minds in the
knowledge and love of God, and of His Son Jesus
Christ our Lord; and the blessing of God Almighty, the Father, the Son, and the Holy Spirit,
be upon you, and remain with you always.   *Amen.*

A LITANY

A General Supplication, in which the People respond after each petition offered by the Minister. It may be used in Morning Worship instead of the General Prayer; as preparation for Holy Communion; or separately.

OUR help is in the name of the Lord, who made heaven and earth.

O God, we have heard with our ears, and our fathers have declared unto us, the noble works that Thou didst in their days, and in the old time ·before them:

> *O Lord, arise, help us, and deliver us for Thy name's sake.*

O God the Father, Creator of heaven and earth:

> *Have mercy upon us.*

O God the Son, Redeemer of the world:

> *Have mercy upon us.*

O God the Holy Ghost, Sanctifier of the faithful:

> *Have mercy upon us.*

O holy, blessed, and glorious Trinity, one God:

> *Have mercy upon us.*

Remember not our offenses, nor the offenses of our forefathers. Spare us, good Lord, spare Thy people, whom Thou hast redeemed with Thy most precious blood:

> *Spare us, good Lord.*

From all blindness of heart; from pride, vainglory, and hypocrisy; from envy, hatred, and malice, and all uncharitableness:

Good Lord, deliver us.

From fleshly lusts that war against the soul; from the deceits of the world; from the counsel of the ungodly; and from all sin:

Good Lord, deliver us.

From sedition and rebellion; from heresy and schism; from hardness of heart, and contempt of Thy Word and commandment:

Good Lord, deliver us.

By the mystery of Thy holy Incarnation; by Thy holy Nativity; by Thy baptism, fasting, and temptation:

Good Lord, deliver us.

By Thine agony and bloody sweat; by Thy cross and Passion; by Thy precious death and burial; by Thy glorious Resurrection and Ascension; and by the coming of the Holy Ghost:

Good Lord, deliver us.

In all time of our tribulation; in all time of our prosperity; in the hour of death, and in the Day of Judgment:

Good Lord, deliver us.

We sinners do beseech Thee to hear us, O Lord God; and that it may please Thee to rule and govern Thy holy Church Universal:

We beseech Thee to hear us, good Lord.

That it may please Thee so to rule the heart of Thy servant, the President of the United States, that he may above all things seek Thy honor and glory:

We beseech Thee to hear us, good Lord.

That it may please Thee to bless and keep the rulers of all lands, giving them grace to execute justice, and to maintain truth:

We beseech Thee to hear us, good Lord.

That it may please Thee to bless and protect all who serve mankind by labor, industry, and learning:

We beseech Thee to hear us, good Lord.

That it may please Thee to give to all nations unity, peace, and concord:

We beseech Thee to hear us, good Lord.

That it may please Thee to give us a heart to love and fear Thee, and diligently to live after Thy commandments:

We beseech Thee to hear us, good Lord.

That it may please Thee to keep us in all time of temptation and heaviness; to comfort and help all the weak-hearted; to raise up those who fall; and finally to give us the victory:

We beseech Thee to hear us, good Lord.

That it may please Thee to help and comfort all who are in danger, necessity, and tribulation; to preserve all who travel by land, by water, or by air, all women in childbirth, all sick persons, and young children; and to show Thy pity upon all prisoners and captives:

We beseech Thee to hear us, good Lord.

That it may please Thee to defend and provide for the fatherless children, and widows, and all who are desolate and oppressed:

We beseech Thee to hear us, good Lord.

That it may please Thee to have mercy upon all men:

We beseech Thee to hear us, good Lord.

O Son of God, Redeemer of the world:

Have mercy upon us.

O Lamb of God, who takest away the sins of the world:

Have mercy upon us.

O Lamb of God, who takest away the sins of the world:

Grant us Thy peace.

Then shall the Minister, and the People with him, say the Lord's Prayer.

OUR Father, who art in heaven; Hallowed be Thy name. Thy kingdom come. Thy will be done; On earth as it is in heaven. Give us this day our daily bread. And forgive us our debts; As we forgive our debtors. And lead us not into temptation; But deliver us from evil; For Thine is the kingdom, and the power, and the glory, for ever. Amen.

Then the Minister shall say:

O GOD, from whom all holy desires, all good counsels, and all just works do proceed: Give unto Thy servants that peace which the world cannot give; that our hearts may be set to obey Thy commandments, and also that, by Thee, we, being defended from the fear of our enemies, may pass our time in rest and quietness; through Jesus Christ our Lord.

Almighty God, who hast given us grace at this time with one accord to make our common supplications unto Thee; and dost promise that when two or three are gathered together in Thy name Thou wilt grant their requests: Fulfill now, O Lord, the desires and petitions of Thy servants, as may be most expedient for them; granting us in this world knowledge of Thy truth, and in the world to come life everlasting. *Amen.*

THE grace of the Lord Jesus Christ, and the love of God, and the communion of the Holy Spirit, be with you all. *Amen.*

A LITANY: THE HOLY SPIRIT

O CREATOR Spirit; Lord and Giver of life and light; Comforter, Sanctifier, and Guide of the souls of men:

Hear us and help us, we beseech Thee.

Spirit of wisdom, infinite, immortal, and unsearchable, proceeding from the Father and the Son, have compassion on our ignorance and lead us by Thy kindly light onward into truth:

Hear us and help us, we beseech Thee.

Spirit of love and perfect service, given beyond measure unto Jesus Christ our Saviour, manifested in His sinless life, His heavenly teaching, and His redeeming death, and glorified in His resurrection, we open our hearts to receive Thy grace:

Hear us and help us, we beseech Thee.

Thou whom the Father is more ready to give than earthly parents are to give good gifts unto their children; Thou whom Christ hath promised to send unto His disciples, come to us, abide in us, and sanctify our souls by truth and love:

Hear us and help us, we beseech Thee.

By the inspiration Thou hast given to Thy holy prophets in all ages; by the guidance Thou hast granted to those in doubt and trouble; by the courage Thou hast restored to the fearful and the strength Thou hast imparted to the weak; by the comfort Thou hast bestowed upon the sorrowful and the hope Thou hast kindled in sad hearts, have mercy on us and supply all our needs:

Hear us and help us, O Holy Spirit.

From pride and vainglory; from self-will and obstinacy; from shallow thoughts and hasty judgments; from impure desires and unkind purposes; from envy, malice, and all uncharitableness; from every wicked way and evil wish, deliver and save us by Thine indwelling grace:

Hear us and help us, O Holy Spirit.

In the growth of wisdom and the increase of love; in loyalty to the truth as Thou givest us to see it, and in deepening good will toward our fellow men; in honesty and honor, in cheerful labor and true gladness of heart, make Thy presence felt within us, and enable us to grow into the likeness of Christ our Lord:

Hear us and help us, O Holy Spirit.

By the promise of the Almighty to pour out His Spirit upon all flesh, we beseech Thee that Thou wouldst visit our nation with divine favor. Uphold, defend, and guide the President and all in authority; unite our hearts in the love of country; and make the land which Thou hast blessed a blessing to the world. Promote among all nations the brotherhood of man; cause war to cease and violence to vanish; bring the whole human family together in the bond of amity, and grant us all a place in that kingdom which is righteousness and peace and joy in the Holy Spirit.

O Thou who art one with the Father and the Son:
Hear us and help us and dwell in us for ever.

THE grace of the Lord Jesus Christ, and the love of God, and the communion of the Holy Spirit, be with you all. *Amen.*

A LITANY: THE CHURCH

O GOD the Father, from whom the whole
family in heaven and earth is named;
O God the Son, given to be head over the
Church;
O God the Holy Spirit, the bond of peace;
O Holy Trinity, eternal love:

Have mercy upon us.

By Thy ministry of healing and forgiveness; by
Thy seeking and saving the lost; by Thy words
of eternal life:

Help us, good Lord.

By the calling and training of the twelve
apostles; by Thy promise to build Thy Church;
by Thy institution of the holy sacraments:

Help us, good Lord.

By the love shown in Thy Crucifixion; by the
power of Thy Resurrection; by the glory of Thy
Ascension; and by the indwelling of Thy Holy
Spirit:

Help us, good Lord.

That it may please Thee to strengthen and
enlarge Thy holy Church in every land, and to
unite all those who profess and call themselves
Christians in faith and hope and charity:

We beseech Thee, good Lord.

That Thy Church may strive, not for its own

safety, but for the world's salvation, seeking only Thy kingdom and Thy righteousness:

We beseech Thee, good Lord.

That Thy Church may proclaim the Gospel throughout the whole earth and make disciples of all nations:

We beseech Thee, good Lord.

That Thou wilt grant to all ministers of Thy Word and sacraments the spirit of wisdom, power, and love, and call many more to the work of Thy ministry:

We beseech Thee, good Lord.

That Thou wilt give to all Thy people grace to understand and to believe Thy Word, and to show forth their faith in their lives:

We beseech Thee, good Lord.

That we may reverently and rightly use Thy sacraments and be strengthened in body and soul by Thy heavenly grace:

We beseech Thee, good Lord.

That Thou wilt remove from us all hatred, prejudice, and narrowness of thought, that we may receive and rejoice in all that Thou revealest:

We beseech Thee, good Lord.

That Thou wilt guide us in all perplexities of belief and conduct, that we may hold fast that which is true, and faithfully confess Thee before men:

We beseech Thee, good Lord.

That, regardless of the praise or contempt of the world, Thy Church may worship and adore Thee in spirit and in truth:

We beseech Thee, good Lord.

AS WE pray for the Church Universal, we pray for God's blessing on the Church in this place.

Here may the faithful find salvation, and the careless be awakened.

Here may the doubting find faith, and the anxious be encouraged.

Here may the tempted find help, and the sorrowful comfort.

Here may the weary find rest, and the strong be renewed.

Here may the aged find consolation, and the young be inspired. *Amen.*

NOW unto Him that is able to do exceeding abundantly above all that we ask or think, according to the power that worketh in us; unto Him be glory in the Church by Christ Jesus, throughout all ages, world without end. *Amen.*

A LITANY: OUR COUNTRY

O GOD the Father, who governest the nations upon earth:

Be merciful unto us.

Remember not, O Lord, the offenses of Thy people, our manifold transgressions and our national sins; deal not with us after our sins, neither reward us according to our wickedness:

Spare us, Father of mercies.

From blindness of heart, from love of ease, from contentment with the second best, from failure to do the good that was in the heart of our fathers and for which they prepared the way:

Save Thy people, Lord.

From presumptuous sins, from pride of possession, from vainglorious boastings, from national hypocrisies:

Save Thy people, Lord.

From the covetousness which is idolatry, from hard bargaining and ruthless competition, and from all the service of mammon and the worship of wealth:

Save Thy people, Lord.

From class warfare and class hatred, from racial antagonisms, from the spirit of party, from the seeking of sectional advantage and forgetfulness of the general good:

Save Thy people, Lord.

From failure to take account of the needs of other nations, from living unto ourselves alone, and from putting our trust in our own strength when our trust should be in Thee:

Save Thy people, Lord.

That we may hallow Thy name, that we may seek first Thy kingdom and Thy righteousness; and that, as Thou givest us to know Thy will, so we may do it:

We beseech Thee to hear us, good Lord.

That we may be mindful of the poor and the oppressed among us; that we may bring up the children of the nation in Thy faith and fear; that we may welcome those who in good faith have come from other lands to seek our fellowship, and receive them in Thy name:

We beseech Thee to hear us, good Lord.

That we make choice of just legislators and faithful counselors, who with a godly spirit may enact always things just, and things wise, and things merciful:

We beseech Thee to hear us, good Lord.

That we may co-operate earnestly and effectively with other nations, and with them labor for the defense and maintenance of public right, for the abolition of war and the establishment of international law, and for whatever else may pertain to the general good:

We beseech Thee to hear us, good Lord.

ALMIGHTY God, who turnest the heart of the fathers to their children, and the heart of the children to their fathers: Receive, we pray Thee, our unfeigned thanks for the good land which Thou hast given us. Forgive our transgressions; cleanse us from things that defile our national life, and grant that this people, which Thou hast abundantly blessed, may keep Thy commandments, walk in Thy ways, and fear Thee. Be gracious to our times, that by Thy bounty both national quietness and Christian devotion may be duly maintained. Let Thy work appear unto Thy servants, and Thy glory unto their children; and let the beauty of the Lord our God be upon us, and establish Thou the work of our hands upon us; yea, the work of our hands, establish Thou it; through Jesus Christ our Lord. *Amen.*

THE grace of the Lord Jesus Christ, and the love of God, and the communion of the Holy Spirit, be with you all. *Amen.*

A LITANY: LABOR

O THOU all-wise Creator of the world, who hast made man in Thine image to have dominion over Thine other creatures, and hast given him the duty to subdue the earth, that it may yield the riches Thou hast hidden therein to supply his need: We thank Thee for the blessing of labor whereby we are made workers together with Thee:

Bless and guide us, we beseech Thee.

By human willfullness and waywardness, ignorance and greed, idleness and oppression, a curse has touched Thy blessing, and the joy of man in work has departed from many. For our part in this sin we beg Thy forgiveness, our Heavenly Father:

Bless and guide us, we beseech Thee.

From pride and avarice and tyranny over the bodies or spirits of men; from the hard heart which disregards the need of a fellow servant, and from the dishonest temper which withholds the fullness of a promised service; from laziness, and self-indulgence, and inhumanity:

O Lord, deliver us.

From injustice and oppression, from conspiracy and violence, from the choice of force instead of reason, from all denial of our common humanity, and our fellowship in Christ; from all contempt of those who toil and suffer; and from all shame of our own work:

O Lord, deliver us.

For all who till the earth and gather the harvest;
For all who go down to the sea and do business
in great waters;
For all who work in offices and in shops;
For all who labor in factories and at furnaces;
For those who toil in the mines:

Hear us, we beseech Thee.

For all who employ and direct labor;
For all who carry responsibility;
For all who enrich life through art and science
and learning;
For pastors and teachers, physicians and sur-
geons;
For nurses and all who minister to the sick;
For women in business and in homes;
For statesmen and all social workers:

Hear us, we beseech Thee.

For all who have lost the reward of their labor;
For those who cannot find work;
For those who will not work;
For the homeless, and the friendless:

Hear us, we beseech Thee.

O LORD, our Heavenly Father, by whose providence the duties of men are varied and ordered: Grant to us all the spirit to labor heartily to
do our work in our several stations, in serving one
Master and looking for one reward. Teach us
to put to good account whatever talents Thou
hast given us, and enable us to redeem our time
by patience and zeal; through Jesus Christ our
Lord. *Amen.*

THE COMMANDMENTS

This Order may be used as a separate service, or as an introduction to the Order of Holy Communion, or with Morning or Evening Worship.

Minister:

Blessed are the undefiled in the way, who walk in the law of the Lord.

People:

Order my steps in Thy Word: and let not any iniquity have dominion over me.

Minister:

Blessed are they that keep His testimonies, and that seek Him with the whole heart.

People:

With my whole heart have I sought Thee: O let me not wander from Thy commandments.

Then the Minister shall say:

Let us pray.

ALMIGHTY God, unto whom all hearts are open, all desires known, and from whom no secrets are hid: Cleanse the thoughts of our hearts by the inspiration of Thy Holy Spirit, that we may perfectly love Thee, and worthily magnify Thy holy name; through Christ our Lord. *Amen.*

Then the Minister, omitting, if he desires, the words in brackets, shall say:

GOD spake all these words, saying,
I am the Lord thy God. Thou shalt have no other gods before Me.

> *Lord, have mercy upon us, and incline our hearts to keep this law.*

Thou shalt not make unto thee any graven image, or any likeness of any thing that is in heaven above, or that is in the earth beneath, or that is in the water under the earth; thou shalt not bow down thyself to them, nor serve them: [for I, the Lord thy God, am a jealous God, visiting the iniquity of the fathers upon the children unto the third and fourth generation of them that hate Me; and showing mercy unto thousands of them that love Me, and keep My commandments.]

> *Lord, have mercy upon us, and incline our hearts to keep this law.*

Thou shalt not take the name of the Lord thy God in vain: for the Lord will not hold him guiltless that taketh His name in vain.

> *Lord, have mercy upon us, and incline our hearts to keep this law.*

Remember the Sabbath Day, to keep it holy. [Six days shalt thou labor, and do all thy work: but the seventh day is the Sabbath of the Lord thy God; in it thou shalt not do any work, thou, nor thy son, nor thy daughter, thy manservant, nor thy maidservant, nor thy cattle, nor thy stranger that is within thy gates: for in six days the Lord made heaven and earth, the sea, and all that in them is, and rested the seventh day; wherefore the Lord blessed the Sabbath Day, and hallowed it.]

> *Lord, have mercy upon us, and incline our hearts to keep this law.*

Honor thy father and thy mother: [that thy days may be long upon the land which the Lord thy God giveth thee.]

> *Lord, have mercy upon us, and incline our hearts to keep this law.*

Thou shalt not kill.

> *Lord, have mercy upon us, and incline our hearts to keep this law.*

Thou shalt not commit adultery.

> *Lord, have mercy upon us, and incline our hearts to keep this law.*

Thou shalt not steal.

> *Lord, have mercy upon us, and incline our hearts to keep this law.*

Thou shalt not bear false witness against thy neighbor.

> *Lord, have mercy upon us, and incline our hearts to keep this law.*

Thou shalt not covet thy neighbor's house, thou shalt not covet thy neighbor's wife, nor his man-servant, nor his maidservant, nor his ox, nor his ass, nor any thing that is thy neighbor's.

> *Lord, have mercy upon us, and write all these Thy laws in our hearts, we beseech Thee.*

Then the Minister shall say:

HEAR also what our Lord Jesus Christ saith:
Thou shalt love the Lord thy God with all
thy heart, and with all thy soul, and with all thy
mind. This is the first and greatest commandment.
And the second is like unto it; Thou shalt love
thy neighbor as thyself.   On these two commandments hang all the Law and the Prophets.

Then the Minister shall say:

Let us pray.

Confession   Minister and People

WE CONFESS to Thee, Almighty God,
Father, Son, and Holy Spirit; That we have
grievously sinned in thought, word, and deed.
Make us truly contrite.   Fill us with holy fear;
And give us grace to amend our lives according
to Thy Word; For the glory of Thy holy name;
Through Jesus Christ our Lord.   Amen.

Assurance of Pardon   Minister

ALMIGHTY God, our Heavenly Father, who of
His great mercy hath promised forgiveness of
sins to all them that with hearty repentance and
true faith turn to Him, have mercy upon you;
pardon and deliver you from all your sins; confirm and strengthen you in all goodness; and bring
you to everlasting life; through Jesus Christ our
Lord.   *Amen.*

Ascription

NOW unto the God of all grace, who hath called
us unto His eternal glory by Christ Jesus,
be glory and dominion for ever and ever.   *Amen.*

III. THE SACRAMENTS AND ORDINANCES OF THE CHURCH

ORDER FOR
THE ADMINISTRATION OF
THE SACRAMENT OF BAPTISM
TO INFANTS

While the Parents are bringing the Children to be baptized a Baptismal Hymn may be sung; or the following Sentences may be read by the Minister:

THE mercy of the Lord is from everlasting to everlasting upon them that fear Him, and His righteousness unto children's children;

To such as keep His covenant, and to those that remember His commandments to do them.

He shall feed His flock like a shepherd: He shall gather the lambs with His arm, and carry them in His bosom.

For the promise is unto you, and to your children, and to all that are afar off, even as many as the Lord our God shall call.

Glory be to the Father, and to the Son, and to the Holy Ghost; as it was in the beginning, is now, and ever shall be, world without end. *Amen.*

The Minister shall say:

DEARLY beloved, the Sacrament of Baptism is of divine ordinance. God our Father, who has redeemed us by the sacrifice of Christ, is also the God and Father of our children. They belong, with us who believe, to the membership of the Church through the covenant made in Christ, and confirmed to us by God in this Sacrament, which is a sign and seal of our cleansing, of our engrafting into Christ, and of our welcome in the house-

hold of God. Our Lord Jesus said, Suffer the
little children to come unto Me, and forbid them
not, for of such is the kingdom of God. Verily
I say unto you, Whosoever shall not receive the
kingdom of God as a little child, he shall not
enter therein. And He took them up in His
arms, and put His hands upon them and blessed
them. Saint Paul also declared that the children
of believers are to be numbered with the holy
people of God.

The Minister shall say:

In presenting your Child for baptism, do you
confess your faith in Jesus Christ as your Lord
and Saviour; and do you promise, in dependence
on the grace of God, to bring up your Child in
the nurture and admonition of the Lord?

Then the answer is given: I do.

Then the Minister shall say:

Let us pray.

MOST merciful and loving Father, we thank
Thee for the Church of Thy dear Son, the
ministry of Thy Word, and the sacraments of grace.
We praise Thee that Thou hast given us so gracious promises concerning our children, and that in
mercy Thou callest them to Thee, marking them
with this Sacrament as a singular token and pledge
of Thy love. Set apart this water from a common
to a sacred use, and grant that what we now do
on earth may be confirmed in heaven. As in
humble faith we present *this Child* to Thee, we
beseech Thee to receive *him*, to endue *him* with

Thy Holy Spirit, and to keep *him* ever as Thine own; through Jesus Christ our Lord. *Amen.*

All present reverently standing, the Minister shall say:

What is the Christian name of this Child?

Then the Minister, taking the Child in his arms, or leaving it in the arms of the Parent, pronouncing the Christian name of the Child, shall pour or sprinkle water upon the head of the Child, saying:

N., I BAPTIZE THEE IN THE NAME OF THE FATHER, AND OF THE SON, AND OF THE HOLY GHOST. *Amen.*

The blessing of God Almighty, Father, Son, and Holy Ghost, descend upon thee, and dwell in thine heart for ever. *Amen.*

Then the Minister shall say to the Congregation:

This Child is now received into Christ's Church: And you the people of this congregation in receiving *this Child* promise with God's help to be *his* sponsor to the end that *he* may confess Christ as *his* Lord and Saviour and come at last to His eternal kingdom. Jesus said, Whoso shall receive one such little child in My name receiveth Me.

Then the Minister shall say:

Let us pray.

ALMIGHTY and everlasting God, who of Thine infinite mercy and goodness hast promised that Thou wilt be not only our God, but also the God and Father of our children: We humbly beseech Thee for *this Child*, that Thy Spirit may be upon *him*, and dwell in *him* for ever. Take *him*, we entreat Thee, under Thy Fatherly care and protection; guide *him* and sanctify *him* both in body and in soul. Grant *him* to grow in wisdom as in stature, and in favor with God and man. Abundantly enrich *him* with Thy heavenly grace: bring *him* safely through the perils of childhood, deliver *him* from the temptations of youth, and lead *him* to witness a good confession, and to persevere therein to the end.

O God our Father, give unto Thy servants to whom Thou hast committed this blessed trust, the assurance of Thine unfailing providence and care. Guide them with Thy counsel as they teach and train their child; and help them to lead their household into an ever-increasing knowledge of Christ, and a more steadfast obedience to His will.

We commend to Thy Fatherly care the children and families of this congregation. Help us in our homes to honor Thee, and by love to serve one another.

And to Thy name be all blessing and glory, through Jesus Christ our Lord. *Amen.*

And now, as our Saviour Christ hath taught us, we humbly pray:

OUR Father, who art in heaven; Hallowed be Thy name. Thy kingdom come. Thy will be done; On earth as it is in heaven. Give us this day our daily bread. And forgive us our debts; As we forgive our debtors. And lead us not into temptation; But deliver us from evil; For Thine is the kingdom, and the power, and the glory, for ever. Amen.

Then the Minister shall say:

THE grace of the Lord Jesus Christ, and the love of God, and the communion of the Holy Spirit, be with you all. *Amen.*

ORDER FOR
THE ADMINISTRATION OF
THE SACRAMENT OF BAPTISM
TO ADULTS

The Person to be baptized shall stand before the Minister, who shall say:

HEAR the words of our Lord Jesus Christ: If any man will come after Me, let him deny himself, and take up his cross, and follow Me.

For whosoever will save his life shall lose it: and whosoever will lose his life for My sake shall find it.

If thou shalt confess with thy mouth the Lord Jesus, and shalt believe in thine heart that God hath raised Him from the dead, thou shalt be saved.

For with the heart man believeth unto righteousness; and with the mouth confession is made unto salvation.

Glory be to the Father, and to the Son, and to the Holy Ghost; as it was in the beginning, is now, and ever shall be, world without end. *Amen.*

DEARLY beloved, attend to the words of the institution of the holy Sacrament of Baptism:

All power is given unto Me in heaven and in earth. Go ye therefore, and teach all nations, baptizing them in the name of the Father, and of the Son, and of the Holy Ghost: teaching them to observe all things whatsoever I have commanded you: and, lo, I am with you alway, even unto the end of the world.

Saint Peter also, on the Day of Pentecost, called upon the people, saying:

Repent, and be baptized every one of you in the name of Jesus Christ for the remission of sins, and ye shall receive the gift of the Holy Ghost. For the promise is unto you, and to your children, and to all that are afar off, even as many as the Lord our God shall call.

The Minister shall then say to the Person to be baptized:

Doubt not, therefore, but earnestly believe, that truly repenting and coming unto Him by faith, He will number you among His people, and that this Baptism with water in His name shall be unto you the sign and seal of the washing away of your sins, your union with Christ, your regeneration by His Holy Spirit, and your engagement to be the Lord's.

DEARLY beloved, you are now faithfully, on your part, in the presence of God and of this congregation, to answer the following questions:

Question: Do you believe in God the Father Almighty, Maker of heaven and earth: and in Jesus Christ His only Son our Lord: and in the Holy Spirit, the Lord and Giver of life?

Answer: I do.

Question: Do you confess your need of the forgiveness of sins and with a humble and contrite heart put your whole trust in the mercy of God, which is in Christ Jesus our Lord?

Answer: I do.

Question: Do you promise to make diligent use of the means of grace, to continue in the peace and fellowship of the people of God, and with the aid of the Holy Spirit to be Christ's faithful disciple to your life's end?

Answer: I do.

Question: Do you desire to be baptized in this faith and to be received into membership in Christ's Church?

Answer: I do.

The Minister shall say:

Let us pray.

ALMIGHTY and everlasting God, whose blessed Son, Jesus Christ our Lord, hath ordained this holy Sacrament: Mercifully look upon us, we beseech Thee, who are met together in His name, and ratify in heaven that which, by His appointment, we do upon earth.

Graciously accept Thy *servant*, we pray Thee, that *he*, coming to Thee in Baptism, may receive remission of sins, and being born again of water and of the Holy Spirit, may die unto sin and live unto righteousness.

Set apart this water from a common to the sacred use to which it is appointed and grant that Thy *servant*, now to be baptized therewith, may receive the fullness of Thy grace, and ever remain in the number of Thy faithful people; through Jesus Christ our Lord. *Amen.*

Then, the Congregation reverently standing, the Person to be baptized kneeling, the Minister, pronouncing his Christian name, shall pour or sprinkle water upon his head, saying:

N., I BAPTIZE THEE IN THE NAME OF THE FATHER, AND OF THE SON, AND OF THE HOLY GHOST. *Amen.*

The blessing of God Almighty, Father, Son, and Holy Spirit, descend upon thee, and dwell in thine heart for ever. *Amen.*

Here each Person who has made his Confirmation Vows, as set forth in the Order for the Confirmation of Baptismal Vows and Admission to the Lord's Supper, together with each one who has received Adult Baptism, shall stand before the Holy Table, and the Minister shall say:

Let us pray.

ALMIGHTY and eternal God, strengthen *this* Thy *servant*, we beseech Thee, with the Holy Spirit the Comforter, and daily increase in *him* Thy manifold gifts of grace: the spirit of wisdom and understanding, the spirit of counsel and might, the spirit of knowledge and of the fear of the Lord; and keep *him* in Thy mercy unto life eternal; through Jesus Christ our Lord.
Amen.

Then the Minister, laying his hand upon the head of each kneeling before him, shall say:

Defend, O Lord, *this* Thy *servant* with Thy heavenly grace; that *he* may continue Thine for ever; and daily increase in Thy Holy Spirit more and more, until *he* come unto Thine everlasting kingdom.

The God of all grace, who hath called you to

His eternal glory, confirm you to the end, that you may be blameless in the day of our Lord Jesus Christ. *Amen.*

Then, all standing, the Minister shall say:

Forasmuch as you have made confession of your faith, I do now, in the name of the Lord Jesus Christ, the great Head of the Church, admit you to the Sacrament of the Lord's Supper and to the fellowship of Christ's Church.

Then the Minister shall give this Charge:

And now as *a member* of Christ's Church, go forth into the world in peace; be of good courage; hold fast that which is good; render to no man evil for evil; strengthen the fainthearted; support the weak; heal the afflicted; honor all men; love and serve the Lord, rejoicing in the power of the Spirit.

AND the blessing of God Almighty, the Father, the Son, and the Holy Spirit, be upon you and remain with you for ever. *Amen.*

ORDER FOR THE CONFIRMATION
OF BAPTISMAL VOWS
AND ADMISSION TO THE
LORD'S SUPPER

The Minister shall say:

DEARLY beloved, we are now to receive to the confirmation of their baptismal vows, and to the Lord's Supper, these Persons about to be named. They have received instruction in the teaching of the Church, and have been examined and admitted to full communion with the Church by the Session, and are now ready to confess publicly the faith into which they were baptized.

The Persons whose names are now read shall stand before the Minister, and he shall say:

BELOVED in the Lord, in your Baptism you received the sign and seal of your union with Christ, and were solemnly engaged to be the Lord's. God in His goodness has brought you to years of responsibility, and you now desire to acknowledge before God and His Church the covenant then made on your behalf, to profess your faith in the Lord Jesus, to consecrate yourselves to Him, and thereby to bind yourselves anew to His service.

Our Lord Jesus Christ hath said, Whosoever shall confess Me before men, him will I confess also before My Father which is in heaven.

Question: Do you confess your faith in God the Father Almighty, Maker of heaven and earth, and in Jesus Christ His only Son our Lord, and do you promise with the aid of the Holy Spirit to be Christ's faithful disciple to your life's end?

Answer: I do.

Question: Do you confirm the vows taken for you in Baptism and with a humble and contrite heart put your whole trust in the mercy of God, which is in Christ Jesus our Lord?

Answer: I do.

Question: Do you promise to make diligent use of the means of grace, to share faithfully in the worship and service of the Church, to give of your substance as the Lord may prosper you, and to give your whole heart to the service of Christ and His kingdom throughout the world?

Answer: I do.

Here each Person who has made his Confirmation Vows, together with each one who has received Adult Baptism, shall stand before the Holy Table, and the Minister shall say:

Let us pray.

ALMIGHTY and eternal God, strengthen *this* Thy *servant*, we beseech Thee, with the Holy Spirit the Comforter, and daily increase in *him* Thy manifold gifts of grace: the spirit of wisdom and understanding, the spirit of counsel and might, the spirit of knowledge and of the

fear of the Lord; and keep *him* in Thy mercy
unto life eternal; through Jesus Christ our Lord.
Amen.

*Then the Congregation standing, the Minister, laying his
hand upon the head of each kneeling before him, shall say:*

Defend, O Lord, this Thy servant with Thy
heavenly grace; that *he* may continue Thine for
ever; and daily increase in Thy Holy Spirit more
and more, until *he* come unto Thine everlasting
kingdom.

The God of all grace, who hath called you to
His eternal glory, confirm you to the end, that
you may be blameless in the day of our Lord
Jesus Christ. *Amen.*

Then, all standing, the Minister shall say:

Forasmuch as you have made confession of your
faith, I do now, in the name of the Lord Jesus
Christ, the great Head of the Church, admit you
to the Sacrament of the Lord's Supper and to the
fellowship of Christ's Church.

Then the Minister shall give this Charge:

And now confirmed as *a member* of Christ's
Church, go forth into the world in peace; be of
good courage; hold fast that which is good; render to no man evil for evil; strengthen the fainthearted; support the weak; heal the afflicted; honor
all men; love and serve the Lord, rejoicing in
the power of the Spirit.

AND the blessing of God Almighty, the Father,
the Son, and the Holy Spirit, be upon you
and remain with you for ever. *Amen.*

ORDER FOR
THE RECEPTION OF COMMUNICANTS
FROM OTHER CHURCHES
OR
ON REAFFIRMATION OF FAITH
OR
AS AFFILIATED MEMBERS

The Minister shall say:

THE following *Persons* have been received by the Session into the membership of this Church on *letters* of dismission and commendation from *other Churches:*

The following *Persons,* who before *have* held membership in *other Churches, have* been received on reaffirmation of *their* faith in Christ:

These Persons named will now present *themselves* for public reception into the fellowship of this Church.

These Persons having presented themselves, the Minister shall say:

Dearly beloved, having before made public confession of your faith in Christ, and having voluntarily transferred to this Church your covenant relation of membership, you now promise to wait diligently upon its ordinances, to study its peace and prosperity, and to walk worthy of the vocation wherewith we are called.

The following *Persons*, while retaining *their* membership in *other Churches*, *are* welcomed as affiliated *members:*

Then the members of the Church shall rise, and the Minister shall say:

IN THE name of the Lord Jesus, we, the officers and members of this Church, bid you welcome to its work and worship, and pledge to you our Christian fellowship. We pray that all of us, thus united in faith and brotherhood, may grow into the likeness of Christ, being faithful in every good work and increasing in the knowledge of God; through Jesus Christ our Lord. *Amen.*

THE Lord bless you, and keep you: the Lord make His face to shine upon you, and be gracious unto you: the Lord lift up His countenance upon you, and give you peace; through Jesus Christ our Lord. *Amen.*

ORDER FOR
THE SERVICE OF PREPARATION
FOR HOLY COMMUNION

Let the Minister say:

Let us worship God.

Then may be sung a Hymn, all the People standing, and then the Minister may read the Call to Worship. Or the service may begin with the Call to Worship.

Call to Worship

WHEREWITH shall I come before the Lord, and bow myself before the high God? He hath showed thee, O man, what is good; and what doth the Lord require of thee, but to do justly, and to love mercy, and to walk humbly with thy God?

The sacrifices of God are a broken spirit: a broken and a contrite heart, O God, Thou wilt not despise.

Let us pray.

ALMIGHTY God, Thou holy One, who art of purer eyes than to behold iniquity: Look upon us in Thy mercy; visit us with such a vision of Thy glory that with humble and penitent hearts we may receive such good gifts as Thou art more ready to give than we to desire; through Jesus Christ our Lord. *Amen.*

Confession

Let us humbly confess our sins unto Almighty God.

136

MOST holy and merciful Father; We acknowledge and confess before Thee; Our sinful nature prone to evil and slothful in good; And all our shortcomings and offenses. Thou alone knowest how often we have sinned; In wandering from Thy ways; In wasting Thy gifts; In forgetting Thy love. We confess our sins against our brethren; The blindness and hardness of our hearts toward those in suffering and want; Our indifference toward justice and mercy; Our arrogance and all the evil ways of our selfishness and pride.

Have mercy upon us, O God, according to Thy loving-kindness; According to the multitude of Thy tender mercies blot out our transgressions. Create in us a clean heart, O God; And renew a right spirit within us. Cast us not away from Thy presence and take not Thy Holy Spirit from us. Restore unto us the joy of Thy salvation; And uphold us with Thy free Spirit; Through Jesus Christ our Lord. Amen.

Assurance of Pardon   *Minister*

ALMIGHTY God, whose nature is to forgive sinners and ever to have compassion on them that turn to Him, grant you perfect remission of all your sins and full assurance of pardon; strengthen and confirm you in all good works; and bring you to everlasting life; through Jesus Christ our Lord. *Amen.*

Then may be read responsively a Penitential Psalm, ending with the Gloria.

Lesson from the Old Testament

Hymn

Lesson from the New Testament

Sermon Preparatory to Holy Communion

Hymn

The Beatitudes

Minister:

Let us examine ourselves in the light of the teaching of our Lord Christ, as given in the Beatitudes.

People:

Blessed are the poor in spirit: for theirs is the kingdom of heaven.

A period of silence.

Minister:

O Lord Jesus Christ, who for our sakes didst become poor that we might be made rich: Increase in us the desire for Thine inestimable gifts of the Spirit. Prevent us from putting our trust in riches. Deliver us from pride in the same. Grant us grace so to use Thy gifts that we may be rich in good works, ready to distribute, and eager to communicate. By the abundant riches of Thy grace, bring us to Thy heavenly kingdom; through Jesus Christ our Lord. *Amen.*

People:

Blessed are they that mourn: for they shall be comforted.

A period of silence.

Minister:

Give us, O Lord, sorrow for our sins, and for
the sins of the whole world; that through our
sorrow there may be joy in the presence of the
angels of God.   Give us, O Lord, the spirit of
Thy Son, that, being well and glad and strong,
we may never lack sympathy for those who suffer
and are sad.   Give us, O Lord, the power when
we suffer pain to look into Thy face, and learn
from Thee to bear it patiently as seeing Him who
is invisible; through Jesus Christ our Lord. *Amen.*

People:

Blessed are the meek: for they shall inherit the
earth.

A period of silence.

Minister:

Teach us, O Lord, not to think of ourselves
more highly than we ought to think.   Help us to
overcome the impulse to put ourselves forward at
the expense of others.   Grant that we may never
boast of ourselves, as though we alone had labored
without Thine aid or the help of others.   Make
us, O Lord, eager to learn to be Thy servants, that
we may work the works of Thy blessed Son; may
we so delight to do Thy will that we may find in
Thy service perfect freedom and fullness of joy;
through Thy Son our Saviour Jesus Christ. *Amen.*

People:

Blessed are they which do hunger and thirst after righteousness: for they shall be filled.

A period of silence.

Minister:

Give us, O Lord, a reverence for the truth, the desire both to think and to speak truly. Save us from all fear of the truth. Grant us all an appreciation of beauty and whatsoever things are lovely. Increase our reverence for them; make us to see in them a part of Thy revelation of Thyself, that beauty becometh Thee no less than truth and righteousness.

Quicken in us, O Lord, the desire to see justice established among men. Do Thou hasten that day, we beseech Thee, when love shall prevail in our social and industrial life, when none shall enrich himself at others' expense, nor live indifferent to others' needs and rights; through Him who gave Himself for us, even Jesus Christ our Lord. *Amen.*

People:

Blessed are the merciful: for they shall obtain mercy.

A period of silence.

Minister:

Help us, O Lord, to look for the good in others, and not the evil. Enable us always to understand before we condemn. Make us quick to forgive, knowing how greatly we stand in need of

forgiveness. Help us, O Lord, to remember how
often men do wrong through want of thought,
rather than from lack of love; and how cunning
are the snares that trip our feet. Make us worthy
to pray that we may be forgiven in the measure
with which we forgive, and finally that we may
obtain Thy mercy; through our Mediator and
Advocate, Jesus Christ. *Amen.*

People:

Blessed are the pure in heart: for they shall
see God.

A period of silence.

Minister:

O most holy God, teach us to reverence our
bodies as temples of the Holy Spirit; and grant
that we may never be satisfied with any standard
of personal purity lower than Thine own. Grant,
O Lord, that we may think clean, generous,
humble thoughts and harbor none that stains the
mind or dims our vision of Thee. So cleanse our
hearts that we may ever behold Thee face to face;
through Jesus Christ our Lord. *Amen.*

People:

Blessed are the peacemakers: for they shall be
called the children of God.

A period of silence.

Minister:

Keep our hearts, O Lord, ever open unto Thee, that being constantly renewed by Thy grace, amid all the perils and dangers, the restlessness and complexity of our day, we may at all times possess the peace of those whose minds are stayed on Thee. Help us to walk as children of the light. Keep us, O Lord, from straining and embittering our earthly relationships; and grant us, we beseech Thee, a courteous and forbearing spirit, that so we may be makers of peace; through Him who so loved us, even Jesus Christ our Lord. *Amen.*

Hymn

Prayer of Adoration

Let us pray.

O MERCIFUL Jesus, who when Thou tookest upon Thee to deliver man didst humble Thyself to be born of a virgin: Vouchsafe evermore to dwell in the heart of us Thy servants; inspire us with Thy purity; strengthen us with Thy might; make us perfect in Thy ways; guide us in Thy truth; and unite us to Thyself and to Thy whole Church by Thy holy mysteries; that we may conquer every adverse power, and be wholly devoted to Thy service and conformed to Thy will; to the glory of God the Father.

Most gracious Father, who callest us to the Holy Table of our Saviour, to show His death and to receive His gift of life: Enable us to come with earnest faith and kindled devotion. Help us to make the memorial of our Saviour's sacrifice with adoration and praise. Open our eyes to behold the vision of His love, and pour into our souls the fullness of His grace. And grant that, yielding ourselves to Thee, we may henceforth live as those who are not their own, but are bought with a price; through Jesus Christ our Lord, to whom with Thee and the Holy Spirit be all honor and glory, world without end. *Amen.*

Benediction

THE grace of the Lord Jesus Christ, and the love of God, and the communion of the Holy Spirit, be with you all. *Amen.*

AN ALTERNATIVE ORDER
FOR THE SERVICE OF PREPARATION
FOR HOLY COMMUNION

Let the Minister say:

Let us worship God.

Then may be sung a Hymn, all the People standing, and then the Minister may read the Call to Worship. Or the service may begin with the Call to Worship.

Call to Worship

OUR help is in the name of the Lord, who made heaven and earth.

O come, let us worship and bow down: let us kneel before the Lord our Maker. For He is our God; and we are the people of His pasture, and the sheep of His hand.

The sacrifices of God are a broken spirit: a broken and a contrite heart, O God, Thou wilt not despise.

Then, the People kneeling or bowing down, the Minister shall say:

Let us pray.

ALMIGHTY God, our Heavenly Father, whose love is unchanging and who dost ever provide us with manifold means of grace: Regard us with Thy favor, as in the fellowship of faith we seek to worship Thee; through Jesus Christ our Lord.
Amen.

Confession

O GOD, who art of purer eyes than to behold
iniquity; But who despisest not the sorrow
of the contrite; Have mercy upon us, we beseech
Thee, according to Thy loving-kindness. Thou
alone knowest how often we have sinned; In
wandering from Thy ways; In wasting Thy gifts;
In forgetting Thy love. O Thou searcher of
hearts, help us to acknowledge with deep contri-
tion the multitude of our transgressions; And
especially those which are the present burden of
our conscience . . . ; In Thy mercy, Thou bringest these things to our remembrance; And dost
not suffer us to continue in them without reproof.
Cleanse us, we beseech Thee, from all iniquity;
And let Thy mercy bring us healing; Through
Jesus Christ our Lord. Amen.

Assurance of Pardon   *Minister*

ALMIGHTY God, who doth freely pardon all
who repent and turn to Him, now fulfill in
every contrite heart the promise of redeeming
grace; remitting all our sins, and cleansing us from
an evil conscience; through the perfect sacrifice of
Christ Jesus our Lord. *Amen.*

*Let the Minister read from the Gospels the following
Lessons from the Life and Passion of our Lord, and let
appropriate verse or verses of Hymns be sung after each
reading:*

The Last Supper

NOW when the even was come, He sat down
with the twelve. And as they did eat, He
said, Verily I say unto you, that one of you shall

betray Me. And they were exceeding sorrowful, and began every one of them to say unto Him, Lord, is it I? And He answered and said, He that dippeth his hand with Me in the dish, the same shall betray Me. The Son of man goeth as it is written of Him: but woe unto that man by whom the Son of man is betrayed! it had been good for that man if he had not been born. Then Judas, which betrayed Him, answered and said, Master, is it I? He said unto him, Thou hast said.

And as they were eating, Jesus took bread, and blessed it, and brake it, and gave it to the disciples, and said, Take, eat; this is My body. And He took the cup, and gave thanks, and gave it to them, saying, Drink ye all of it; for this is My blood of the new testament, which is shed for many for the remission of sins. But I say unto you, I will not drink henceforth of this fruit of the vine, until that day when I drink it new with you in My Father's kingdom.

—Matthew 26 : 20–29.

Hymn

Gethsemane

THEN cometh Jesus with them unto a place called Gethsemane, and saith unto the disciples, Sit ye here, while I go and pray yonder. And He took with Him Peter and the two sons of Zebedee, and began to be sorrowful and very heavy. Then saith He unto them, My soul is exceeding sorrowful, even unto death: tarry ye here, and watch with Me. And He went a little farther, and fell on His face, and prayed, saying,

O My Father, if it be possible, let this cup pass from Me: nevertheless not as I will, but as Thou wilt. And He cometh unto the disciples, and findeth them asleep, and saith unto Peter, What, could ye not watch with Me one hour? Watch and pray, that ye enter not into temptation: the spirit indeed is willing, but the flesh is weak. He went away again the second time, and prayed, saying, O My Father, if this cup may not pass away from Me, except I drink it, Thy will be done. And He came and found them asleep again: for their eyes were heavy. And He left them, and went away again, and prayed the third time, saying the same words. Then cometh He to His disciples, and saith unto them, Sleep on now, and take your rest: behold, the hour is at hand, and the Son of man is betrayed into the hands of sinners.

—*Matthew* 26 : 36–45.

Hymn

The Trial Before Caiaphas

AND they that had laid hold on Jesus led Him away to Caiaphas the high priest, where the scribes and the elders were assembled. But Peter followed Him afar off unto the high priest's palace, and went in, and sat with the servants, to see the end. Now the chief priests, and elders, and all the council, sought false witness against Jesus, to put Him to death; but found none: yea, though many false witnesses came, yet found they none. At the last came two false witnesses, and said, This fellow said, I am able to destroy the temple of God, and to build it in three days. And the

high priest arose, and said unto Him, Answerest
Thou nothing? what is it which these witness
against Thee? But Jesus held His peace. And
the high priest answered and said unto Him, I
adjure Thee by the living God, that Thou tell us
whether Thou be the Christ, the Son of God.
Jesus saith unto him, Thou hast said: nevertheless
I say unto you, Hereafter shall ye see the Son
of man sitting on the right hand of power, and
coming in the clouds of heaven. Then the high
priest rent his clothes, saying, He hath spoken
blasphemy; what further need have we of witnesses? behold, now ye have heard His blasphemy.
What think ye? They answered and said, He is
guilty of death.

—Matthew 26 : 57–66.

Hymn

The Trial Before Pilate

AND straightway in the morning the chief priests
held a consultation with the elders and scribes
and the whole council, and bound Jesus, and
carried Him away, and delivered Him to Pilate.
And Pilate asked Him, Art Thou the King of the
Jews? And He answering said unto him, Thou
sayest it. And the chief priests accused Him of
many things: but He answered nothing. And
Pilate asked Him again, saying, Answerest Thou
nothing? behold how many things they witness
against Thee. But Jesus yet answered nothing;
so that Pilate marveled.

Now at that feast he released unto them one
prisoner, whomsoever they desired. And there
was one named Barabbas, which lay bound with

them that had made insurrection with him, who had committed murder in the insurrection. And the multitude crying aloud began to desire him to do as he had ever done unto them. But Pilate answered them, saying, Will ye that I release unto you the King of the Jews? For he knew that the chief priests had delivered Him for envy. But the chief priests moved the people, that he should rather release Barabbas unto them. And Pilate answered and said again unto them, What will ye then that I shall do unto Him whom ye call the King of the Jews? And they cried out again, Crucify Him. Then Pilate said unto them, Why, what evil hath He done? And they cried out the more exceedingly, Crucify Him. And so Pilate, willing to content the people, released Barabbas unto them, and delivered Jesus, when he had scourged Him, to be crucified.

—Mark 15 : 1–15.

Hymn

The Crucifixion

AND when they were come unto a place called Golgotha, that is to say, a place of a skull, they gave Him vinegar to drink mingled with gall: and when He had tasted thereof, He would not drink. And they crucified Him, and parted His garments, casting lots: that it might be fulfilled which was spoken by the prophet, They parted My garments among them, and upon My vesture did they cast lots. And sitting down they watched Him there; and set up over His head His accusation written, THIS IS JESUS THE KING OF THE JEWS. Then were there two thieves crucified with Him, one on the right hand, and another on the left. And they that passed by reviled Him, wagging their heads, and saying, Thou that destroyest the temple, and buildest it in three days, save Thyself. If Thou be the Son of God, come down from the cross. Likewise also the chief priests mocking Him, with the scribes and elders, said, He saved others; Himself He cannot save. If He be the King of Israel, let Him now come down from the cross, and we will believe Him. He trusted in God; let Him deliver Him now, if He will have Him: for He said, I am the Son of God. The thieves also, which were crucified with Him, cast the same in His teeth.

Now from the sixth hour there was darkness over all the land unto the ninth hour. And about the ninth hour Jesus cried with a loud voice, saying, Eli, Eli, lama sabachthani? that is to say, My God, My God, why hast Thou forsaken Me? Some of them that stood there, when they heard that, said, This man calleth for Elias. And straightway one of them ran, and took a sponge, and filled it with vinegar, and put it on a reed, and gave Him to drink. The rest said, Let be, let us see whether Elias will come to save Him. Jesus, when He had cried again with a loud voice, yielded up the ghost.

—*Matthew* 27 : 33–50.

Hymn

The Risen Christ

THEN the same day at evening, being the first day of the week, when the doors were shut where the disciples were assembled for fear of the

Jews, came Jesus and stood in the midst, and saith unto them, Peace be unto you. And when He had so said, He showed unto them His hands and His side. Then were the disciples glad, when they saw the Lord. Then said Jesus to them again, Peace be unto you: as My Father hath sent Me, even so send I you. And when He had said this, He breathed on them, and saith unto them, Receive ye the Holy Ghost: Whose soever sins ye remit, they are remitted unto them; and whose soever sins ye retain, they are retained.

—John 20:19–23.

Hymn

The Living Bread

VERILY, verily, I say unto you, He that believeth on Me hath everlasting life. I am that bread of life. Your fathers did eat manna in the wilderness, and are dead. This is the bread which cometh down from heaven, that a man may eat thereof, and not die. I am the living bread which came down from heaven: if any man eat of this bread, he shall live for ever: and the bread that I will give is My flesh, which I will give for the life of the world.

—John 6:47–51.

Hymn

Thanksgiving

WE GIVE Thee thanks, O Lord, for Thy great goodness to us and to all men, for Thy faithfulness which never faileth, for Thy mercies which are more than we can number, and for Thy

Fatherly hand ever upon us, in health and sickness, in joy and sorrow, in life and death.

Above all, with Thy whole Church throughout the world, we adore Thee for Thy love in the redemption of mankind by our Lord Jesus Christ.

We bless Thee for Thy gift of the Holy Spirit; for the Church filled with His presence; for our baptism and nurture in the faith; and for Thy blessed assurance of everlasting life. For these and all Thy gifts, glory be to Thee, Lord God Almighty. *Amen.*

Supplication

MOST gracious Father, who callest us to the Holy Table of our Saviour, to show His death and to receive His gift of life: Enable us to come with earnest faith and kindled devotion. Help us to make the memorial of our Saviour's sacrifice with adoration and praise. Open our eyes to behold the vision of His love, and pour into our souls the fullness of His grace. And grant that, yielding ourselves to Thee, we may henceforth live as those who are not their own, but are bought with a price; through Jesus Christ our Lord. *Amen.*

Intercession

ALMIGHTY God, whose tender mercies are over all Thy works: Hear us as we pray for all mankind.

Grant, we beseech Thee, that Thy Church, being gathered together in unity by Thy Holy Spirit, may manifest Thy power among all peoples, to the glory of Thy name.

And to all Thy people give Thy heavenly grace,

especially to this congregation, that with willing heart and due reverence they may hear and receive Thy holy Word. Prepare them to behold wondrous things out of Thy law and at Thy Holy Table to eat of that Living Bread which giveth life indeed. Increase in them faith, hope, and charity.

[O most merciful Father, strengthen and bless these Thy servants, who come for the first time to Thy Holy Table; daily increase in them Thy manifold gifts of grace: the spirit of wisdom and understanding, the spirit of counsel and might, the spirit of knowledge and true godliness; give unto them the mind of Christ and keep them ever in the communion and fellowship of the faithful, that in the end they may obtain everlasting life; through Jesus Christ our Lord.]

Father of mercies and great Physician of our souls and bodies, we remember before Thee the sick . . . , the suffering . . . , the lonely . . . , the bereaved . . . , and the dying . . . , especially those whom we remember in our hearts before Thee. . . . Visit them with Thy healing and consolation and grant them Thy peace; through Jesus Christ our Lord, to whom, with Thee and the Holy Spirit, be all honor and glory, world without end. *Amen.*

Sermon

Dedication

Let us pray.

To be said by Minister and People:

MOST gracious God, who art at this time calling us to prepare ourselves for coming to Thy Holy Table; Grant us grace from the heart freely to forgive one another. Accept us as we dedicate ourselves to Thee; And grant that; Feeding on Christ by faith; We may be strengthened by Thy Holy Spirit; And enabled to live in Thy fellowship; Now and evermore. Amen.

Hymn

Benediction

THE God of peace, that brought again from the dead our Lord Jesus, that great Shepherd of the sheep, through the blood of the everlasting covenant, make you perfect in every good work to do His will, working in you that which is well-pleasing in His sight; through Jesus Christ, to whom be glory for ever and ever. *Amen.*

ORDER FOR THE
CELEBRATION OF THE SACRAMENT
OF THE LORD'S SUPPER OR
HOLY COMMUNION

Let the Holy Table be covered with a cloth of fair white linen. Let there be at least one large Chalice for lifting, and one piece of Bread, sufficiently large for the Minister's taking and breaking in the sight of the People.

Let the Minister say:

Let us worship God.

Then may be sung a Hymn, all the People standing, and then the Minister may read the Call to Worship. Or the service may begin with the Call to Worship.

Call to Worship

WHAT shall we render unto the Lord for all His benefits toward us? We will take the cup of salvation, and call upon the name of the Lord.

Christ our Passover is sacrificed for us; therefore let us keep the feast.

O taste and see that the Lord is good. Blessed is the man who trusteth in Him.

Let us pray.

ALMIGHTY God, unto whom all hearts are open, all desires known, and from whom no secrets are hid: Cleanse the thoughts of our hearts by the inspiration of Thy Holy Spirit, that we may perfectly love Thee, and worthily magnify Thy holy name; through Christ our Lord. *Amen.*

Then may be said the Ten Commandments as given on pages 116, 117, or the Lord's Summary as given on page 118.

Then may be said or sung:

Lord have mercy.

Christ have mercy.

Lord have mercy.

Then shall the Minister say:

Ye who do truly and earnestly repent of your sins, and are in love and charity with your neighbors, and intend to lead a new life, following the commandments of God, and walking from henceforth in His holy ways: Draw near with faith, and take this Holy Sacrament to your comfort; and make your humble confession to Almighty God.

Confession   *Minister and People*

ALMIGHTY God, Father of our Lord Jesus Christ, Maker of all things, Judge of all men; We acknowledge and confess our manifold sins; Which we, from time to time, most grievously have committed; By thought, word, and deed; Against Thy divine majesty. We do earnestly repent; And are heartily sorry for these our misdoings; The remembrance of them is grievous unto us. Have mercy upon us; Have mercy upon us, most merciful Father; For Thy Son our Lord Jesus Christ's sake; Forgive us all that is past; And grant that we may ever hereafter serve and please Thee in newness of life; To the honor and glory of Thy name; Through Jesus Christ our Lord. Amen.

Assurance of Pardon

ALMIGHTY God, our Heavenly Father, who of His great mercy hath promised forgiveness of sins to all those who with hearty repentance and true faith turn unto Him, have mercy upon you; pardon and deliver you from all your sins; confirm and strengthen you in all goodness; and bring you to everlasting life; through Jesus Christ our Lord. *Amen.*

Gloria in Excelsis, the Te Deum, or other Canticle or Hymn of Praise, shall be said or sung.

The Epistle shall be read, and before reading, the Minister shall say:

Hear the Word of God, as it is written in . . . . , the . . . . chapter, at the . . . . verse.

After the Epistle shall be said:

The Lord bless to us the reading of His holy Word, and to His name be glory and praise.

The Gospel shall be read, and before the reading, the Minister shall say:

Hear the Word of God, as it is written in The Gospel According to Saint . . . . , chapter . . . . , beginning at the . . . . verse.

Before the reading of the Gospel shall be said or sung by all:

Glory be to Thee, O Lord.

After the reading of the Gospel shall be said or sung by all:

Praise be to Thee, O Christ.

Then shall be said the Apostles' Creed, or the Nicene Creed may be said or sung.

Let us pray.

ALMIGHTY and everliving God, who by Thy holy apostle hast taught us to make prayers and supplications, and to give thanks for all men: We humbly beseech Thee to inspire continually the Universal Church with the spirit of truth, unity, and concord; and grant that all those who confess Thy holy name may agree in the truth of Thy holy Word, and live in unity and godly love.

We beseech Thee also to lead all nations in the way of righteousness and peace and so to direct all rulers and governors that they may truly and impartially administer justice, to the punishment of wickedness and vice, and to the maintenance of Thy true religion and virtue.

Give grace, O Heavenly Father, to all ministers of the Gospel, that they may, both by their life and by their doctrine, set forth Thy true and living Word, and rightly and duly administer Thy sacraments.

And to all Thy people give Thy heavenly grace; and especially to this congregation here present, that with meek heart and due reverence they may hear and receive Thy holy Word, truly serving Thee in holiness and righteousness all the days of their life.

[We pray for all those who come to Thy Holy Table for the first time, beseeching Thee to perfect the good work Thou hast begun in them, and to keep them ever faithful to Thee.]

And we most humbly beseech Thee, O Lord, to comfort and relieve all those who are in trouble . . ., sorrow . . ., need . . ., sickness . . ., bereavement . . ., or any other adversity, especially those known to us, whom we remember in our hearts before Thee. . . . Visit them with Thy love and consolation, and grant them Thy peace.

And here we give Thee most high praise and hearty thanks for all Thy saints who have been chosen vessels of Thy grace and the lights of the world in their several generations; and we pray that, rejoicing in their fellowship and following their good examples, we may be partakers with them of Thy heavenly kingdom. Grant this, O Father, for Jesus Christ's sake, our only Mediator and Advocate. *Amen.*

Hymn

Before the Sermon may be said:

IN THE name of the Father, and of the Son, and of the Holy Spirit. *Amen.*

Sermon

After the Sermon this Ascription may be said:

UNTO Him that loved us, and washed us from our sins in His own blood, and hath made us kings and priests unto God and His Father; to Him be glory and dominion for ever and ever. *Amen.*

The Offerings shall be given, during which the Minister shall go to the Holy Table. (Here, if there be such, shall follow Adult Baptism, Confirmation, and Admission of Members.)

Then shall the Minister give the Invitation:

BELOVED in the Lord, hear what gracious words our Saviour Christ saith unto all who truly turn to Him:

Come unto Me, all ye that labor and are heavy-laden, and I will give you rest.

Take My yoke upon you, and learn of Me; for I am meek and lowly in heart: and ye shall find rest unto your souls.

I am the Bread of Life: he that cometh to Me shall never hunger; and he that believeth on Me shall never thirst. Him that cometh to Me I will in no wise cast out.

Blessed are they which do hunger and thirst after righteousness: for they shall be filled.

Hymn

The Elders having taken their places, and the Elements being reverently uncovered, the presiding Minister shall say:

THE GRACE OF THE LORD JESUS CHRIST BE WITH YOU ALL.

HEAR the Words of the Institution of the Holy Supper of our Lord Jesus Christ, as they are delivered by the Apostle Paul:

I have received of the Lord that which also I delivered unto you, That the Lord Jesus the same night in which He was betrayed took bread: and when He had given thanks, He brake it, and said, Take, eat: this is My body, which is broken for you: this do in remembrance of Me. After the same manner also He took the cup, when He had supped, saying, This cup is the New Covenant in My blood: this do ye, as oft as ye drink it, in remembrance of Me. For as often as ye eat this bread, and drink this cup, ye do show the Lord's death till He come.

As the Lord Jesus, the same night in which He was betrayed, took bread, I take these Elements

*Here the presiding Minister shall lay his hand upon the
Plate and the Chalice*

of bread and wine, to be set apart from all common
uses to this holy use and mystery; and as
He gave thanks and blessed, let us draw nigh
unto God, and present unto Him our prayers and
thanksgivings.

The Lord be with you.

And with thy spirit.

Lift up your hearts.

We lift them up unto the Lord.

Let us give thanks unto our Lord God.

It is meet and right so to do.

It is very meet, right, and our bounden duty
that we should at all times and in all places give
thanks unto Thee, O Holy Lord, Father Almighty,
Everlasting God; who didst create the heavens
and the earth and all that in them is; who didst
make man in Thine own image and whose tender
mercies are over all Thy works.*

Therefore, with angels and archangels and all
the company of heaven, we worship and adore Thy
glorious name, evermore praising Thee and saying:

*Holy, Holy, Holy, Lord God of Hosts;
Heaven and earth are full of Thy glory:
Glory be to Thee, O Lord Most High.*

**Here may follow the Preface proper to the season of the
Christian Year, pages 166–168.*

All glory and thanksgiving be to Thee, Almighty
God, our Heavenly Father, for that Thou, of Thy
great mercy, didst give Thine only Son Jesus
Christ to take our nature upon Him, and to suffer
death upon the cross for our redemption; who
made there a full, perfect, and sufficient sacrifice
for the sins of the whole world and did institute
and, in His holy Gospel, command us to continue
a perpetual memorial of His death and sacrifice
until His coming again.

Wherefore, having in remembrance His Incarnation and holy life, His Passion and precious
death, His Resurrection and glorious Ascension,
and His continual intercession, we Thy humble
servants, pleading His eternal sacrifice, do set
forth, with these Thy holy gifts, which we now
offer unto Thee, the memorial Thy Son hath
commanded us to make.

And we most humbly beseech Thee, O merciful
Father, to bless and sanctify with Thy Holy Spirit
both us and these Thy gifts of bread and wine,
that the bread which we break may be the communion of the body of Christ, and the cup of
blessing which we bless, the communion of the
blood of Christ.

And here we offer and present unto Thee ourselves, our souls and bodies, to be a reasonable,
holy, and living sacrifice; and we beseech Thee
mercifully to accept this our sacrifice of praise
and thanksgiving, as, in the communion of all the
faithful in heaven and on earth, we pray Thee to
fulfill in us, and in all men, the purpose of Thy
redeeming love; through Jesus Christ our Lord,

by whom, and with whom, in the unity of the Holy Spirit, all honor and glory be unto Thee, O Father Almighty, world without end. *Amen.*

And now, as our Saviour Christ hath taught us, we humbly pray:
Our Father, . . .

Then shall the presiding Minister say:

According to the holy institution of our Lord Jesus Christ, and in remembrance of Him, we do this: For in the night in which He was betrayed, HE TOOK BREAD,

Here the presiding Minister shall take the Bread into his hands

and when he had blessed, and given thanks, HE BRAKE IT,

Here he shall break the Bread

and said, TAKE, EAT: THIS IS MY BODY WHICH IS BROKEN FOR YOU: THIS DO IN REMEMBRANCE OF ME. AFTER THE SAME MANNER ALSO, HE TOOK THE CUP

Here he shall raise the Cup

saying: THIS CUP IS THE NEW COVENANT IN MY BLOOD: THIS DO YE, AS OFT AS YE DRINK IT, IN REMEMBRANCE OF ME.

O Lamb of God, who takest away the sins of the world: Have mercy upon us.
O Lamb of God, who takest away the sins of the world: Grant us Thy peace.

Then the Minister shall himself receive in both kinds; and then shall he serve the Elders, who shall thereafter serve the People.

In giving the Bread the Minister shall say:

Take ye, eat ye; this is the body of Christ which is broken for you: This do in remembrance of Him.

And, in giving the Cup:

This cup is the New Covenant in the blood of Christ, which is shed for many unto remission of sins: Drink ye, all, of it.

When all have received, and the Bread and Wine have been replaced on the Holy Table and reverently covered, the presiding Minister shall say:

THE PEACE OF THE LORD JESUS CHRIST BE WITH YOU ALL.

Then shall he call the People to thanksgiving, saying:

Let us pray.

ALMIGHTY and everliving God, we most heartily thank Thee that in Thy great love Thou hast fed us at Thy Table with this spiritual food, and hast assured us of Thy goodness toward us; and that we are members of the mystical Body of Thy Son, the blessed company of all faithful people, and heirs of Thine everlasting kingdom. And we beseech Thee, O Heavenly Father, so to assist us with Thy grace that we may continue in this holy fellowship, and live henceforth to Thy glory; through Jesus Christ our Lord, who liveth and reigneth, and is worshiped and glorified, with Thee, O Father and the Holy Spirit, world without end. *Amen.*

*Then may be sung a Hymn of Praise, or the Nunc Dimittis
may be read responsively or sung.*

Benediction

THE peace of God, which passeth all understanding, keep your hearts and minds in the
knowledge and love of God, and of His Son
Jesus Christ our Lord; and the blessing of God
Almighty, the Father, the Son, and the Holy Spirit,
be upon you, and remain with you always.   *Amen.*

*After the celebration, reverent disposition of the Elements
which remain shall be made by the Minister and Elders.*

PROPER PREFACES
FOR THE CHRISTIAN YEAR

The following Prayers or Proper Prefaces are for use in connection with the Order of the Holy Communion on these days or seasons of the Christian Year.

ADVENT. And we praise Thee for Jesus Christ Thy Son our Saviour, by whom Thou hast sent a new light to shine upon the world, that we who rejoice in that light may be found cleansed from our sins and without fear when He shall come again to judge the world in righteousness. Therefore, with angels, etc. . . .

CHRISTMAS. And especially at this time we praise Thee, because Thou didst give Jesus Christ Thine only Son to be born for us of Mary, that through Him we might have power to become the sons of God. Therefore, with angels, etc. . . .

EPIPHANY. And we praise Thee for Jesus Christ our Lord, who in the likeness of men manifested forth Thy glory, that He might bring all men out of darkness into His marvelous light. Therefore, with angels, etc. . . .

LENT. And we praise Thee for Jesus Christ our Lord, who was in all points tempted like as we are, yet without sin; by whose grace we are enabled to subdue the sinful desires of the flesh, and live no longer unto ourselves, but unto Him who died for us and rose again. Therefore, with angels, etc. . . .

THURSDAY BEFORE EASTER.   And we praise Thee
for Jesus Christ our Lord, who the night before
He suffered did institute this holy Sacrament,
to be a pledge of His love and a memorial of
His Passion, that we being partakers of these
holy mysteries might receive the benefits of His
redemption.   Therefore, with angels, etc. . . .

EASTER.   But chiefly are we bound to praise Thee
for the glorious resurrection of Thy Son Jesus
Christ our Lord, who is the very Lamb of God,
which was offered for us, and hath taken away
the sins of the world; who by His death hath
destroyed death, and by His rising to life again
hath brought to us everlasting life.   Therefore,
with angels, etc. . . .

ASCENSION.   And we praise Thee for Jesus Christ
our Lord, who ascended up on high, the one
Mediator between God and man; who abideth
for ever in that glory which He had with Thee,
and in that nature which He took of us, that
He might bring us to the fellowship of His
Godhead.   Therefore, with angels, etc. . . .

WHITSUNDAY.   And we praise Thee for Jesus
Christ our Lord, who having ascended up on
high, and sitting at Thy right hand, sent forth
the promise of the Holy Spirit upon the whole
Church, that the everlasting Gospel should be
preached among all men to bring them out of
darkness into the clear light of Thy truth.
Therefore, with angels, etc. . . .

TRINITY. And we praise Thee for Jesus Christ
our Lord, with Thee and the Holy Spirit one
God, the same in substance, equal in power
and glory. Therefore, with angels, etc. . . .

ALL SAINTS. And we praise Thee for Jesus Christ
our Lord, who in the blessedness of Thy saints
hath given us a glorious pledge of the hope of
our calling; that, being compassed about with
so great a cloud of witnesses, we may run with
patience the race that is set before us, and
with them receive the crown of glory that fadeth
not away. Therefore, with angels, etc. . . .

ANOTHER ORDER
FOR THE CELEBRATION OF THE
SACRAMENT OF THE LORD'S SUPPER
OR HOLY COMMUNION

Let the Holy Table be covered with a cloth of fair white linen. Let there be at least one large Chalice for lifting, and one piece of Bread, sufficiently large for the Minister's taking and breaking in the sight of the People.

Before coming to the Table let the Minister give the Invitation in these or other suitable words:

DEARLY beloved, all that humbly put their trust in Christ, and desire His help that they may lead a holy life, all that are truly sorry for their sins and would be delivered from the burden of them, are invited and encouraged in His name to come to this Sacrament. Let us, therefore, so come that we may find refreshing and rest unto our souls.

As we draw near to the Lord's Table to celebrate the Holy Communion of the body and blood of Christ, we are gratefully to remember that our Lord instituted this Sacrament:

For the perpetual memory of His dying for our sakes and the pledge of His undying love;

As a bond of our union with Him and with each other as members of His mystical Body;

As a seal of His promises to us and a renewal of our obedience to Him;

For the blessed assurance of His presence with us who are gathered here in His name;

And as a pledge of His coming again.

Seeing, therefore, what great benefits Christ has prepared for us in this Communion, for this cause let us bow our knees unto the Father, of whom the whole family in heaven and earth is named,

That He would grant us, according to the riches of His glory, to be strengthened with might by His Spirit in the inner man; that Christ may dwell in our hearts by faith;

That we, being rooted and grounded in love, may be able to comprehend with all saints what is the breadth, and length, and depth, and height, and to know the love of Christ, which passeth knowledge, that we may be filled with all the fullness of God.

Now unto Him that is able to do exceeding abundantly above all that we ask or think, according to the power that worketh in us; unto Him be glory in the Church by Christ Jesus, throughout all ages, world without end. *Amen.*

Hymn

Then the Minister shall say:

LET us reverently attend to the Words of the Institution of the Holy Supper of our Lord Jesus Christ, as they are delivered by the Apostle Paul:

I have received of the Lord that which also I delivered unto you, That the Lord Jesus the same night in which He was betrayed took bread: and when He had given thanks, He brake it, and said, Take, eat: this is My body, which is broken for you: this do in remembrance of Me. After the same manner also He took the cup, when He had supped, saying, This cup is the New Covenant in My blood: this do ye, as oft as ye drink it, in remembrance of Me.   For as often as ye eat this bread, and drink this cup, ye do show the Lord's death till He come.

And now, in His name, I take these Elements

Here the Minister may lay his hand upon the Plate and the Cup

to be set apart by prayer and thanksgiving to the holy use for which He has appointed them.

Then the Minister shall say:

Let us pray.

If so desired, the Prayers and Thanksgivings may be offered in the form following, the People reverently kneeling or bowing down:

O GOD, who by the life and death and rising again of Thy dear Son hast consecrated for us a new and living way into the holiest of all: Cleanse our minds, we beseech Thee, by the inspiration of Thy Holy Spirit, that, drawing near unto Thee with a pure heart and conscience undefiled, we may receive these Thy gifts without sin, and worthily magnify Thy holy name; through Jesus Christ our Lord.   *Amen.*

Then the People, still kneeling or bowing down, shall make these responses:

Minister: The Lord be with you.

People: And with thy spirit.

Minister: Lift up your hearts.

People: We lift them up unto the Lord.

Minister: Let us give thanks unto the Lord our
         God.

People: It is meet and right so to do.

Then the Minister, proceeding, shall say:

It is very meet, right, and our bounden duty
that we should at all times give thanks unto Thee,
O Lord, our Heavenly Father, for all Thy bounties known and unknown; but chiefly are we bound
to praise Thee for Thy great love wherewith Thou
hast drawn us to Thyself in Christ and made us
to sit in heavenly places with Him, who is our
Peace.

Therefore, with angels and archangels and all
the company of heaven, we laud and magnify Thy
glorious name, evermore praising Thee and saying:

*Here let the People, still kneeling or bowing down, join
aloud, saying:*

Holy, Holy, Holy, Lord God of Hosts; Heaven
and earth are full of the majesty of Thy glory.
Hosanna in the highest. Blessed is He that
cometh in the name of the Lord. Hosanna in
the highest.

Then the Minister shall proceed, saying:

MOST gracious God, the Father of our Lord
Jesus Christ, whose once offering up of
Himself upon the cross we commemorate before
Thee: We earnestly desire Thy Fatherly goodness
to accept this our sacrifice of praise and thanks-
giving:

And we pray Thee to bless and sanctify with
Thy Word and Spirit these Thine own gifts of
bread and wine which we set before Thee, that

we may receive by faith Christ crucified for us, and so feed upon Him that He may be made one with us and we with Him.

And here we offer and present unto Thee ourselves, our souls and bodies, to be a reasonable, holy, and living sacrifice; and we beseech Thee mercifully to accept this our sacrifice of praise and thanksgiving, as, in fellowship with all the faithful in heaven and on earth, we pray Thee to fulfill in us, and in all men, the purpose of Thy redeeming love;

Through Jesus Christ our Lord; to whom, with Thee and the Holy Spirit, be the glory and the praise, both now and evermore. *Amen.*

The Bread and Wine being thus set apart by Prayer and Thanksgiving, the Minister shall say:

The Lord Jesus took bread,

Here he shall take some of the Bread into his hands

And when He had blessed it, He broke it,

Here he shall break the Bread in view of the People

And gave it to His disciples, as I, ministering in His name, give this bread to you: saying, Take, eat; this is My body, broken for you: this do in remembrance of Me.

Then the Minister, who is himself to communicate, is to give the Bread to the Elders to be distributed.

When the People have communicated, the Elders shall return the Plates to the hands of the Minister, who shall then administer to them. And after they have communicated, he shall say:

After the same manner our Saviour took the cup,

Here he shall raise the Cup

And, having given thanks, as hath been done in His name, He gave it to His disciples; saying, This cup is the New Covenant in My blood. Drink ye, all, of it.

Then the Minister, who is himself to communicate, is to give the Cup to the Elders to be distributed.

When the People have communicated and the Minister has administered the Cup to the Elders, he shall say:

Let us pray.

WE GIVE Thee thanks, O Lord, for Thy rich mercy and invaluable goodness, vouchsafed to us in this sacred Communion, wherein we have assurance that we are very members of the mystical Body of Thy Son, and heirs through hope of Thine everlasting kingdom. So enrich us by Thy continual grace that the life of Jesus may be made manifest in our mortal body, and Thy kingdom be furthered through all such good works as Thou hast prepared for us to walk in.

O Almighty God, who hast built Thy Church upon the foundation of the apostles and prophets, Jesus Christ Himself being the head cornerstone: Grant, we beseech Thee, that, being gathered together in unity by Thy Holy Spirit, Thy Church may manifest Thy power among all peoples to the glory of Thy name; through Jesus Christ our Lord, who liveth and reigneth with Thee and the same Spirit, one God, world without end.

Eternal Light, immortal Love, we bless Thy name for all Thy servants who have kept the faith and finished their course and are at rest with Thee. Help us to abide in their fellowship and to follow their example, that we with them may sit down at the marriage supper of the Lamb, which is in heaven. *Amen.*

Then the People shall rise and sing:

Hymn

Then, the People reverently kneeling or bowing down, the Minister shall pronounce:

Benediction

THE God of peace, that brought again from the dead our Lord Jesus, that great Shepherd of the sheep, through the blood of the everlasting covenant, make you perfect in every good work to do His will, working in you that which is well-pleasing in His sight; through Jesus Christ, to whom be glory for ever and ever. *Amen.*

After the celebration, reverent disposition of the Elements which remain shall be made by the Minister and Elders.

ORDER FOR THE CELEBRATION
OF HOLY COMMUNION
FOR THE SICK

Let the Minister give the Invitation in these words:

BELOVED in the Lord, hear what gracious words our Saviour Christ saith unto all who truly turn to Him:

Come unto Me, all ye that labor and are heavy-laden, and I will give you rest.

Take My yoke upon you, and learn of Me; for I am meek and lowly in heart: and ye shall find rest unto your souls.

I am the Bread of Life: he that cometh to Me shall never hunger; and he that believeth on Me shall never thirst. Him that cometh to Me I will in no wise cast out.

Then the Minister shall say:

LET us reverently attend to the Words of the Institution of the Holy Supper of our Lord Jesus Christ, as they are delivered by the Apostle Paul:

I have received of the Lord that which also I delivered unto you, That the Lord Jesus the same night in which He was betrayed took bread: and when He had given thanks, He brake it, and said, Take, eat: this is My body, which is broken for you: this do in remembrance of Me. After the same manner also He took the cup, when He had supped, saying, This cup is the New Covenant in My blood: this do ye, as oft as ye drink it, in remembrance of Me.   For as often as ye eat this bread, and drink this cup, ye do show the Lord's death till He come.

And now, in His name, I take these Elements

Here the Minister may lay his hand upon the Plate and the Cup

to be set apart by prayer and thanksgiving to the holy use for which He has appointed them.

Then the Minister shall say:

Let us pray.

MOST gracious God, the Father of our Lord Jesus Christ, whose once offering up of Himself upon the cross we commemorate before Thee: We earnestly desire Thy Fatherly goodness to accept this our sacrifice of praise and thanksgiving:

And we pray Thee to bless and sanctify with Thy Word and Spirit these Thine own gifts of bread and wine which we set before Thee, that we may receive by faith Christ crucified for us, and so feed upon Him that He may be made one with us and we with Him.

And here we offer and present unto Thee ourselves, our souls and bodies, to be a reasonable, holy, and living sacrifice; and we beseech Thee mercifully to accept this our sacrifice of praise and thanksgiving, as, in fellowship with all the faithful in heaven and on earth, we pray Thee to fulfill in us, and in all men, the purpose of Thy redeeming love;

Through Jesus Christ our Lord; to whom, with Thee and the Holy Spirit, be the glory and the praise, both now and evermore.   *Amen.*

The Bread and Wine being thus set apart by Prayer and Thanksgiving, the Minister shall say:

The Lord Jesus took bread,

Here he shall take some of the Bread into his hands

And when He had blessed it, He broke it,

Here he shall break the Bread

And gave it to His disciples, as I, ministering in His name, give this bread to you: saying, Take, eat; this is My body, broken for you: this do in remembrance of Me.

Then the Minister, who is himself to communicate, is to administer the Bread

Then the Minister shall say:

After the same manner our Saviour took the cup,

Here he shall raise the Cup

And, having given thanks, as hath been done in His name, He gave it to His disciples; saying, This cup is the New Covenant in My blood. Drink ye, all, of it.

Then the Minister, who is himself to communicate, is to administer the Cup

Then the Minister shall say:

Let us pray.

WE THANK Thee, O God, for Thy great mercy given to us in this Sacrament, whereby we are made partakers of Christ. So enrich us by the Holy Spirit that the life of Jesus may be made manifest in us, and the remainder of our days may be spent in Thy love and service.

O Lord, holy Father, by whose loving-kindness our souls and bodies are renewed: Mercifully look upon this Thy servant, that, every cause of sickness being removed, *he* may be restored to soundness of health; through Jesus Christ our Lord. *Amen.*

Benediction

THE peace of God, which passeth all understanding, keep your hearts and minds in the knowledge and love of God, and of His Son Jesus Christ our Lord; and the blessing of God Almighty, the Father, the Son, and the Holy Spirit, be upon you, and remain with you always. *Amen.*

After the celebration, reverent disposition of the Elements which remain shall be made.

SCRIPTURE FOR USE IN
THE VISITATION OF THE SICK

The eternal God is thy Refuge,
And underneath are the everlasting arms.

O taste and see that the Lord is good:
Blessed is the man that trusteth in Him.

He that dwelleth in the secret place of the
Most High
Shall abide under the shadow of the Almighty.
I will say of the Lord, He is my Refuge and
my Fortress:
My God; in Him will I trust.

Thou wilt keep him in perfect peace, whose
mind is stayed on Thee: because he trusteth in
Thee. Trust ye in the Lord for ever: for in the
Lord Jehovah is everlasting strength.

Hast thou not known? hast thou not heard, that
the everlasting God, the Lord, the Creator of the
ends of the earth, fainteth not, neither is weary?
there is no searching of His understanding. He
giveth power to the faint; and to them that have
no might He increaseth strength.

Fear thou not; for I am with thee: be not dismayed; for I am thy God: I will strengthen thee;
yea, I will help thee; yea, I will uphold thee with
the right hand of My righteousness.

For the mountains shall depart, and the hills be removed; but My kindness shall not depart from thee, neither shall the covenant of My peace be removed, saith the Lord that hath mercy on thee.

Come unto Me, all ye that labor and are heavy-laden, and I will give you rest. Take My yoke upon you, and learn of Me; for I am meek and lowly in heart: and ye shall find rest unto your souls. For My yoke is easy, and My burden is light.

For this thing I besought the Lord thrice, that it might depart from me. And He said unto me, My grace is sufficient for thee: for My strength is made perfect in weakness. Most gladly therefore will I rather glory in my infirmities, that the power of Christ may rest upon me.

Be careful for nothing; but in every thing by prayer and supplication with thanksgiving let your requests be made known unto God. And the peace of God, which passeth all understanding, shall keep your hearts and minds through Christ Jesus.

Wherefore seeing we also are compassed about with so great a cloud of witnesses, let us lay aside every weight, and the sin which doth so easily beset us, and let us run with patience the race that is set before us, looking unto Jesus the Author and Finisher of our faith; who for the joy that was set before Him endured the cross, despising the shame, and is set down at the right hand of the throne of God.

In this was manifested the love of God toward us, because that God sent His only-begotten Son into the world, that we might live through Him. Herein is love, not that we loved God, but that He loved us, and sent His Son to be the propitiation for our sins.

The Lord is my Shepherd . . . —*Psalm* 23 (see p. 197).
I will lift up mine eyes unto the hills . . . —*Psalm* 121 (see pp. 196, 197).
Let not your heart be troubled . . . —*John*, *ch.* 14 (see pp. 202, 203).
As many as are led by the Spirit . . . —*Romans*, *ch.* 8 (see pp. 199, 200).

ORDER FOR
THE SOLEMNIZATION OF MARRIAGE

*The Persons to be married shall present themselves before
the Minister, the Man standing at the right hand of the
Woman.   Then, all present reverently standing, the Minister shall say:*

DEARLY beloved, we are assembled here in
the presence of God, to join this Man and
this Woman in holy marriage; which is instituted
of God, regulated by His commandments, blessed
by our Lord Jesus Christ, and to be held in honor
among all men.   Let us therefore reverently remember that God has established and sanctified
marriage, for the welfare and happiness of mankind.   Our Saviour has declared that a man shall
leave his father and mother and, cleave unto his
wife.   By His apostles, He has instructed those
who enter into this relation to cherish a mutual
esteem and love; to bear with each other's infirmities and weaknesses; to comfort each other in
sickness, trouble, and sorrow; in honesty and industry to provide for each other, and for their
household, in temporal things; to pray for and
encourage each other in the things which pertain
to God; and to live together as the heirs of the
grace of life.

Forasmuch as these two Persons have come
hither to be made one in this holy estate, if there
be any here present who knows any just cause
why they may not lawfully be joined in marriage,
I require him now to make it known, or ever after
to hold his peace.

Then, speaking unto the Persons who are to be married, the Minister shall say:

I CHARGE you both, before the great God, the Searcher of all hearts, that if either of you know any reason why ye may not lawfully be joined together in marriage, ye do now confess it. For be ye well assured that if any persons are joined together otherwise than as God's Word allows, their union is not blessed by Him.

Then, if no impediment appear, the Minister shall say:

Let us pray.

ALMIGHTY and ever-blessed God, whose presence is the happiness of every condition, and whose favor hallows every relation: We beseech Thee to be present and favorable unto these Thy servants, that they may be truly joined in the honorable estate of marriage, in the covenant of their God. As Thou hast brought them together by Thy providence, sanctify them by Thy Spirit, giving them a new frame of heart fit for their new estate; and enrich them with all grace, whereby they may enjoy the comforts, undergo the cares, endure the trials, and perform the duties of life together as becometh Christians, under Thy heavenly guidance and protection; through our Lord Jesus Christ. *Amen.*

Then the Minister, calling the Man by his Christian name, shall say:

N., wilt thou have this Woman to be thy wife, and wilt thou pledge thy troth to her, in all love and honor, in all duty and service, in all faith and tenderness, to live with her, and cherish her, according to the ordinance of God, in the holy bond of marriage?

The Man shall answer:

I will.

Then the Minister, calling the Woman by her Christian name, shall say:

N., wilt thou have this Man to be thy husband, and wilt thou pledge thy troth to him, in all love and honor, in all duty and service, in all faith and tenderness, to live with him, and cherish him, according to the ordinance of God, in the holy bond of marriage?

The Woman shall answer:

I will.

Then the Minister may say:

Who giveth this Woman to be married to this Man?

Then the Father, or Guardian, or Friend, of the Woman shall put her right hand in the hand of the Minister, who shall cause the Man with his right hand to take the Woman by her right hand and to say after the Minister as follows:

I, *N.*, take thee, *N.*; To be my wedded wife; And I do promise and covenant; Before God and these witnesses; To be thy loving and faithful husband; In plenty and in want; In joy and in sorrow; In sickness and in health; As long as we both shall live.

Then shall they loose their hands; and the Woman, with her right hand taking the Man by his right hand, shall likewise say after the Minister:

I, *N.*, take thee, *N.*; To be my wedded husband; And I do promise and covenant; Before God and these witnesses; To be thy loving and faithful wife; In plenty and in want; In joy and in sorrow; In sickness and in health; As long as we both shall live.

Then if a ring be provided, it shall be given to the Minister, who shall return it to the Man, who shall then put it upon the fourth finger of the Woman's left hand, saying after the Minister:

This ring I give thee; In token and pledge; Of our constant faith; And abiding love.

Or,

With this ring I thee wed; In the name of the Father; And of the Son; And of the Holy Spirit. Amen.

Before giving the ring, the Minister may say:

Bless, O Lord, this ring, that he who gives it and she who wears it may abide in Thy peace, and continue in Thy favor, unto their life's end; through Jesus Christ our Lord. *Amen.*

If a second ring be provided, a similar order shall be followed, the Woman saying the same words after the Minister.

Then the Minister shall say:

Let us pray.

MOST merciful and gracious God, of whom the whole family in heaven and earth is named: Bestow upon these Thy servants the seal of Thine approval, and Thy Fatherly benediction; granting unto them grace to fulfill, with pure and steadfast affection, the vow and covenant between them made. Guide them together, we beseech Thee, in the way of righteousness and peace, that, loving and serving Thee, with one heart and mind, all the days of their life, they may be abundantly enriched with the tokens of Thine everlasting favor, in Jesus Christ our Lord. *Amen.*

Then the Minister and People shall say:

OUR Father, who art in heaven; Hallowed be Thy name. Thy kingdom come. Thy will be done; On earth as it is in heaven. Give us this day our daily bread. And forgive us our debts; As we forgive our debtors. And lead us not into temptation; But deliver us from evil; For Thine is the kingdom, and the power, and the glory, for ever. Amen.

Then shall the Minister say unto all who are present:

BY THE authority committed unto me as a Minister of the Church of Christ, I declare that *N.* and *N.* are now Husband and Wife, according to the ordinance of God, and the law of the State: in the name of the Father, and of the Son, and of the Holy Spirit. Amen.

Then, causing the Husband and Wife to join their right hands, the Minister shall say:

Whom therefore God hath joined together, let no man put asunder.

It is fitting that the Bride and Groom kneel to receive the Benediction:

THE Lord bless you, and keep you: the Lord make His face to shine upon you, and be gracious unto you: the Lord lift up His countenance upon you, and give you peace: both now and in the life everlasting. *Amen.*

Or,

GOD the Father, God the Son, God the Holy Spirit, bless, preserve, and keep you; the Lord mercifully with His favor look upon you, and fill you with all spiritual benediction and grace; that ye may so live together in this life that in the world to come ye may have life everlasting.
Amen.

ORDER FOR THE
BLESSING OF A CIVIL MARRIAGE

Before blessing a civil marriage the Minister must satisfy himself that the Persons seeking this blessing have been lawfully married.

The Minister shall say:

DEARLY beloved, we are assembled here in the presence of God, to invoke the blessing of our Heavenly Father upon your marriage. Let us therefore reverently remember that God has established and sanctified marriage, for the welfare and happiness of mankind. Our Saviour has declared that a man shall leave his father and mother and cleave unto his wife. By His apostles, He has instructed those who enter into this relation to cherish a mutual esteem and love; to bear with each other's infirmities and weaknesses; to comfort each other in sickness, trouble, and sorrow; to provide for each other, and for their household, in temporal things; to pray for and encourage each other in the things which pertain to God; and to live together as the heirs of the grace of life.

The Minister shall say:

Let us pray.

ALMIGHTY and ever-blessed God, whose presence is the happiness of every condition, and whose favor hallows every relation: We beseech Thee to be present and favorable unto these Thy servants. As Thou hast brought them together by Thy providence, sanctify them by Thy Spirit, giving them a new frame of heart fit for their new estate; and enrich them with all grace, whereby they may enjoy the comforts, undergo the cares, endure the trials, and perform the duties of life together as becometh Christians, under Thy heavenly guidance and protection; through our Lord Jesus Christ. *Amen.*

Then the Minister shall cause the Man with his right hand to take the Woman by her right hand and, calling him by name, shall say:

N., do you acknowledge this Woman to be your wedded wife, and do you promise and covenant, before God and these witnesses, to be her loving and faithful husband, in plenty and in want, in joy and in sorrow, in sickness and in health, as long as you both shall live?

The Man shall answer:

I do.

Then shall they loose hands; and the Minister shall cause the Woman with her right hand to take the Man by his right hand and, calling her by name, shall say:

N., do you acknowledge this Man to be your wedded husband, and do you promise and covenant, before God and these witnesses, to be his loving and faithful wife, in plenty and in want, in joy and in sorrow, in sickness and in health, as long as you both shall live?

The Woman shall answer:

I do.

If a ring be provided, it shall be given to the Minister, who shall return it to the Man, who shall then put it upon the fourth finger of the Woman's left hand, saying after the Minister:

This ring I give thee; In the name of the Father; And of the Son; And of the Holy Spirit. Amen.

Then the Minister shall say:

Let us pray.

MOST merciful and gracious God, of whom the whole family in heaven and earth is named: Bestow upon these Thy servants the seal of Thine approval, and Thy Fatherly benediction; granting unto them grace to fulfill, with pure and steadfast affection, the vow and covenant between them made. Guide them together, we beseech Thee, in the way of righteousness and peace, that, loving and serving Thee, with one heart and mind, all the days of their life, they may be abundantly enriched with the tokens of Thine everlasting favor, in Jesus Christ our Lord. *Amen.*

Then the Minister and People shall say:

OUR Father, who art in heaven; Hallowed be Thy name. Thy kingdom come. Thy will be done; On earth as it is in heaven. Give us this day our daily bread. And forgive us our debts; As we forgive our debtors. And lead us not into temptation; But deliver us from evil; For Thine is the kingdom, and the power, and the glory, for ever. Amen.

*It is fitting that the Bride and Groom kneel to receive the
Benediction:*

GOD the Father, God the Son, God the Holy
Spirit, bless, preserve, and keep you; the
Lord mercifully with His favor look upon you,
and fill you with all spiritual benediction and
grace; that ye may so live together in this life
that in the world to come ye may have life everlasting. *Amen.*

THE FUNERAL SERVICE

The Minister may use one or more of these Sentences from Holy Scripture.

OUR help is in the name of the Lord, who made heaven and earth.

The eternal God is thy Refuge, and underneath are the everlasting arms.

Like as a father pitieth his children, so the Lord pitieth them that fear Him.

As one whom his mother comforteth, so will I comfort you; and ye shall be comforted.

Peace I leave with you, My peace I give unto you: not as the world giveth, give I unto you. Let not your heart be troubled, neither let it be afraid.

God is our Refuge and Strength, a very present Help in trouble. Therefore will not we fear.

I am the Resurrection, and the Life, saith the Lord: he that believeth in Me, though he were dead, yet shall he live: and whosoever liveth and believeth in Me shall never die.

Then let the Minister say:

Let us pray.

ETERNAL God, our Heavenly Father, who lovest us with an everlasting love, and canst turn the shadow of death into the morning: Help us now to wait upon Thee with reverent and believing hearts. In the silence of this hour speak to us of eternal things, that through patience and comfort of the Scriptures we may have hope, and be lifted above our darkness and distress into the light and peace of Thy presence; through Jesus Christ our Lord. *Amen.*

Minister and People:

OUR Father, who art in heaven; Hallowed be Thy name. Thy kingdom come. Thy will be done; On earth as it is in heaven. Give us this day our daily bread. And forgive us our debts; As we forgive our debtors. And lead us not into temptation; But deliver us from evil; For Thine is the kingdom, and the power, and the glory, for ever. Amen.

Then let one or more of the following Psalms be read or chanted.

LORD, Thou hast been our dwelling place In all generations.
Before the mountains were brought forth,
Or ever Thou hadst formed the earth and the world,
Even from everlasting to everlasting, Thou art God.
For a thousand years in Thy sight
Are but as yesterday when it is past,
And as a watch in the night.
Thou carriest them away as with a flood; they are as a sleep:
In the morning they are like grass which groweth up.
In the morning it flourisheth, and groweth up;
In the evening it is cut down, and withereth.

The days of our years are threescore years and ten;
And if by reason of strength they be fourscore
    years,
Yet is their strength labor and sorrow;
For it is soon cut off, and we fly away.
So teach us to number our days,
That we may apply our hearts unto wisdom.
And let the beauty of the Lord our God be upon
    us:
And establish Thou the work of our hands upon
    us;
Yea, the work of our hands establish Thou it.
                            —*Psalm* 90.

Out of the depths have I cried unto Thee, O Lord.
Lord, hear my voice:
Let Thine ears be attentive
To the voice of my supplications.
If Thou, Lord, shouldest mark iniquities,
O Lord, who shall stand?
But there is forgiveness with Thee,
That Thou mayest be feared.
I wait for the Lord, my soul doth wait,
And in His word do I hope.
My soul waiteth for the Lord
More than they that watch for the morning:
I say, more than they that watch for the morning.
                            —*Psalm* 130.

Lord, make me to know mine end,
And the measure of my days, what it is;
That I may know how frail I am.
Behold, Thou hast made my days as an hand-
    breadth;
And mine age is as nothing before Thee.

Hear my prayer, O Lord, and give ear unto my
    cry;
Hold not Thy peace at my tears:
For I am a stranger with Thee,
And a sojourner, as all my fathers were.

—Psalm 39.

God is our Refuge and Strength,
A very present Help in trouble.
Therefore will not we fear, though the earth be
    removed,
And though the mountains be carried into the
    midst of the sea;
Though the waters thereof roar and be troubled,
Though the mountains shake with the swelling
    thereof.
There is a river, the streams whereof shall make
    glad the city of God,
The holy place of the tabernacles of the Most High.
God is in the midst of her; she shall not be moved:
God shall help her, and that right early.
The Lord of Hosts is with us;
The God of Jacob is our Refuge.

—Psalm 46.

I will lift up mine eyes unto the hills,
From whence cometh my help.
My help cometh from the Lord,
Which made heaven and earth.
He will not suffer thy foot to be moved:
He that keepeth thee will not slumber.

Behold, He that keepeth Israel
Shall neither slumber nor sleep.
The Lord is thy keeper:
The Lord is thy shade upon thy right hand.
The sun shall not smite thee by day,
Nor the moon by night.
The Lord shall preserve thee from all evil:
He shall preserve thy soul.
The Lord shall preserve thy going out and thy
    coming in
From this time forth, and even for evermore.

—*Psalm* 121.

The Lord is my Shepherd; I shall not want.
He maketh me to lie down in green pastures:
He leadeth me beside the still waters.
He restoreth my soul:
He leadeth me in the paths of righteousness for
    His name's sake.
Yea, though I walk through the valley of the
    shadow of death,
I will fear no evil: for Thou art with me;
Thy rod and Thy staff they comfort me.
Thou preparest a table before me in the presence
    of mine enemies:
Thou anointest my head with oil;
My cup runneth over.
Surely goodness and mercy shall follow me all
    the days of my life:
And I will dwell in the house of the Lord for ever.

—*Psalm* 23.

At the close of the Psalter, the Minister shall say:

GLORY be to the Father, and to the Son, and to the Holy Ghost;

As it was in the beginning, is now, and ever shall be, world without end. *Amen.*

A Hymn or Anthem may here be sung.

Then let the Minister read from the New Testament, choosing if he will from the following passages, and before the reading let him say:

Hear the Word of God as it is written in the New Testament:

NOW is Christ risen from the dead, and become the firstfruits of them that slept. For since by man came death, by man came also the resurrection of the dead. For as in Adam all die, even so in Christ shall all be made alive. But every man in his own order: Christ the firstfruits; afterward they that are Christ's at His coming. Then cometh the end, when He shall have delivered up the kingdom to God, even the Father; when He shall have put down all rule and all authority and power. For He must reign, till He hath put all enemies under His feet. The last enemy that shall be destroyed is death.

But some man will say, How are the dead raised up? and with what body do they come? Thou foolish one, that which thou sowest is not quickened, except it die: and that which thou sowest, thou sowest not that body that shall be. But God giveth it a body as it hath pleased Him, and to every seed his own body.

So also is the resurrection of the dead. It is sown in corruption; it is raised in incorruption: it is sown in dishonor; it is raised in glory: it is sown in weakness; it is raised in power: it is sown a natural body; it is raised a spiritual body. There is a natural body, and there is a spiritual body.

Now this I say, brethren, that flesh and blood cannot inherit the kingdom of God; neither doth corruption inherit incorruption. For this corruptible must put on incorruption, and this mortal must put on immortality. So when this corruptible shall have put on incorruption, and this mortal shall have put on immortality, then shall be brought to pass the saying that is written, Death is swallowed up in victory. O death, where is thy sting? O grave, where is thy victory?

Thanks be to God, which giveth us the victory through our Lord Jesus Christ. Therefore, my beloved brethren, be ye steadfast, unmovable, always abounding in the work of the Lord, forasmuch as ye know that your labor is not in vain in the Lord.

—I Corinthians, ch. 15.

The Spirit itself beareth witness with our spirit, that we are the children of God: and if children, then heirs; heirs of God, and joint-heirs with Christ; if so be that we suffer with Him, that we may be also glorified together.

For I reckon that the sufferings of this present time are not worthy to be compared with the glory which shall be revealed in us.

And we know that all things work together for good to them that love God, to them who are the called according to His purpose.

What shall we then say to these things? If God be for us, who can be against us? He that spared not His own Son, but delivered Him up for us all, how shall He not with Him also freely give us all things? It is Christ that died, yea rather, that is risen again, who is even at the right hand of God, who also maketh intercession for us. Who shall separate us from the love of Christ? shall tribulation, or distress, or persecution, or famine, or nakedness, or peril, or sword? Nay, in all these things we are more than conquerors through Him that loved us. For I am persuaded, that neither death, nor life, nor angels, nor principalities, nor powers, nor things present, nor things to come, nor height, nor depth, nor any other creature, shall be able to separate us from the love of God, which is in Christ Jesus our Lord.
—*Romans, ch. 8.*

Our light affliction, which is but for a moment, worketh for us a far more exceeding and eternal weight of glory; while we look not at the things which are seen, but at the things which are not seen: for the things which are seen are temporal; but the things which are not seen are eternal.

For we know that if our earthly house of this tabernacle were dissolved, we have a building of God, an house not made with hands, eternal in the heavens.
—*II Corinthians, chs. 4; 5.*

I would not have you to be ignorant, brethren, concerning them which are asleep, that ye sorrow not, even as others which have no hope.   For if we believe that Jesus died and rose again, even so them also which sleep in Jesus will God bring with Him.   Wherefore comfort one another with these words.

—I Thessalonians, ch. 4.

After this I beheld, and, lo, a great multitude, which no man could number, of all nations, and kindreds, and people, and tongues, stood before the throne, and before the Lamb, clothed with white robes, and palms in their hands; and cried with a loud voice, saying, Salvation to our God which sitteth upon the throne, and unto the Lamb.   And all the angels stood round about the throne, and about the elders and the four living creatures, and fell before the throne on their faces, and worshiped God, saying,

Amen: Blessing, and glory, and wisdom, and thanksgiving, and honor, and power, and might, be unto our God for ever and ever. Amen.

And one of the elders answered, saying unto me, What are these which are arrayed in white robes? and whence came they?   And I said unto him, Sir, thou knowest.   And he said to me, These are they which came out of great tribulation, and have washed their robes, and made them white in the blood of the Lamb.   Therefore are they before the throne of God, and serve Him day and night in His temple: and He that sitteth on the throne shall dwell among them.   They shall hunger no more, neither thirst any more; neither shall the sun light on them, nor any heat. For the Lamb which is in the midst of the throne shall feed them, and shall lead them unto living fountains of waters: and God shall wipe away all tears from their eyes.

—*Revelation, ch.* 7.

And I saw a new heaven and a new earth: for the first heaven and the first earth were passed away; and there was no more sea. And I John saw the holy city, new Jerusalem, coming down from God out of heaven, prepared as a bride adorned for her husband. And I heard a great voice out of heaven saying, Behold, the tabernacle of God is with men, and He will dwell with them, and they shall be His people, and God Himself shall be with them, and be their God. And God shall wipe away all tears from their eyes; and there shall be no more death, neither sorrow, nor crying, neither shall there be any more pain: for the former things are passed away.

And there shall be no more curse: but the throne of God and of the Lamb shall be in it; and His servants shall serve Him: and they shall see His face; and His name shall be in their foreheads. And there shall be no night there; and they need no candle, neither light of the sun; for the Lord God giveth them light: and they shall reign for ever and ever.

—*Revelation, chs.* 21; 22.

Jesus said: Let not your heart be troubled: ye believe in God, believe also in Me. In My Father's house are many mansions: if it were not so, I would have told you.   I go to prepare a place for you.   And if I go and prepare a place for you, I will come again, and receive you unto Myself; that where I am, there ye may be also.   And whither I go ye know, and the way ye know.   I am the way, the truth, and the life: no man cometh unto the Father, but by Me.

These things have I spoken unto you, being yet present with you.   But the Comforter, which is the Holy Ghost, whom the Father will send in My name, He shall teach you all things, and bring all things to your remembrance, whatsoever I have said unto you.   Peace I leave with you, My peace I give unto you: not as the world giveth, give I unto you.   Let not your heart be troubled, neither let it be afraid.

—John, ch. 14.

At the close of the reading from the Holy Scriptures the Minister shall say:

The Lord bless unto us the reading of His holy Word, and to His name be glory and praise.

AT THE FUNERAL OF A CHILD

AND Jesus called a little child unto Him, and set him in the midst of them, and said, Verily I say unto you, Except ye be converted, and become as little children, ye shall not enter into the kingdom of heaven.   Whosoever therefore shall humble himself as this little child, the same is greatest in the kingdom of heaven.   And whoso shall receive one such little child in My name receiveth Me.

Take heed that ye despise not one of these little ones; for I say unto you, That in heaven their angels do always behold the face of My Father which is in heaven. Even so it is not the will of your Father which is in heaven, that one of these little ones should perish.

—Matthew, ch. 18.

And they brought young children to Him, that He should touch them: and His disciples rebuked those that brought them. But when Jesus saw it, He was much displeased, and said unto them, Suffer the little children to come unto Me, and forbid them not: for of such is the kingdom of God. Verily I say unto you, Whosoever shall not receive the kingdom of God as a little child, he shall not enter therein. And He took them up in His arms, put His hands upon them, and blessed them.

—Mark, ch. 10.

Here, if desired, an address may be made.

Then the Minister may use such of the following Prayers as are fitting.

Adoration

O THOU eternal God, the Father of our spirits, in whose presence there is no darkness and no death: We worship and adore Thee, the everliving God.

O Thou Lord Jesus Christ, the Resurrection and the Life, who hast tasted death for every man and who hast brought life and immortality to light: We praise Thy name for the victory over death and the grave.

O Thou Holy Spirit, the Author and Giver of life, the Comforter of those who sorrow: In Thee is our sure confidence and our everlasting hope.

Before Thee we worship and adore, saying: Blessing and glory and wisdom and thanksgiving and honor and power and might be unto our God, for ever and ever. *Amen.*

Confession

ALMIGHTY and everlasting God, who alone amid the changes of this mortal life abidest ever the same: We confess before Thee the uncertainty of our life upon the earth. Thou hast made our days as a handbreadth; and our age is as nothing before Thee. All flesh is as grass; and all the goodliness thereof as the flower of the field. The grass withereth; the flower fadeth; but the Word of our God shall stand for ever. Therein is our hope, for Thou art our Father. We confess, even in the valley of the shadow of death, that Thou art with us. O Lord, make us to know our end, and the measure of our days what it is, that we may know how frail we are. Hear our prayer, and give ear unto our cry. Hold not Thy peace at our tears; for we are strangers with Thee and sojourners, as all our fathers were. But Thou art the same, and Thy years shall have no end. *Amen.*

Thanksgiving

GOD of all grace, who didst send Thy Son our Saviour Jesus Christ to bring life and immortality to light: Most humbly and heartily we give Thee thanks that by His death He destroyed the power of death; and by His glorious resurrection opened the kingdom of heaven to all believers. Grant us assuredly to know that because He lives we shall live also, and that neither death nor life, nor things present nor things to come, shall be able to separate us from Thy love, which is in Christ Jesus our Lord.

O merciful God, the Father of our Lord Jesus Christ, who is the Resurrection and the Life, our Comfort in sorrow and our Peace in dying: We thank Thee that Thou art the eternal home and dwelling place of all who seek Thee. We bless Thee for the hope Thou hast given us, telling of a light that never fades, and of a life that cannot know the bitterness of death, where Christ and those we love await with Thee our coming; through Jesus Christ our Lord.

O God, who art the Strength of Thy saints and who redeemest the souls of Thy servants: We bless Thy name for all those who have died in the Lord, and who now rest from their labors, having received the end of their faith, even the salvation of their souls. Especially we call to remembrance Thy loving-kindness and Thy tender mercies to this Thy servant. For all Thy goodness that withheld not *his* portion in the joys of this earthly life, and for Thy guiding hand along the way of *his* pilgrimage, we give Thee thanks and praise. Especially we bless Thee for Thy grace that kindled in *his* heart the love of Thy dear name; that enabled *him* to fight the good fight, to endure unto the end, and to obtain the victory, yea, to become more than conqueror, through Him that loveth us. We magnify Thy holy name that, *his* trials and temptations being ended; sickness and death being passed, with all the dangers and difficulties of this mortal life, *his* spirit is at home in Thy presence; at whose right hand dwelleth eternal peace. Through Jesus Christ our Lord. *Amen.*

Supplication

O GOD, whose days are without end, and whose mercies cannot be numbered: Make us deeply sensible of the shortness and uncertainty of human life, and let Thy Holy Spirit lead us through this present world in holiness and righteousness all the days of our life; that, when we shall have served Thee in our generation, we may be gathered unto our fathers, having the testimony of a good conscience; in the communion of Thy holy Church; and in the confidence of a certain faith; in the comfort of a reasonable religious and holy hope; in favor with Thee, our God; and in perfect charity with the world.   All which we ask through Jesus Christ our Lord.

We beseech Thee, Almighty God, that we, being inspired by the example of Thy saints, may run with patience the race that is set before us, looking unto Jesus, the Author and Finisher of our faith; so that, when this mortal life is ended, we may be gathered with those whom we have loved, in the kingdom of Thy glory, where there shall be no more death, neither sorrow nor crying, neither shall there be any more pain, for the former things are passed away; through Jesus Christ our Lord. *Amen.*

Intercession

FATHER of mercies, and God of all comfort: Look in Thy tender love and compassion, we beseech Thee, on Thy sorrowing servants. Enable them to find in Thee their refuge and strength, a very present help in trouble, and to know the love of Christ which passeth knowledge. Grant them faith and hope in Him who by death hath conquered death, and by rising again hath opened the gates of everlasting life; even Jesus Christ our Lord.

O Gòd, who healest the broken in heart, and bindest up their wounds: Look down in tender pity and compassion upon Thy servants whose joy has been turned into mourning. Leave them not comfortless, but grant that they may be drawn closer one to another by their common sorrow. As Thou hast given them this new tie to bind them to the world unseen, so grant unto them that where their treasure is, there may their hearts be also. Fill their souls with the light and comfort of Thy presence. Grant unto them such a vision of that life wherein all mysteries shall be revealed, and all tears be wiped away, that they may be able to endure as seeing Thee who art invisible. So dwell with them and be their God, until the day break and the shadows flee away; through Jesus Christ our Lord.

O Lord of life, who dwellest in eternity, and who hast planted in our hearts the faith and hope which look beyond our mortal life to another, even a heavenly country: We give thanks to Thee this day for the bright shining light of immortality in Jesus Christ.   As He has showed us the blessedness of heaven on earth, and has called us into a kingdom not of this world, so may our life be made ever richer in the things that do not pass away.   Raise us up, we pray Thee, in the power of His Spirit, from the death of sin to the life of righteousness.   Prepare us to follow Him, in hope and trust, through all the darkness of the grave into the world of light whither He has led the way, in the sure and certain hope of eternal life; through Him who is the Resurrection and the Life, even Jesus Christ our Lord.

O Thou who hast ordered this wondrous world and who knowest all things in earth and heaven: So fill our hearts with trust in Thee that by night and by day, at all times and in all seasons, we may without fear commit those who are dear to us to Thy never-failing love for this life and the life to come.   *Amen.*

Communion of Saints

O LORD God, the Light of the faithful, the Strength of those who labor, and the Repose of the blessed dead: We give Thee thanks for Thy saints who have witnessed in their lives a good confession, for all the faithful departed, and for those dear to our own hearts who have entered into rest. . . . Grant us grace so to follow their good example that we may be one with them in spirit, and, at the last, together with them, be made partakers of Thine eternal kingdom; through Jesus Christ our Lord.

Eternal Lord God, who holdest all souls in life:
Shed forth, we beseech Thee, on Thy whole
Church in heaven and on earth the bright shining
of Thy light and heavenly comfort. Receive our
thanksgiving for those who have loved and served
Thee and are now at rest; and grant that we,
following their good example, may at the last enter
with them into the fullness of Thine unending
joy; through Jesus Christ our Lord. *Amen.*

Benediction

THE God of peace, that brought again from
the dead our Lord Jesus, that great Shepherd
of the sheep, through the blood of the everlasting
covenant, make you perfect in every good work
to do His will, working in you that which is well-
pleasing in His sight; through Jesus Christ, to
whom be glory for ever and ever. *Amen.*

A GENERAL PRAYER

O GOD, our Father, from whom we come,
unto whom we return, and in whom we live
and move and have our being: We praise Thee
for Thy good gift of life; for its wonder and mystery, its friendships and fellowships. We thank
Thee for the ties that bind us one to another.
We bless Thee for Thy loving and patient dealings with us, whereby Thou dost ever teach us
Thy way; for the meaning that lies hidden in the
heart of sorrow, disappointment, and grief; and
for Thy guiding hand along the way of our
pilgrimage.

We give thanks to Thee for this, Thy servant,
recalling all in *him* that made others love *him*.

We bless Thee for the good and gracious influences in *his* home and training, for all that ministered to *his* best life. We thank Thee for the goodness and truth that have passed from *his* life into the lives of others, and have made the world richer for *his* presence. (*Here may be made mention of characteristics or service.*)

We bless Thy name for the revelation of Thyself and of Thy love in our Lord Jesus Christ, and for the hope set before us in the Gospel. We thank Thee that deep in the human heart is an unquenchable trust that life does not end with death; that the Father, who made us, will care for us beyond the bounds of vision, even as He has cared for us in this earthly world. We praise Thy name that our hope has been so wondrously confirmed in the life and words and resurrection of our Lord and Saviour Jesus Christ.

Grant us, we beseech Thee, the comfort of Thy presence, and the ministry of Thy Holy Spirit. Renew within us the gifts of faith, patience, and enduring love. Help us to walk amid the things of this world with eyes open to the beauty and glory of the eternal; that so, among the sundry and manifold changes of this life, our hearts may surely there be fixed where true joys are to be found; through Jesus Christ our Lord. *Amen.*

AT THE FUNERAL OF A CHILD

O GOD, our Heavenly Father, whose goodness is everlasting and whose mercies never fail: Thine is the beauty of childhood and Thine the light that shines in the face of age. We com-

mend to Thee those who mourn.   Grant that
Thy strength and consolation may be given them
and endue them with all holy thoughts and a
living hope.   Grant that the words of Thy Son,
our Saviour, which speak of His care for little
children, may breathe peace into their troubled
hearts.   Grant that their thoughts and affections
may follow their heart's desire, and may they be
assured that the love in which they rejoiced for
a season is not lost, that the child that has been
taken out of their sight is with Thee, safe in the
eternal love and care; through Jesus Christ our
Lord.   *Amen.*

Almighty God, our Heavenly Father: We thank
Thee for the love that cares for us in life and
watches over us in death.   May we in faith and
hope give back to Thee the life which in love was
given us.   We bless Thy name for our Saviour's
joy in little children and for the assurance that of
such is the kingdom of heaven.   We believe that
in death as in life they are in His holy keeping.
In our sorrow make us strong to commit ourselves
and those we love to Thy never-failing care.   In
our perplexity may we trust where we cannot
understand, knowing that the eternal God is our
Refuge and underneath are the everlasting arms.
In our loneliness make our remembrance grateful,
and may we never forget that the God whom
fatherhood and motherhood interpret will keep
that which we have committed unto Him until
the eternal morning breaks; through Jesus Christ
our Lord.   *Amen.*

O Lord of boundless love, the only Comforter

of the afflicted: Send, we beseech Thee, Thy peace
and comfort into the hearts of Thy sorrowing
servants, that they may earnestly seek after Thee,
who turnest the shadow of death into the light of
morning. Lift up their hearts above earth's darkness to the light and love of Thy presence, that
where their treasure is their heart may be also;
through Jesus Christ our Lord. *Amen.*

AT THE GRAVE

I AM the resurrection, and the life, saith the
Lord: he that believeth in Me, though he were
dead, yet shall he live: and whosoever liveth and
believeth in Me shall never die.

For we know that if our earthly house of this
tabernacle were dissolved, we have a building of
God, a house not made with hands, eternal in
the heavens.

Fear not; I am the first and the last, saith the
Lord: I am He that liveth, and was dead; and,
behold, I am alive for evermore.

Thou wilt keep him in perfect peace, whose
mind is stayed on Thee: because he trusteth in
Thee.

Lord, to whom shall we go? Thou hast the
words of eternal life.

Thanks be unto God who giveth us the victory.

Then shall be said the words of the Committal.

UNTO the mercy of Almighty God, we commend the soul of our *brother* departed and
we commit *his* body to the ground,* earth to
earth, ashes to ashes, dust to dust, in the sure

*Or, *his* body to the deep;
Or, *his* ashes to their resting place.

and certain hope of the resurrection to eternal life; through Jesus Christ our Lord. *Amen.*

Blessed are the dead who die in the Lord from henceforth: yea, saith the Spirit, that they may rest from their labors; and their works do follow them.

Then the Minister shall offer one of the following Prayers, and shall follow with the Lord's Prayer and the Benediction.

O LORD, support us all the day long, until the shadows lengthen and the evening comes, and the busy world is hushed, and the fever of life is over, and our work is done. Then in Thy mercy grant us a safe lodging, and a holy rest, and peace at the last; through Jesus Christ our Lord. *Amen.*

ALMIGHTY God, who by the death of Thy dear Son Jesus Christ hast destroyed death, by His rest in the tomb hast sanctified the graves of the saints, and by His glorious resurrection hast brought life and immortality to light: Receive, we beseech Thee, our unfeigned thanks for that victory over death and the grave which He hath obtained for us and for all who sleep in Him. Keep us in everlasting fellowship with all that wait for Thee on earth, and with all that are with Thee in heaven, in union with Him who is the Resurrection and the Life, who liveth and reigneth with Thee and the Holy Spirit, ever one God, world without end. *Amen.*

Benediction

THE peace of God, which passeth all understanding, keep your hearts and minds in the
knowledge and love of God, and of His Son Jesus
Christ our Lord; and the blessing of God Almighty, the Father, the Son, and the Holy Spirit,
be upon you, and remain with you always.   *Amen.*

FORM AND ORDER FOR
THE RECOGNITION OF CANDIDATES
FOR THE HOLY MINISTRY

The recognition of Candidates for the Holy Ministry shall take place in the presence of the Presbytery, duly constituted.

The Moderator, or other Presiding Minister, shall say:

OUR help is in the name of the Lord, who made heaven and earth.

How beautiful upon the mountains are the feet of him that bringeth good tidings, that publisheth peace!

Lift up your eyes, and look on the fields; for they are white already to harvest. The harvest truly is plenteous, but the laborers are few; pray ye therefore the Lord of the harvest, that He will send forth laborers into His harvest.

IN THE name of the Lord Jesus Christ, the great Head of the Church, we are now to receive under the care of the Presbytery of . . . . , N., who *has* been approved by *his* Church Session and by the Presbytery as *a Candidate* for the Holy Ministry of The United Presbyterian Church in the United States of America.

The Holy Scriptures require that trial be previously had of them who are to be ordained to the Ministry of the Gospel, that this sacred office may not be committed to unworthy men; and that the Churches may have an opportunity to form a true judgment respecting those who are to minister to them in holy things. For this purpose Presbyteries are authorized to enroll as candidates for licensure and ordination such persons as in their judgment give promise of usefulness in this sacred office, after the training and trial of their talents prescribed in the Constitution of the Church.

The Candidate shall stand before the Moderator, who shall say:

The Presbytery of . . . . , having approved your testimonials and sustained your examination, now requires you to make answer to the following questions:

DO YOU, as far as you know your own heart, believe yourself to be called to the office of the Christian Ministry?

The Candidate shall answer:

I do.

Do you promise in reliance upon the grace of God to maintain a Christian character and conduct, and to be diligent and faithful in making full preparation for the Holy Ministry?

The Candidate shall answer:

I do.

· Do you promise to submit yourself to the proper supervision of the Presbytery in matters that concern your preparation for the Holy Ministry?

The Candidate shall answer:

I do.

Do you desire now to be received by this Presbytery as a Candidate for the Holy Ministry in

The United Presbyterian Church in the United States of America?

The Candidate shall answer:

I do.

The Candidate shall then kneel, and the Moderator shall say:

Let us pray.

ALMIGHTY and eternal God, graciously accept this Thy servant as in faith and humility he dedicates himself to the service of Thy kingdom. Bestow upon him the grace of Thy Holy Spirit, that he may be instructed in the deep things of Thy truth, enabled by purity of life to adorn the doctrine of God our Saviour, and guided into ever fuller knowledge of Jesus Christ Thy Son, whom to know is life, whom to serve is freedom, whom to love is joy. Spare him, if it please Thee, that in due season, enriched in grace, learning, and experience, he may be ordained to the office of the Holy Ministry. Teach him to have a steadfast care of his own soul; conserve in him the gifts of Thy love; that, holding fast his profession without wavering, he may finish his course with joy, and finally, of Thy mercy, receive a full reward in Thine eternal and glorious kingdom; through Jesus Christ our Lord. *Amen.*

And now, as our Saviour Christ hath taught us, we humbly pray:

Our Father, . . .

Then the Candidate, together with the Presbytery, shall stand, and the Moderator shall say:

IN THE name of the Lord Jesus Christ, the great Head of the Church, I do now by the authority of this Presbytery declare that you are acknowledged and received as a candidate for licensure and ordination in The United Presbyterian Church in the United States of America, and I do now direct that your name be recorded on the roll of this Presbytery as a candidate for the Holy Ministry.

The Moderator shall then extend to the Candidate the right hand of Christian fellowship, and afterward he shall say:

THE Lord bless you, and keep you: the Lord make His face to shine upon you, and be gracious unto you: the Lord lift up His countenance upon you, and give you peace; through Jesus Christ our Lord. *Amen.*

FORM AND ORDER FOR
THE LICENSING OF CANDIDATES
FOR THE HOLY MINISTRY

The licensing of Candidates for the Holy Ministry should follow a specially appointed Service of Worship, or it may follow at an appointed time after the approval of Candidates at a regular session of Presbytery. An ordained minister, who is the Moderator of the Presbytery or other minister, shall preside.

The Moderator shall say:

PRAISE waiteth for Thee, O God, in Zion: and unto Thee shall the vow be performed.

Blessed is the man whom Thou choosest, and causest to approach unto Thee, that he may dwell in Thy courts: we shall be satisfied with the goodness of Thy house, even of Thy holy temple.

The harvest truly is plenteous, but the laborers are few; pray ye therefore the Lord of the harvest, that He will send forth laborers into His harvest.

The Moderator shall say:

Let us pray.

ETERNAL God, Fountain of life and light, who in old times didst raise up prophets to lead Thy people, and who by Thy Son our Saviour didst send abroad into the world apostles, evangelists, pastors, and teachers: We beseech Thee to provide in our day truehearted, wise, and faithful men, filled with prophetic fire and apostolic zeal, to preach the Gospel of Christ and minister to men according to His example, by whose words Thy Church may be quickened and empowered, and through whose service Thy will may be done on earth as it is in heaven. *Amen.*

Then the Moderator shall say:

BRETHREN in Christ: God by His Holy Spirit calls men to serve Him according to the gifts bestowed upon them, and to chosen servants He grants this grace that they should make known the riches of Christ by the preaching of the Gospel. Unto His Church commandment has been given not only to pray for the increase of the ministry, but also to prove and try those who seek the sacred office, that men of pure heart, good conduct, sound learning, and true Christian experience, able to speak to edification, be found for the service of the sanctuary. Therefore, it is proper that those who desire to give themselves to this ministry should not only prepare themselves by study, prayer, and good works, but should also have opportunity to make trial of their gifts by the experience of preaching, and to approve themselves to the Churches as workmen fitted rightly to divide the Word of truth. According to the Constitution of this Church the oversight of these matters is committed to the Presbytery, which is to examine every candidate for the sacred office in regard to his religious experience, his motives in seeking the ministry, and his proficiency in that knowledge which is necessary as a teacher of the truth as it is in Jesus Christ our Lord.

The Candidate shall stand before the Moderator, and make answer to each of the following questions:

DO YOU believe in One God, Father, Son, and Holy Spirit—and do you confess anew the Lord Jesus Christ as your Saviour and Lord, and acknowledge Him Head over all things to the Church, which is His body?

Answer:

I do so believe.

Do you believe the Scriptures of the Old and New Testaments to be the Word of God, the only infallible rule of faith and practice?

Answer:

I do so believe.

Do you sincerely receive and adopt the Confession of Faith and Catechisms of this Church, as containing the system of doctrine taught in the Holy Scriptures?

Answer:

I do so receive it.

Do you promise to study the peace, unity, and purity of the Church?

Answer:

I do.

Do you promise to submit yourself, in the Lord, to the government of this Presbytery, or of any other into the bounds of which you may be called?

Answer:

I do.

The Candidate shall kneel, and the Moderator shall say:

Let us pray.

O GOD, the Father eternal, who hast made
Thy risen and ever-glorious Son, Jesus Christ,
Head over all things to Thy Church: Bestow upon
this Thy *servant*, whom we bless in Thy name,
the sevenfold gifts of Thy Holy Spirit, that *he* may
be endued with power to preach Thy Gospel,
and may prove *his* fitness to serve Thee in the
ministry of the Word. Grant unto *him* riches of
heavenly wisdom, and guidance of divine love,
that *he* may live near to God and near to man,
in fellowship with Thy Son. Strengthen *his* faith,
confirm *his* courage, and deepen *his* joy in work
for Thee, renewing in *his* heart and on *his* lips
the glad tidings of salvation, and giving unto *him*
the great reward of those that turn many to righteousness. So may the time of *his* probation bear
fruit unto everlasting life, and lead *him* into the
full assurance that Thou hast called and blessed
him for the Ministry of the Gospel. *Amen.*

*The Candidate and the Presbytery shall stand, and the
Moderator shall say:*

IN THE name of the Lord Jesus Christ, and by
the authority which He has given to the Church
for its edification, we do license you to preach the
Gospel as a probationer for the Holy Ministry
wherever God in His providence may call you:
and for this purpose may the blessing of God rest
upon you and the Spirit of Christ fill your heart.
Amen.

The Moderator shall here present a Bible provided by the Presbytery for this purpose, and he shall say:

Take now this Bible, of which you are appointed an interpreter; and be diligent to study the things that are written therein, that, as much as in you lies, you may faithfully and truly teach the Gospel of the grace of God, and be an example of faith and holy living.

NOW unto Him that is able to keep you from falling, and to present you faultless before the presence of His glory with exceeding joy; to the only wise God our Saviour, be glory and majesty, dominion and power, both now and ever.

Amen.

THE grace of the Lord Jesus Christ, and the love of God, and the communion of the Holy Spirit, be with you all. *Amen.*

FORM AND ORDER
FOR THE ORDINATION TO THE
HOLY MINISTRY

Ordination to the Holy Ministry must take place in connec-
tion with a duly constituted meeting of Presbytery, or
Commission of Presbytery, and should follow a regular
service of Public Worship. An ordained minister, who is
the Moderator of the Presbytery or of the Commission,
or other minister of the same Presbytery, shall preside.

The Ordinand shall stand before the Moderator, who shall
say:

OUR help is in the name of the Lord, who
made heaven and earth.

How beautiful upon the mountains are the feet
of him that bringeth good tidings, that publisheth peace!

Go ye therefore, and teach all nations, baptizing them in the name of the Father, and of the
Son, and of the Holy Ghost.

Let us pray.

O LORD our God, who hast founded Thy
Church upon earth, and hast promised to
abide with it for ever: Enlighten and sanctify it,
we beseech Thee, by Thy Holy Spirit.

We pray for all ministers of Thy Word and
sacraments, that Thou wouldst increase in them
Thy grace, that with joy and assurance they may
guard and feed Thy flock, looking to the great
Shepherd and Bishop of souls; even Jesus Christ
our Lord. *Amen.*

The Moderator shall say:

IN THE NAME OF THE LORD JESUS CHRIST, the great Head of the Church, who, being ascended on high, hath given gifts unto men for the edifying of the Body of Christ, we are met here as a Presbytery (or Commission of Presbytery) to ordain *N.* to the office of the Holy Ministry by prayer and the laying on of the hands of the Presbytery, to whom this act of ordination doth belong.

In the act of ordination The United Presbyterian Church in the United States of America, as part of the Holy Catholic or Universal Church, worshiping one God—Father, Son, and Holy Spirit—affirms anew its belief in the Gospel of the sovereign grace and love of God, wherein through Jesus Christ, His only Son, our Lord, incarnate, crucified, and risen, He freely offers to all men, upon repentance and faith, the forgiveness of sins, renewal by the Holy Spirit, and eternal life, and calls them to labor in the fellowship of faith for the advancement of the kingdom of God throughout the world.

The United Presbyterian Church acknowledges the Word of God as contained in the Scriptures of the Old and New Testaments to be the only rule of faith and life. It accepts the Confession of Faith, together with the Larger and Shorter Catechisms, and the Apostles' Creed, as containing the system of doctrine taught in the Scriptures. It adheres to the Form of Government, Book of Discipline, and the Directory for Worship as defining the government and worship of the Church. It administers in the name of the Father, the Son, and the Holy Spirit, the sacraments of Baptism and the Lord's Supper.

Knowing these things, you come of your own commitment to be ordained to this office of the Holy Ministry. You will now make answer to the following questions which the Presbytery, in the name of Christ and His Church, requires of you:

DO YOU believe in One God, Father, Son, and Holy Spirit—and do you confess anew the Lord Jesus Christ as your Saviour and Lord, and acknowledge Him Head over all things to the Church, which is His body?

Answer:

I do so believe.

Do you believe the Scriptures of the Old and New Testaments to be the Word of God, the only infallible rule of faith and practice?

Answer:

I do so believe.

Do you sincerely receive and adopt the Confession of Faith and Catechisms of this Church, as containing the system of doctrine taught in the Holy Scriptures?

Answer:

I do.

Do you approve of the government and discipline of The United Presbyterian Church in the United States of America?

Answer:

I do.

Do you promise subjection to your brethren in the Lord?

Answer:

I do.

Have you been induced, as far as you know your own heart, to seek the office of the Holy Ministry from love of God and a sincere desire to promote His glory in the Gospel of His Son?

Answer:

I have been thus induced.

Do you promise to be zealous and faithful in maintaining the truths of the Gospel and the purity and peace of the Church, whatever persecution or opposition may arise unto you on that account?

Answer:

I do so promise.

Do you engage to be faithful and diligent in the exercise of all your duties as a Christian and a minister of the Gospel, whether personal or relative, private or public; and to endeavor by the grace of God to adorn the profession of the Gospel in your manner of life, and to walk with exemplary piety before the flock of which God shall make you overseer?

Answer:

I do so engage, relying on God's grace.

At the Ordination of an Evangelist, Teacher, Editor, etc.,
the following additional question must be asked:

DO YOU now undertake the work of a minister without pastoral charge (Evangelist, Teacher, Editor, etc.), and do you promise, in reliance upon God for strength, to be faithful in the discharge of all the duties incumbent upon you as a minister of the Gospel of the Lord Jesus Christ?

Answer:

I am willing, and I do so promise, the Lord being my Helper.

The Ordinand shall kneel, and the Presiding Minister shall say:

Let us pray.

ALMIGHTY God and everlasting Father, who dost govern all things in heaven and earth by Thy wisdom, and hast from the beginning ordained for Thy Church the ministry of reconciliation, giving some apostles, and some prophets, and some evangelists, and some pastors and teachers, for the perfecting of the saints, for the work of the ministry, for the edifying of the Body of Christ: SEND DOWN THY HOLY SPIRIT UPON THIS THY SERVANT, WHOM WE, IN THY NAME AND IN OBEDIENCE TO THY HOLY WILL, DO NOW BY THE LAYING ON OF OUR HANDS

Here the Presiding Minister shall lay his hand upon the head of the Ordinand, in which act the Ministers of the Presbytery present shall join

ORDAIN AND APPOINT TO THE OFFICE OF THE HOLY MINISTRY IN THY CHURCH, COMMITTING UNTO HIM AUTHORITY TO PREACH THE WORD, ADMINISTER THE

SACRAMENTS, AND TO BEAR RULE IN THY CHURCH.
Bestow upon him the grace of Thy Holy Spirit,
confirming in heaven what we do in Thy Church
on earth, and owning him as a true Minister of
the Gospel of Thy Son. Like his Master, may he
sanctify himself, that others may be sanctified
through the truth. Let the same mind be in him
which was also in Christ Jesus. May he quicken
and nourish Thy people in the faith of the Gospel.
Increase his own faith in Thee, our God. Abiding
in the fellowship of Thy Son, may his speech be
full of sincerity and truth. May he by his words
and works show forth the power of the Gospel, to
the saving of men and the glory of Thy holy name.
Grant this, O Heavenly Father, for the sake of Thy
dear Son Jesus Christ; in whose name we pray:

Our Father, . . .

*Prayer being ended, the one ordained shall rise from his
knees, and the Minister who presides shall first, and afterward all the Ministers of the Presbytery present in their
order, take him by the right hand, saying:*

We give you the right hand of fellowship, to
take part in this ministry with us.

The Presiding Minister shall then say:

I NOW pronounce and declare that A.B. has been
regularly ordained to the Gospel Ministry,
agreeably to the Word of God, and according to
the Constitution of The United Presbyterian
Church in the United States of America, and that
as such he is entitled to all support, encourage-

ment, honor, and obedience in the Lord: In the name of the Father, and of the Son, and of the Holy Ghost. Amen.

After which, this or other solemn charge shall be given to the newly ordained Minister:

The Charge

MY BROTHER: You have now been ordained to the office of the Holy Ministry and by the authority of Presbytery you have been commissioned to preach the Word, to administer the sacraments, and to perform those other duties appointed by the Church. I now charge you, in the name of the Lord Jesus, the great Head of the Church, to be faithful to this your high calling. I exhort you, in the name of our Lord Jesus Christ, that you have in remembrance into how high a dignity, and to how weighty an office, you have been set apart: that is to say, to be a messenger, watchman, and steward of the Lord; to teach, and to admonish, to feed and provide for the Lord's flock; to seek for Christ's sheep that are dispersed abroad, and for His children who are in the midst of this evil world, that they may be saved through Christ for ever.

Have always, therefore, in remembrance how great a treasure is committed to your charge. For they are the sheep of Christ which He bought with His death, and for whom He shed His blood. The Church and congregation which you must serve is His Body. And if it shall happen that the same Church, or any member thereof, do take any hurt or hindrance by reason of your negligence, you know the greatness of the fault. Wherefore, consider with yourself the end of the ministry toward the children of God, toward the Church, the Body of Christ; and never cease your labor, your care and diligence, until you have done all that lieth in you to bring all such as are or shall be committed to your charge unto agreement in the faith and knowledge of God.

Forasmuch then as your office is both of so great excellency and of so great difficulty, with great care and study you ought to apply yourself, as well to show yourself dutiful and thankful unto that Lord, who hath placed you in so high a dignity; as also to beware that you neither yourself offend nor be occasion that others offend. Howbeit, you cannot have a mind and will thereto of yourself; for the will and ability are given of God alone: therefore you ought, and have need, to pray earnestly for His Holy Spirit. And seeing that you cannot by any other means compass the doing of so weighty a work, pertaining to the salvation of man, but with doctrine and exhortation taken out of the Holy Scriptures, and with a life agreeable to the same, consider how studious you ought to be in reading and learning the Scriptures, and in framing the manners both of yourself and of them that specially pertain unto you, according to the rule of the same Scriptures.

We have good hope that you have well weighed these things long before this time; and that you have clearly determined, by God's grace, to give yourself to this Holy Ministry, whereunto it hath pleased God to call you: so that you will apply yourself wholly to this one thing, and draw all your cares and studies this way; and that you will continually pray to God the Father, by the mediation of our only Saviour Jesus Christ, for the heavenly assistance of the Holy Spirit; that, by daily reading and weighing the Scriptures, you may wax riper and stronger in your ministry; and that you may so endeavor yourself, from time to time, to sanctify the lives of yourself and others, and to fashion them after the rule and doctrine of Christ, that you may be a wholesome and godly example and pattern for the people to follow.

We commend you to God, and to the Word of His grace, which is able to build you up and to give you an inheritance among all them which are sanctified; through Jesus Christ our Lord. *Amen.*

Hymn

The Congregation shall be dismissed with the Benediction by the newly ordained Minister:

NOW unto Him that is able to keep you from falling, and to present you faultless before the presence of His glory with exceeding joy; to the only wise God our Saviour, be glory and majesty, dominion and power, both now and ever.
Amen.

THE grace of the Lord Jesus Christ, and the love of God, and the communion of the Holy Spirit, be with you all. *Amen.*

FORM AND ORDER FOR
THE INSTALLATION OF A MINISTER

The Service of Installation shall be conducted by the Presbytery, or by a Commission appointed by it, or by its General Council when voted by the Presbytery, and in connection with a regular Service of Worship. An ordained minister, who is the Moderator of the Presbytery or other minister, shall preside. In the installation of a minister previously ordained, a ruling elder who is Moderator of the Presbytery may preside. After the sermon, the Moderator shall say:

OUR help is in the name of the Lord, who made heaven and earth.

I beseech you that ye walk worthy of the vocation wherewith ye are called, with all lowliness and meekness, with long-suffering, forbearing one another in love; endeavoring to keep the unity of the Spirit in the bond of peace.

He gave some apostles; and some prophets; and some evangelists; and some pastors and teachers; for the perfecting of the saints, for the work of the ministry, for the edifying of the Body of Christ.

IN THE name of the Lord Jesus Christ, the great Head of the Church, we have met to induct into the pastoral charge of this congregation *N.* The call of this congregation has been placed in his hands and he has signified to the Presbytery his willingness to accept thereof. We are here by appointment and order of the Presbytery; and by its authority do now proceed to constitute and install him, in the name of the Lord Jesus Christ, as the Pastor of this congregation.

The Minister to be installed shall stand before the Moderator, who shall say:

You will now make answer to the following questions which the Presbytery, in the name of Christ and His Church, requires of you.

ARE you now willing to take charge of this Church as its Pastor (to accept the responsibility of Associate Pastor in this Church), agreeably to your declaration in accepting its call?

Answer: I am now willing.

Do you conscientiously believe and declare, as far as you know your own heart, that, in taking upon you this charge, you are influenced by a sincere desire to promote the glory of God, and the good of the Church?

Answer: I so believe and declare.

Do you solemnly promise that, by the assistance of the grace of God, you will endeavor faithfully to discharge all the duties of a Pastor to this Church, and will be careful to maintain a deportment in all respects becoming a minister of the Gospel of Christ, agreeably to your ordination engagements?

Answer: I do.

Then the Moderator shall propose to the People the following questions and the People shall make affirmative answer by raising the right hand:

DO YOU, the People of this Church, continue to profess your readiness to receive A.B., whom you have called to be your Pastor (or Associate Pastor)?

Do you promise to receive the word of truth from his mouth with meekness and love and to submit to him in the due exercise of discipline?

Do you promise to encourage him in his labors, and to assist his endeavors for your instruction and spiritual edification?

And do you engage to continue to him while he is your Pastor (or Associate Pastor) that competent worldly maintenance which you have promised, and to furnish him with whatever you may see needful for the honor of religion and for his comfort among you?

All standing, the Moderator shall say:

I NOW pronounce and declare that A.B. has been regularly elected [ordained] and installed Pastor (Associate Pastor) of this Church, agreeably to the Word of God, and according to the Constitution of The United Presbyterian Church in the United States of America, and that as such he is entitled to all support, encouragement, honor, and obedience in the Lord: In the name of the Father, and of the Son, and of the Holy Ghost. Amen.

The Moderator shall say:

Let us pray.

ALMIGHTY God and everlasting Father, who dost govern all things in heaven and earth by Thy wisdom, and hast from the beginning ordained for Thy Church the ministry of reconciliation: We thank Thee for Thy goodness to us this day in establishing this pastorate: and we beseech Thee to continue Thy loving-kindness to this congregation, and to Thy servant who has now been set over them in holy things. Bless him in full measure with the gifts of Thy Spirit, that he may truly and effectively preach the Gospel. So endue him with purity of life that he may be an example to this flock; and grant that in all things he may faithfully serve Thee, to the glory of Thy great name.

O Lord God, the Sanctifier of the faithful: Visit, we pray Thee, this people with Thy love and favor; prepare their hearts to receive Thy Word; enlighten their minds more and more with the light of the everlasting Gospel; increase in them true religion; nourish them in all goodness; arouse them to works that shall establish among men righteousness and love and truth, according to Thy holy will; and of Thy great mercy keep them in the unity of the Spirit and in the bonds of love; through Jesus Christ our Lord; whom, with Thee and the Holy Spirit, one God, we worship and glorify, world without end. *Amen.*

Then shall follow, according to the direction of the Presbytery, a solemn charge to the Pastor and to the People. The following forms may be used if desired, after which the service shall be concluded by the singing of a Hymn and the pronouncing of the Benediction.

Charge to the Pastor

BROTHER in Christ: You now have been inducted into the charge of this congregation. The members of this Church have called you to be their Minister, and you have accepted their call, and by the authority of Presbytery you have been commissioned to preach the Word and administer the sacraments. In the name of the Lord Jesus Christ, the great Head of the Church, I charge you to give full proof of your ministry, to follow after righteousness, godliness, faith, love, patience, meekness.

Yours is the first and highest office in the Church for both dignity and usefulness, and you will remember how varied and manifold are the duties and responsibilities to which you are called.

You are a bishop, and as overseer of Christ's flock you will have a watchful regard for your people. You will be their guide and leader, and they will follow you as they see you follow Christ.

You are a pastor. You will shepherd the Church of Christ which He purchased with His own blood. You will respond to the Master's command: "Feed My sheep"; "Feed My lambs." This will require, on your part, diligence in study and fidelity in the care of your people.

You are a minister. You are a servant of Christ and a servant of His people, a servant of the Gospel and a servant of the Church. No calling is higher, for the Lord Jesus Himself said: Whosoever will be chief among you, let him be your servant.

You are a presbyter. You will be faithful and diligent in your responsibilities not only in your Church but in your Presbytery. You will not neglect the welfare of your brethren in other Churches, and you will be concerned for the work of the kingdom beyond your own parish.

You are an ambassador. You will faithfully declare the whole counsel of God. You will proclaim the holy birth, the perfect life, the atoning death, the glorious resurrection, the everliving presence of the Lord Jesus. How great is this responsibility as set forth by Saint Paul: We are ambassadors for Christ, as though God did beseech you by us: we pray you in Christ's stead, be ye reconciled to God.

You are a steward.   You are entrusted with the mysteries of God, and it will be your obligation faithfully to proclaim the Word of God, to administer the Holy Sacraments instituted by Christ, and so to uphold the work and worship of the Church that He who is the great Head of the Church may be glorified.

I charge you therefore before God, and the Lord Jesus Christ, who shall judge the quick and the dead at His appearing and His kingdom: preach the Word; be instant in season, out of season; reprove, rebuke, exhort, with all long-suffering and doctrine.   Suffer hardship; do the work of an evangelist; fulfill thy ministry.

And may the very God of peace sanctify you wholly, and preserve you blameless unto the coming of our Lord Jesus Christ.   *Amen.*

Charge to the People

BELOVED in the Lord: You have now entered into a contract and solemn covenant with this Presbytery and with your Pastor that you will faithfully perform the things which you have promised.   With careful consideration and prayerful decision you have satisfied yourselves as to the qualifications of your Pastor for this high office. You have called him, and he has answered your petition, and the Presbytery has confirmed it.   We pray that God, who is able to make all grace abound unto you, may grant you all sufficiency in everything that ye may abound in every good work.

You will, therefore, at all times remember the things which you have covenanted to perform.

As you have called him to be your Pastor you will continue to receive and welcome him as such. You have promised to be good hearers and to receive the Word of truth which he preaches with meekness and love. You will, therefore, be considerate in your judgment. You have promised to be ready to receive discipline at his hands. This is one of the functions of the Church. Your Pastor is charged to preach the Word; be urgent in season, out of season; reprove, rebuke, exhort, with all long-suffering and teaching. You have promised to encourage him in his work and to help him in his endeavor to help yourselves. This will require thought and planning on your part. You carry responsibility with him for the spiritual upbuilding of the Church. You are his fellow workers. You are laborers together with him. You will pray for him and with him. You have promised to make it your particular duty so to provide for him in material things that he may be free to give his whole time to the Church and to the Presbytery without distraction or unnecessary anxiety.

You have promised, further, to make it your concern that everything that can be done to advance the honor of religion in this place shall be done by you. This is a high obligation. It places upon you the solemn duty to see that nothing takes place here that would in any way harm the Church, or the cause of Christ, and it encourages you in your effort to honor the Church and to adorn your profession of the Gospel. Remember always that you are the Body of Christ, and severally members thereof. There is one Body, and one Spirit, one Lord, one faith, one baptism, one

God and Father of all, who is above all, and
through all, and in you all.

May the blessing of God rest upon you, and
unto Him that is able to do exceeding abundantly
above all that we ask or think, according to the
power that worketh in us; unto Him be glory in
the Church by Christ Jesus, throughout all ages,
world without end.   *Amen.*

Hymn

Benediction

*The Congregation shall be dismissed with the Benediction
by the newly installed Minister.*

THE peace of God, which passeth all understanding, keep your hearts and minds in the
knowledge and love of God, and of His Son Jesus
Christ our Lord; and the blessing of God Almighty, the Father, the Son, and the Holy Spirit,
be upon you, and remain with you always.   *Amen.*

*At the close of the service the Members of the Congregation
shall come forward and extend their affectionate welcome
to the Pastor.*

FORM AND ORDER
FOR THE INSTALLATION OF
AN ASSISTANT PASTOR

This service should be held in connection with the regular Order of Worship. When an invitation for the service of an Assistant Pastor has been accepted by him at the hand of his Presbytery, immediate steps for his installation shall be taken in the Church to which he has been duly invited by the Pastor and Session. In the installation of an Assistant Pastor, the Moderator of the Presbytery, or a Minister of the Presbytery whom he shall appoint, shall propose to him the questions.

The Moderator or Presiding Minister shall say:

AS THE Moderator of the Presbytery (or Minister appointed by the Moderator of the Presbytery), I have the honor to present to you the Reverend N., who has been approved by the Pastor, invited by the Session, and approved by the Presbytery, to be Assistant Pastor.

Addressing the Assistant Pastor, the Moderator or Presiding Minister shall propose the following questions:

ARE you now willing to assume the duties of Assistant Pastor agreeably to your declaration upon accepting the invitation of the Session of this Church?

Answer:

I am.

Do you conscientiously believe and declare, as far as you know your own heart, that, in taking upon you this office, you are influenced by a sincere desire to promote the glory of God and the good of the Church?

242

Answer:

I do.

Do you solemnly promise that, by the assistance of the grace of God, you will endeavor faithfully to serve this congregation under the Session, and will be careful to maintain a deportment in all respects becoming a servant of Jesus Christ, agreeably to your ordination engagements?

Answer:

I do so promise.

The Presiding Minister shall then propose to the People these questions, and the People shall respond by raising the right hand.

DO YOU, the People of this Church, profess your readiness to receive . . . . , who has been invited by the Session to be Assistant Pastor?

Do you promise to encourage him in his labors and to assist his endeavors for your instruction and spiritual edification?

IN THE name of the Lord Jesus Christ, the great Head of the Church, we welcome you as Assistant Pastor in this congregation. And may the blessing of God the Father, the Son, and the Holy Spirit, rest upon you and abide with you always. *Amen.*

The Minister shall say:

Let us pray.

ALMIGHTY God, the Source of goodness, the Fountain of light and life: We beseech Thee to hear our prayer in behalf of Thy servant appointed to minister in this Church. Direct all his counsels by Thy wisdom. Give him diligence

and zeal in the service of Thy kingdom. Ever renew
in his heart faith and hope and love. So may the
mind of Christ dwell in him and rule him that he
may be a right and inspiring example to all who
know him. Prosper all whereto he sets his hand,
and give good success to his endeavor.

O Lord God, the Sanctifier of the faithful: Visit,
we pray Thee, this people with Thy love and
favor; prepare their hearts to receive Thy Word;
enlighten their minds more and more with the
light of the everlasting Gospel; increase in them
true religion; nourish them in all goodness; arouse
them to works that shall establish among men
righteousness and love and truth, according to
Thy holy will; and of Thy great mercy keep them
in the unity of the Spirit and in the bonds of love;
through Jesus Christ our Lord; whom, with Thee
and the Holy Spirit, one God, we worship and
glorify, world without end. *Amen.*

The Minister shall say:

THE Lord bless you, and keep you: the Lord
make His face to shine upon you, and be gracious unto you: the Lord lift up His countenance
upon you, and give you peace; through Jesus
Christ our Lord. *Amen.*

FORM AND ORDER FOR THE
ORDINATION OF RULING ELDERS

The Ordination of Ruling Elders should take place in connection with a regular service of worship. The Ruling Elders to be ordained standing before the Minister, he shall say:

GRACE, mercy, and peace, from God the Father and Christ Jesus our Lord.

BELOVED in Christ: In apostolic times there were elders, to whom were entrusted the oversight and leadership of the Christian Churches, and concerning whom the Apostle Paul advised that they that ruled well should be counted worthy of double honor. Therefore, this Church has from the beginning included in its government not only Ministers and Pastors, who are to preach the Gospel and administer the sacraments in the name of Christ and as His representatives, but also Ruling Elders chosen by the people to represent them, and to be joined with Pastors and Ministers in the exercise of government and discipline in the Church.

These Ruling Elders in each congregation, together with the Pastor, constitute the Session, to which it is committed to admit and exclude members, and to supervise the worship, provide for the teaching, direct the activities, and promote the spiritual interests of the Church. The Elders are also to represent the congregation in Presbyteries, Synods, and General Assemblies, when commissioned thereto. And it is the duty of the Elders to set the example of a godly conduct and character, and to assist the Pastor as he may desire in his ministry to the people.

The congregation of this Church, in the mode most approved and in use in this congregation, having elected *A., B., C., D.* to the office of Ruling Elder, and *they* having signified *their* willingness to serve, we do now, in the name of the Lord Jesus Christ, proceed to *their* ordination.

The Minister shall say:

You will now make answer to the following questions which the Constitution of this Church requires of you:

DO YOU believe in One God, Father, Son, and Holy Spirit—and do you confess anew the Lord Jesus Christ as your Saviour and Lord, and acknowledge Him Head over all things to the Church, which is His body?

Answer:
> I do so believe.

Do you believe the Scriptures of the Old and New Testaments to be the Word of God, the only infallible rule of faith and practice?

Answer:
> I do so believe.

Do you sincerely receive and adopt the Confession of Faith and Catechisms of this Church, as containing the system of doctrine taught in the Holy Scriptures?

Answer:
> I do.

Do you approve of the government and discipline of The United Presbyterian Church in the United States of America?

Answer:

I do.

Do you accept the office of Ruling Elder in this Church, and promise faithfully to perform all the duties thereof and to endeavor by the grace of God to adorn the profession of the Gospel in your life, and to set a worthy example before the Church of which God has made you an officer?

Answer:

I do.

Do you promise subjection to your brethren in the Lord?

Answer:

I do.

Do you promise to study the peace, unity, and purity of the Church?

Answer:

I do.

The Minister shall then address the following questions to the Members of the Church, bidding them respond by raising the right hand:

DO YOU, the Members of this Church, acknowledge and receive *these persons* as *Ruling Elders* and do you promise to yield *them* all that honor, encouragement, and obedience in the Lord to which *their* office, according to the Word of God and the Constitution of this Church, entitles *them?*

The Elders to be ordained shall kneel and, the Congregation standing, the Minister shall say:

Let us pray.

O ETERNAL and ever-blessed God, Father of our Lord Jesus Christ, who of Thine infinite mercy hast chosen to Thyself a Church, which Thou hast ever ruled by the inspiration of Thy Holy Spirit; and yet hast used the service of men, as in preaching Thy Word and ministering Thy sacraments, so also in guiding Thy flock and providing for the poor: We commend unto Thee those whom we now ordain to the office of the Eldership.

Here the Minister and the Session shall lay their hands on the heads of the Elders to be ordained, and the Minister shall say:

SET APART, O LORD, THESE THY SERVANTS, TO THE WORK WHEREUNTO THEY HAVE BEEN CALLED BY THE VOICE OF THE CHURCH. ENDUE THEM PLENTEOUSLY WITH HEAVENLY WISDOM. GRANT THEM THY GRACE, THAT THEY MAY BE GOOD MEN, FULL OF THE HOLY SPIRIT AND OF FAITH, RULING IN THE FEAR OF GOD. GIVE THEM THAT FAVOR AND INFLUENCE WITH THE PEOPLE WHICH COME FROM FOLLOWING CHRIST. SO FILL THEM WITH HIS SPIRIT THAT THEY MAY LEAD THIS CONGREGATION IN HIS SERVICE. MAKE THEM FAITHFUL UNTO DEATH, AND WHEN THE CHIEF SHEPHERD SHALL APPEAR, MAY THEY RECEIVE A CROWN OF GLORY THAT FADETH NOT AWAY. *Amen.*

The Elders shall stand, and the Minister shall say:

IN THE name of the Lord Jesus Christ, the great Head of the Church, I now declare you duly ordained and set apart to the sacred office of Ruling Elder.

I charge you in the name of the Lord Jesus to be faithful to this your office, and may the blessing of God Almighty, the Father, the Son, and the Holy Spirit, rest upon you and abide with you always. *Amen.*

I charge you also, the Members of this congregation, to be faithful to *these Elders* whom you have chosen to rule over you in the Lord; and that you render *them* all due obedience, co-operation, and support, and follow *them* so far as you see *them* follow Christ.

The members of the Session shall take the hand of the newly ordained Elders and say:

We give you the right hand of fellowship to take part of this office with us.

Then the Minister shall say:

NOW our Lord Jesus Christ Himself, and God, even our Father, which hath loved us, and hath given us everlasting consolation and good hope through grace, stablish you in every good word and work. *Amen.*

FORM AND ORDER FOR THE
INSTALLATION OF RULING ELDERS
WHO HAVE BEEN ORDAINED

When an Elder has terminated his connection with his Session by removal to another Church, or by resignation, or when he is re-elected under the rotary system, he is to be installed before he can regularly exercise the duties of his office.

The following Order may be used separately. If used in connection with the Order for the Ordination of Ruling Elders, it may be introduced immediately before the Benediction which concludes that Order.

The Minister shall say:

BELOVED in Christ: Having already been solemnly ordained to the office of Ruling Elder, you do now present *yourselves* in response to the voice of this congregation, to be installed again for the discharge of the active duties of your office.

You will therefore now give answer to the following questions:

DO YOU accept the office of Ruling Elder in this congregation, and promise faithfully to perform all the duties thereof?

Answer:

I do.

Do you promise to study the peace, unity, and purity of the Church?

Answer:

I do.

The Elders-elect having answered these questions in the affirmative, the Minister shall address to the Members of the Church this question, to which they shall respond by raising the right hand:

DO YOU, the Members of this Church, acknowledge and receive *these persons* as *Ruling Elders,* and do you promise to yield *them* all that honor, encouragement, and obedience in the Lord to which *their* office, according to the Word of God and the Constitution of this Church, entitles *them?*

Then the Minister shall say:

IN THE name of the Lord Jesus Christ, the great Head of the Church, I do now declare you to be inducted into the office of Ruling Elder in this congregation, and may the blessing of God Almighty, Father, Son, and Holy Spirit, rest upon you and remain with you always.

Amen.

Then the Minister shall say:

NOW our Lord Jesus Christ Himself, and God, even our Father, which hath loved us, and hath given us everlasting consolation and good hope through grace, stablish you in every good word and work. *Amen.*

FORM AND ORDER
FOR THE ORDINATION OF DEACONS

*The Ordination of Deacons should take place in connection
with a regular service of worship. The Deacons to be
ordained standing before the Minister, he shall say:*

OUR help is in the name of the Lord, who
made heaven and earth.

Pure religion and undefiled before God and the
Father is this, To visit the fatherless and widows
in their affliction, and to keep oneself unspotted
from the world.

BELOVED in Christ: In the Christian Churches
of apostolic times there were deacons, whose
office was held in honor, and who were highly es-
teemed for their services to the Church, in company with the elders. From early days it was a
peculiar part of the duties of these office-bearers
to be the instruments of the Church's ministry of
compassion. This Church, therefore, has recog-
nized the office and work of the deacon as in accord with apostolic practice. In the course of
time new forms of work have been given to this
office, and it has grown in value to the Church,
while to it there has always attached its ancient
character as the representative of the Church's
purpose to follow Christ in compassion and in
ministry to the bodily needs of men.

*These persons, A., B., C., D., here present, hav-
ing been chosen, in the mode most approved and*

in use in this congregation, to the office of Deacon, and having signified *their* willingness to serve, we do therefore, in the name of the Lord Jesus Christ, now proceed to *their* ordination.

Then the Minister, addressing the Deacons-elect, shall say:

Forasmuch as you have declared your willingness to take this office upon you, I now require you to answer the following questions, appointed by the Church to be put to those who are to be ordained as Deacons:

DO YOU believe in One God, Father, Son, and Holy Spirit—and do you confess anew the Lord Jesus Christ as your Saviour and Lord, and acknowledge Him Head over all things to the Church, which is His body?

Answer: I do so believe.

Do you believe the Scriptures of the Old and New Testaments to be the Word of God, the only infallible rule of faith and practice?

Answer: I do so believe.

Do you sincerely receive and adopt the Confession of Faith and Catechisms of this Church, as containing the system of doctrine taught in the Holy Scriptures?

Answer: I do.

Do you approve of the government and discipline of The United Presbyterian Church in the United States of America?

Answer: I do.

Do you accept the office of Deacon in this Church, and promise faithfully to perform all the duties thereof, and to endeavor by the grace of God to adorn the profession of the Gospel in your life, and to set a worthy example before the Church of which God has made you an officer?

Answer: I do.

Do you promise subjection to your brethren in the Lord?

Answer: I do.

Do you promise to study the peace, unity, and purity of the Church?

Answer: I do.

The Deacons-elect having answered these questions in the affirmative, the Minister shall address to the Members of the Church the following question, to which they will respond by raising the right hand:

DO YOU, the Members of this Church, acknowledge and receive *these brethren* as *Deacons,* and do you promise to yield *them* all that honor, encouragement, and obedience in the Lord to which *their* office, according to the Word of God and the Constitution of this Church, entitles *them?*

The Deacons to be ordained shall kneel and, the Congregation standing, the Minister and the Session shall lay their hands upon the Deacons to be ordained and the Minister shall say: Let us pray.

O LORD JESUS, who didst come not to be ministered unto but to minister; who for our sakes became poor, that we through Thy poverty might be rich; who didst love the Church, and give Thyself up for it: Set apart and consecrate *these* Thy *servants* to the office of Deacon. Give *them* Thine own spirit of compassion for human needs. Inspire *them* with devotion to the

Church.   Guide and sustain *them* in all *their* service until *their* work on earth is done; and bestow upon *them* the great rewards of Thy heavenly kingdom.   *Amen.*

Then the Minister shall say:

IN THE name of the Lord Jesus Christ, and by the authority committed to me in His Church, I hereby declare you duly set apart and ordained to the office of Deacon.

I now charge you, in the name of the Lord Jesus, to be faithful in this your office.

I also charge you, Christian people, to be faithful to *these Deacons*, remembering *them* in your prayers, providing for *their* ministry to the needy by your liberal gifts, and supporting all *their* service to the Church.

Where there is an existing Board of Deacons, it is proper that the Members of that body shall take the hand of the newly ordained Deacons and say:

We give you the right hand of fellowship, to take part of this office with us.

If Deacons who have been already ordained are to be installed at the same service, the Order for Installation may be here introduced.

Then the Minister shall say:

NOW our Lord Jesus Christ Himself, and God, even our Father, which hath loved us, and hath given us everlasting consolation and good hope through grace, stablish you in every good word and work.   *Amen.*

FORM AND ORDER FOR
THE INSTALLATION OF DEACONS
WHO HAVE BEEN ORDAINED

Deacons who have been re-elected after the expiration of their terms of office are to be installed.

The following Order may be used separately. If used in connection with the Order for the Ordination of Deacons, it may be introduced immediately before the Benediction which concludes that Order.

The Minister shall say:

THE congregation of this Church, in the mode most approved and in use in this congregation, having elected *A., B., C., D.* to the office of Deacon, and *they* having signified *their* willingness to serve, we do now, in the name of the Lord Jesus Christ, proceed to *their* installation.

The Deacons to be installed standing before the Minister, he shall say:

BELOVED in Christ: Having already been solemnly ordained to the office of Deacon, you do now present *yourselves*, in response to the voice of this congregation, to be installed again for the discharge of the active duties of your office.

You will therefore now give answer to these questions:

DO YOU accept the office of Deacon in this congregation, and promise faithfully to perform all the duties thereof?

Answer:

I do.

Do you promise to study the peace, unity, and purity of the Church?

Answer:

I do.

The Deacons-elect having answered these questions in the affirmative, the Minister shall address to the Members of the Church the following question, to which they shall respond by raising the right hand:

DO YOU, the Members of this Church, acknowledge and receive *these persons* as *Deacons*, and do you promise to yield *them* all that honor, encouragement, and obedience in the Lord, to which *their* office, according to the Word of God, and the Constitution of this Church, entitles *them?*

Then the Minister shall say:

IN THE name of the Lord Jesus Christ, the great Head of the Church, I do now declare you to be inducted into the office of Deacon in this congregation, and may the blessing of God Almighty, Father, Son, and Holy Spirit, rest upon you and remain with you always.   *Amen.*

Then the Minister shall say:

NOW our Lord Jesus Christ Himself, and God, even our Father, which hath loved us, and hath given us everlasting consolation and good hope through grace, stablish you in every good word and work.   *Amen.*

THE FORM AND ORDER FOR
THE SETTING APART OF
A COMMISSIONED CHURCH WORKER

By action of the General Assembly, a member of the United Presbyterian Church who has expressed the desire to dedicate his life to the service of Christ and the Church, and who has fulfilled the educational requirements requisite to this office, may be set apart by Presbytery as a Commissioned Church Worker.

The Moderator shall say:

GO YE therefore, and teach all nations, baptizing them in the name of the Father, and of the Son, and of the Holy Ghost: Teaching them to observe all things whatsoever I have commanded you: and, lo, I am with you alway, even unto the end of the world.

Take My yoke upon you, and learn of Me; for I am meek and lowly in heart: and ye shall find rest unto your souls. For My yoke is easy, and My burden is light.

IN THE name of the Lord Jesus Christ, the great Head of the Church, we are now to receive as Commissioned Church Worker *N.*, who has been recommended by *his* Church Session and who has been examined and approved by this Presbytery.

The Church Worker shall stand before the Moderator and shall answer the following questions:

DO YOU believe in One God, Father, Son, and Holy Spirit—and do you confess anew the Lord Jesus Christ as your Saviour and Lord, and acknowledge Him Head over all things to the Church, which is His body?

Answer: I do so believe.

Do you believe the Scriptures of the Old and New Testaments to be the Word of God, the only infallible rule of faith and practice?

Answer: I do so believe.

Do you sincerely receive and adopt the Confession of Faith and Catechisms of this Church as containing the system of doctrine taught in the Holy Scriptures?

Answer: I do.

Do you approve of the government and discipline of The United Presbyterian Church in the United States of America?

Answer: I do.

Have you been induced, as far as you know your own heart, to seek the office of Commissioned Church Worker from love to God and a sincere desire to promote His glory in the Gospel of His Son?

Answer: I have been thus induced.

Do you promise faithfully to perform all the duties of a Commissioned Church Worker, and to study the peace, unity, and purity of the Church?

Answer: I do.

Do you promise to submit yourself in the Lord to the government of this Presbytery, or of any other Presbytery in the bounds of which you may serve, as a Commissioned Church Worker?

Answer: I do.

The Church Worker shall kneel, and the Moderator say:
Let us pray.

ALL glory, praise, and thanksgiving be unto Thee, O Lord our God, for that Thou didst reveal Thy love for the children of men in sending Thy beloved Son for their redemption, and hast from the beginning raised up chosen servants to tell abroad the message of Thy grace.

We give Thee thanks for the devotion of *this* Thy *servant* whom we now, in Thy name, send forth to bear this message of redeeming grace. Accept *his* love and devotion; and increase in *him*, we beseech Thee, the gifts of Thy Holy Spirit, that *he* may commend by teaching and example the grace of the Lord Jesus. Give *him* understanding, sympathy, and patience; guard *him* in peril of body and of soul; be Thou *his* strength and *his* joy; cheer *him* with Thy continual presence; and make *him* glad with the fruits of *his* labor.

And we beseech Thee to help us who send *him* forth to encourage *him* in *his* labors and to bear *him* up continually with prayer; through Jesus Christ our Lord. *Amen.*

Then the Church Worker, together with the Presbytery, shall stand, and the Moderator shall say:

IN THE name of the Lord Jesus Christ, the great Head of the Church, I do now by the authority of the Presbytery declare that you are a Commissioned Church Worker and I do now direct that your name be so recorded by this Presbytery.

Benediction

THE Lord bless you, and keep you: the Lord make His face to shine upon you, and be gracious unto you: the Lord lift up His countenance upon you, and give you peace; through Jesus Christ our Lord. *Amen.*

FORM AND ORDER FOR
THE RECOGNITION OF TRUSTEES

The duties of Trustees of a particular Church corporation shall be confined exclusively to the management of the corporate affairs of said particular Church corporation.

The Trustees elected to office shall stand before the Minister, who shall say:

EXCEPT the Lord build the house, they labor in vain that build it: except the Lord keep the city, the watchman waketh but in vain.

It is required in stewards, that a man be found faithful.

He that is faithful in that which is least is faithful also in much.

A., B., C., D., beloved *Brethren:* You have been duly elected *Trustees* of this congregation. Your office is consecrated by its importance to the Church's welfare. You will always bear in mind that what you do will in high degree determine the Church's usefulness to the kingdom of God. You will look upon your office as an opportunity to serve His kingdom. May you have joy in being faithful *stewards* for Him, knowing that in dedicating your time and talents to the good of His Church you are *workers* together with God. Your office being thus acknowledged, you are asked to express your purpose regarding it by making answer to these questions:

DO YOU promise to give to the corporate affairs of this congregation diligent service?

Answer:

I do.

261

DO YOU promise to study the peace, unity, and purity of the Church?

Answer:

I do.

The Minister shall then propose to the Congregation this question, and the Congregation shall make response by raising the right hand:

DO YOU receive and recognize *these brethren* as *Trustees* of this Church, and do you promise to *them* full support in *their* work?

The Minister shall say:

IN THE name of the Lord Jesus Christ, the great Head of the Church, I now welcome you to the office of Trustee in this congregation, and may the blessing of God, the Father, Son, and Holy Spirit, rest upon you and abide with you always. *Amen.*

The Minister shall say:

Let us pray.

O LORD our God, who art the only Founder and Keeper of Thy Church: We thank Thee that Thou hast called Thy *servants* to share in the work of Thy kingdom. Grant *them* grace to give *themselves* wholly to this *their* task and service. Grant *them* sincerity and singleness of mind. Hold ever before *them* the example of *their* Master, who pleased not Himself, but gave Himself up for us all, that, sharing His ministry and consecration, *they* may enter into His joy. Guide *them* in *their* work for Thy Church. Prosper *their* counsels and *their* labors. Reward *their* fidelity with the knowledge that Thou art using *them* for the accomplishment of Thy purpose in Jesus Christ our Lord. *Amen.*

The Minister shall say:

THE Lord bless you, and keep you: the Lord make His face to shine upon you, and be gracious unto you: the Lord lift up His countenance upon you, and give you peace; through Jesus Christ our Lord. *Amen.*

FORM AND ORDER FOR
THE ORGANIZATION OF A CHURCH

The Moderator of the Presbytery, if the Presbytery be in session, or the Minister who is the chairman of the duly authorized commission of the Presbytery shall preside. This Order should be observed in connection with a regular Service of Worship. The Presiding Minister shall say:

IN THE name of the Lord Jesus Christ, and by virtue of the authority of the Presbytery of . . . . , we have assembled for the purpose of organizing a Church of Christ, according to the Constitution of The United Presbyterian Church in the United States of America.

The United Presbyterian Church in the United States of America, as part of the Holy Catholic or Universal Church, worshiping one God—Father, Son, and Holy Spirit—affirms anew its belief in the Gospel of the sovereign grace and love of God, wherein through Jesus Christ, His only Son, our Lord, incarnate, crucified, and risen, He freely offers to all men, upon repentance and faith, the forgiveness of sins, renewal by the Holy Spirit, and eternal life, and calls them to labor in the fellowship of faith for the advancement of the kingdom of God throughout the world.

The United Presbyterian Church acknowledges the Word of God as contained in the Scriptures of the Old and New Testaments to be the only rule of faith and life. It accepts the Confession of Faith, together with the Larger and Shorter Catechisms, and the Apostles' Creed, as containing the system of doctrine taught in the Scriptures. It adheres to the Form of Government, the Book of Discipline, and the Directory for Worship as defining the government and worship of the Church. It administers, in the name of the Father, Son, and Holy Spirit, the sacraments of Baptism and the Lord's Supper.

The Moderator, or Presiding Minister, shall say:

Let us pray.

ALMIGHTY and everlasting God, who hast revealed Thy glory by Christ among all nations: Preserve the works of Thy mercy, that Thy Church, which is spread throughout the world, may persevere with steadfast faith in the confession of Thy name; through Jesus Christ our Lord. *Amen.*

Then shall be received those Persons having letters of dismissal from other Churches, together with those making confession or reaffirmation of their faith. Those not having been baptized shall receive the Sacrament of Baptism.

Then shall the Moderator, or Presiding Minister, read to those admitted to Church membership the following Covenant, to which they shall subscribe either by signing their names or by raising the right hand:

The Covenant

WE THE undersigned persons desire to be constituted and organized as a Church, which is to be known as . . . . Church. We do covenant and agree to walk together as disciples of Jesus Christ in a Church relation according to the provisions of the Constitution of The United Presbyterian Church in the United States of America. We promise to maintain this Church by our attendance at its services, our support of its work, our gifts, our efforts, and our prayers, and to seek in its fellowship to glorify the name and further the cause of our Lord Jesus Christ.

Then shall follow the election, ordination, and installation of Ruling Elders and Deacons, according to the Constitution of The United Presbyterian Church in the United States of America. Then, all standing, the Moderator, or Presiding Minister, shall say:

FORASMUCH as you have covenanted together to enter into communicant membership with the Church of Christ in this place and have chosen Ruling Elders, now in the name of Jesus Christ, the great Head of the Church, and by the authority of the Presbytery of . . . . , I hereby declare that . . . . Church has been duly organized. And may the blessing of God, the Father, Son, and Holy Spirit, rest upon you and abide with you always. *Amen.*

The original roll of members presented to the Presiding Minister, together with the Covenant subscribed at this time, shall be deposited with the officers of the Church and a copy of the same submitted to the Presbytery.

FORM AND ORDER FOR
THE LAYING OF THE CORNERSTONE
OF A CHURCH

The People, being assembled at the place where the Church is to be built, shall stand, and the Minister shall say:

OUR help is in the name of the Lord,
Who made heaven and earth.

Except the Lord build the house,
They labor in vain that build it.

Let the following be read responsively:

Blessed be Thou, Lord God of Israel our father, for ever and ever.

Thine, O Lord, is the greatness, and the power, and the glory, and the victory, and the majesty: for all that is in the heaven and in the earth is Thine.

Thine is the kingdom, O Lord, and Thou art exalted as Head over all.

Both riches and honor come of Thee, and Thou reignest over all.

And in Thine hand is power and might; and in Thine hand it is to make great, and to give strength unto all.

Now therefore, our God, we thank Thee, and praise Thy glorious name.

But who am I, and what is my people, that we should be able to offer so willingly after this sort?

For all things come of Thee, and of Thine own have we given Thee.

Glory be to the Father, and to the Son, and to the Holy Ghost;

As it was in the beginning, is now, and ever shall be, world without end. Amen.

Then the Minister shall say:

Let us pray.

O LORD JESUS CHRIST, who art the one foundation and the chief cornerstone of Thy Church: Bless what we now do in Thy name, and let this stone planted in this foundation be to us and to our children the symbol and pledge of Thy presence. Direct us, O Lord, in all our doings, with Thy most gracious favor, and further us with Thy continual help; that in all our works, begun, continued, and ended in Thee, we may glorify Thy holy name, and finally, by Thy mercy, obtain everlasting life; through Jesus Christ our Lord. *Amen.*

Then the following Scripture may be read:

The Epistle. I Cor. 3:10-17.

The Gospel. Matt. 7:24-27.

A Hymn shall be sung and then, all standing, the Apostles' Creed may be said:

I BELIEVE in God the Father Almighty, Maker of heaven and earth;

And in Jesus Christ His only Son our Lord; Who was conceived by the Holy Ghost; Born of the Virgin Mary; Suffered under Pontius Pilate; Was crucified, dead, and buried; He descended into hell; The third day He rose again from the dead; He ascended into heaven; And sitteth on the right hand of God the Father Almighty; From thence He shall come to judge the quick and the dead.

I believe in the Holy Ghost; The Holy Catholic Church; The Communion of Saints; The Forgiveness of sins; The Resurrection of the body; And the Life everlasting. Amen.

Here shall follow the LAYING OF THE STONE. *After such documents and other articles as are to be preserved have been deposited in the stone, the Minister, or other Person appointed for the purpose, assisted by the Builder, shall lay the stone in its place. Then the Minister, placing his hand on it, shall say:*

IN THE name of the Father, and of the Son, and of the Holy Spirit, we lay this stone of the building to be here erected under the name of . . . . Church, and devoted to the worship of Almighty God.

Other foundation can no man lay than that is laid, which is Jesus Christ.

Then the Minister shall say:

Let us pray.

ALMIGHTY and everlasting God, who hast built the living temple of Thy Church upon the foundation of the apostles and prophets, Jesus Christ Himself being the chief cornerstone: We beseech Thee to confirm and bless that which we have now done in Thy name. Establish this stone which we have laid, and prosper the work to which we have set our hands, for the upbuilding of Thy Church and the glory of Thy kingdom.

O Thou who art everywhere present in all places of Thy dominion to accept and further the services of all Thy creatures: Remember for good, we beseech Thee, those who have faithfully offered to Thee of their substance for the furthering of this work. Shield and defend those who labor with their hands upon this building, that there be no hurt or loss of life; and grant that the work, which through Thy mercy is now begun, may be carried forward without hindrance and brought in due time to a happy end. And when this house, built to Thine honor, stands complete in strength and beauty, let Thy glory, we beseech Thee, dwell in it for ever, that by the worship of Thy name and the comfort of Thy Word and sacraments, Thy people may be built up for the indwelling of Thy Holy Spirit. So grant that, being devoted to Thee with their whole heart and united to each other with a pure will, they may ever be found both steadfast in faith and active in work for the honor of Thy name.

All this we ask through Jesus Christ our Lord, who liveth and reigneth with Thee, O Father, in the unity of the Holy Spirit, one God, world without end. *Amen.*

Our Father, . . .

An Address may be given, after which an Offering may be received and dedicated.

Then a Hymn may be sung, and the Minister shall pronounce the Benediction:

THE grace of the Lord Jesus Christ, and the love of God, and the communion of the Holy Spirit, be with you all. *Amen.*

FORM AND ORDER FOR
THE DEDICATION OF A CHURCH

At the appointed time of Dedication, the Officiating Ministers shall proceed to the main door of the Church on the outside, and, knocking at the door, the Presiding Minister shall say:

OPEN to me the gates of righteousness: I will go into them, and I will praise the Lord.

The door shall be opened by a Representative of the Church, the Congregation standing. The Officiating Ministers, preceded by the Choir, shall form the procession, singing the hymn "The Church's one Foundation."

The Congregation being seated, the Presiding Minister shall say:

PEACE be to this house, and to all who worship therein.

Peace be to those that enter, and to those that go out therefrom.

Peace be to those that love it, and that love the name of Jesus Christ our Lord.

Lift up your heads, O ye gates;
Even lift them up, ye everlasting doors;
And the King of glory shall come in.
Who is this King of glory?
The Lord of hosts,
He is the King of glory.

Then shall be sung, the Congregation standing:

Glory be to the Father, and to the Son, and to the Holy Ghost;

As it was in the beginning, is now, and ever shall be, world without end. Amen.

Here the Scriptures may be read:

  From the Old Testament: I Kings 8 : 22, 23, 27–30.

  The Epistle: I Cor. 3 : 10–23.

  The Gospel: Matt. 16 : 13–20.

Then, all standing, the Presiding Minister shall say:

  Let us make confession of our faith.

I BELIEVE in God the Father Almighty, Maker of heaven and earth;
  And in Jesus Christ His only Son our Lord; Who was conceived by the Holy Ghost; Born of the Virgin Mary; Suffered under Pontius Pilate; Was crucified, dead, and buried; He descended into hell; The third day He rose again from the dead; He ascended into heaven; And sitteth on the right hand of God the Father Almighty; From thence He shall come to judge the quick and the dead.
  I believe in the Holy Ghost; The Holy Catholic Church; The Communion of Saints; The Forgiveness of sins; The Resurrection of the body; And the Life everlasting. Amen.

Then the Presiding Minister shall say:

  Let us pray.

O LORD GOD, almighty and most merciful, whom the heaven, even the heaven of heavens, cannot contain, much less temples built with hands, but who also dwellest with men, and delightest Thyself in the assemblage of Thy people: Cleanse our hearts, we beseech Thee, from all evil thought and desire, and vouchsafe Thy divine presence and blessing, that those things may please Thee which we do at this present, and also that we may at length obtain Thy favor with life everlasting in Thy heavenly kingdom; through Jesus Christ our Lord. *Amen.*

Then shall the Representative of the Church say to the Presiding Minister:

I deliver to you the keys of this building, erected for The United Presbyterian Church in the United States of America, and pray you now to dedicate it to the worship of Almighty God.

Then the Presiding Minister shall say:

IN THE name of The United Presbyterian Church in the United States of America, we accept the keys of this Church, in token of the trust committed to us.

God our Heavenly Father, having in His grace, which is in our Lord Jesus, brought to its consummation our work of preparing for the honor of His holy name a house within whose walls His Gospel is to be truly preached, His sacraments are to be faithfully administered, and prayer and praise are to be offered unto Him, we are now gathered in His presence for the purpose of consecrating this house, by a solemn act of worship, to its proper and sacred use.

The United Presbyterian Church in the United States of America, as part of the Holy Catholic or Universal Church, worshiping one God—Father, Son, and Holy Spirit—affirms anew its belief in the Gospel of the sovereign grace and love of God, wherein through Jesus Christ, His only Son, our Lord, incarnate, crucified, and risen,

He freely offers to all men, upon repentance and faith, the forgiveness of sins, renewal by the Holy Spirit, and eternal life, and calls them to labor in the fellowship of faith for the advancement of the kingdom of God throughout the world.

The United Presbyterian Church acknowledges the Word of God as contained in the Scriptures of the Old and New Testaments to be the only rule of faith and life. It accepts the Confession of Faith, together with the Larger and Shorter Catechisms, and the Apostles' Creed, as containing the system of doctrine taught in the Scriptures. It adheres to the Form of Government, the Book of Discipline, and the Directory for Worship as defining the government and worship of the Church. It administers, in the name of the Father, the Son, and the Holy Spirit, the sacraments of Baptism and the Lord's Supper.

An Anthem or Hymn may here be sung.

All standing, the Presiding Minister shall say:

DEARLY beloved Brethren: Forasmuch as it pleased Almighty God to put it into the heart of His servants to build this house for His worship, let us now fulfill the godly purpose for which we are assembled of dedicating it to the honor of God's most holy name.

GOD and Father of our Lord Jesus Christ, our Father who art in heaven:
To Thee we dedicate this house.

Lord Jesus, Son of God, Saviour of the world, Head of the Body which is the Church:
To Thee we dedicate this house.

Spirit of God, given to be our abiding Teacher, Sanctifier, and Comforter; Lord and Giver of life:

To Thee we dedicate this house.

Then the Presiding Minister shall say:
Let us pray.

O ETERNAL God, whom the heaven of heavens cannot contain, but who dost graciously manifest Thyself to Thy people who assemble in Thy name: Vouchsafe to be present with us who are here gathered together to dedicate this house to Thy glory, separating it henceforth from all unhallowed and common uses. Be with us as we set it apart entirely to Thy service, for the offering to Thee of the sacrifices of prayer and praise, for the reading and preaching of Thy holy Word, for the celebration of Thy holy sacraments, for the blessing of Thy people in Thy name, and for all other sacred ordinances. Accept, we beseech Thee, this willing service at our hands, and grant that this house may be a habitation of Thy glory, so that all who seek Thy presence here may behold Thine everlasting light, and be satisfied with Thine eternal love; through Jesus Christ our Lord. *Amen.*

Grant, O Lord, that by Thy holy Word, which shall be read and preached in this place, the hearers thereof may both perceive and know what things they ought to do, and also may have grace and power faithfully to fulfill the same. *Amen.*

Grant, O Lord, that those who shall be dedicated unto Thee in this house by baptism may be sanctified by Thy Holy Spirit, and, being made living members of Christ's Church, may ever remain in the number of Thy faithful children. *Amen.*

Grant, O Lord, that those who in this place shall in their own persons renew the promises made for them at their baptism may so receive Thy Holy Spirit that they may ever be enabled to keep their vows, and grow in grace until they come to Thine everlasting kingdom. *Amen.*

Grant, O Lord, that those who shall receive in this place the blessed Sacrament of the body and blood of Christ may do so with a penitent heart, lively faith, and perfect charity; and, being filled with Thy grace and heavenly benediction, may be made partakers of the Living Bread, and heirs through hope of everlasting life. *Amen.*

Grant, O Lord, that those who in this place shall be joined together in marriage may faithfully perform the vow and covenant between them made, and remain in perfect love together unto their lives' end. *Amen.*

Here may the faithful find salvation, and the careless be awakened.

Here may the doubting find faith, and the anxious be encouraged.

Here may the tempted find help, and the sorrowful comfort.

Here may the weary find rest, and the strong be renewed.

Here may the aged find consolation, and the young be inspired. *Amen.*

NOW unto Him that is able to do exceeding abundantly above all that we ask or think, according to the power that worketh in us; unto Him be glory in the Church by Christ Jesus, throughout all ages, world without end.

Amen.

Our Father, . . .

The People standing, the Presiding Minister shall say:

IN THE name of the Father, and of the Son, and of the Holy Ghost, I do now declare this house to be for ever set apart from all profane and common uses, and consecrated to the worship and service of Almighty God: to whom be glory and majesty, dominion and power, for ever and ever. *Amen.*

An Anthem or Hymn may here be sung.

Then shall follow the Sermon.

Then shall follow the Ascription of Praise, the Offering, and the Dedication of Offering.

Then shall be sung Old Hundredth, "All people that on earth do dwell," followed by the Benediction:

THE peace of God, which passeth all understanding, keep your hearts and minds in the knowledge and love of God, and of His Son Jesus Christ our Lord; and the blessing of God Almighty, the Father, the Son, and the Holy Spirit, be upon you, and remain with you always. *Amen.*

FORM AND ORDER FOR
THE DEDICATION OF AN ORGAN

At an appropriate place in a Service of Worship, during which the organ has not been used, the Minister shall say:

IN THE name of the Father, and of the Son, and of the Holy Ghost. *Amen.*

Then let the following be read responsively, the People standing:

PRAISE ye the Lord.

Praise God in His sanctuary:
   Praise Him in the firmament of His power.

Praise Him for His mighty acts:
   Praise Him according to His excellent greatness.

Honor and majesty are before Him:
   Strength and beauty are in His sanctuary.

Give unto the Lord, O ye kindreds of the people:
   Give unto the Lord glory and strength.

Give unto the Lord the glory due unto His name:
   Bring an offering, and come into His courts.

O worship the Lord in the beauty of holiness:
   Fear before Him, all the earth.

Then the Minister shall say:

BELOVED in Christ: Forasmuch as God has put into our hearts to build this instrument of music as an aid to our worship of Him in this holy place, it is right that we should now dedicate it to Him and set it apart to the holy use for which it is designed.

Then the Minister and the People, still standing, shall join responsively in the Act of Dedication:

TO THE glory of God, Author of all goodness and beauty, Giver of all skill of mind and hand:

We dedicate this organ.

In faith in our Lord Jesus Christ, who has inspired men to offer in His praise their best in music and song:

We dedicate this organ.

Moved by the Holy Spirit, our Guide in the worship of God and our Helper in the understanding of truth and beauty:

We dedicate this organ.

To kindle the flame of devotion, that the people of God who here assemble may worship the Father in spirit and in truth:

We dedicate this organ.

To bear up the melody of psalm and hymn and spiritual song in such wise that men may go forth from this house of God with high resolve to do His holy will:

We dedicate this organ.

To comfort the sorrowful and cheer the faint, to bring purity and peace into human hearts, and to lead all who hear it in the way of eternal life:

We dedicate this organ.

Then the Minister shall say:

Let us pray.

O GOD our Father, most holy and most high, unto whom we have access by one Spirit through our Lord Jesus Christ: We give unto Thee, as Thou art worthy to receive, the utmost we can render of power and riches and might and honor and glory and blessing. We thank Thee that Thou hast so made us that by music our hearts can be lifted up to Thee. Forasmuch as Thou hast brought us together to rejoice in the hallowing of the instrument of Thy praise, graciously receive at our hands, we beseech Thee, this organ which we offer for Thy service. As Thou didst move Thy people to prepare it that they might more worthily worship Thee, grant that they and all those who hereafter shall enjoy the benefit of this good work may serve Thee with gladness and show forth Thy praise in triumphant songs. Let Thy glory fill this place, and Thy Spirit so dwell in the hearts of Thy people that they shall sing with the spirit and with the understanding also, and that in Thy house they may become meet to be partakers of the inheritance of the saints in light, who sing the new song.

These things we ask in the name of Jesus Christ our Lord, to whom, with Thee, O Father, and with the Holy Spirit, praise is given for ever and ever. *Amen.*

Then the Minister shall say:

BLESSING, and glory, and wisdom, and thanksgiving, and honor, and power, and might, be unto our God for ever and ever.   *Amen.*

Then shall be sung, the organ sounding, a Hymn of Praise.

FORM AND ORDER FOR
THE DEDICATION OF MEMORIALS,
GIFTS, AND CHURCH FURNISHINGS

At the appointed time in the regular order of worship the Service of Dedication shall take place at that part of the Church where the Memorial or Gift is to be dedicated, using for each Memorial or Gift the Prayer designated.

The People standing, the Minister shall say:

OUR help is in the name of the Lord, who made heaven and earth.

Give unto the Lord, O ye kindreds of the people, give unto the Lord glory and strength.

Honor and majesty are before Him: strength and beauty are in His sanctuary.

Let us pray.

BLESSED and glorious Lord God Almighty, by whose power, wisdom, and love all things are sanctified, enlightened, and made perfect: Be merciful unto us and bless us, we beseech Thee, and cause Thy face to shine upon us, that what we now do may please Thee, and show forth the honor of Thy name. Let Thy work appear unto Thy servants, and Thy glory unto their children. And let the beauty of the Lord our God be upon us; and establish Thou the work of our hands upon us; yea, the work of our hands establish Thou it; through Jesus Christ our Lord. *Amen.*

Acts of Dedication

This Order of Dedication, together with the appropriate Prayer for each occasion, may be followed:

282

*The Minister shall call upon the Person appointed to per-
form the unveiling:*

We ask *N.* now to unveil the Memorial [*or*
Gift].

*The Minister is then asked by the Donor, in such words
as these, to receive the Memorial or Gift:*

In memory of *N.* [*or* in the name of *N.*], we
ask you to receive this Memorial [*or* Gift] and
to dedicate it to the glory and praise of God.

The Minister shall respond:

We accept this Memorial [*or* Gift] as a sacred
trust, and shall treasure it with reverence and
gratitude.

And now in the faith of our Lord Jesus Christ,
we dedicate this Memorial [*or* Gift] to the glory
of God,

IN THE NAME OF THE FATHER, AND OF THE
SON, AND OF THE HOLY GHOST.   *Amen.*

SPECIAL PRAYERS

I

Prayer for the Dedication of a Window

ALMIGHTY God, who art the true light of
faithful souls and the perfect brightness of
Thy saints, and who fillest heaven and earth with
Thy divine majesty, but who dost accept the
offerings of Thy children: Graciously receive at
our hands this Window which we dedicate unto
Thee [in memory of Thy servant], to the beautifying of this sanctuary, to the blessing and edifying of this Thy people, and to the glory of Thy
great name.   *Amen.*

*When Gifts are to be dedicated, the following Prayer may
be added to the Prayer of Dedication:*

WE THANK Thee that Thou didst put it into
the heart of Thy *servant* to give of *his* substance to advance the goodly order of Thy house
and to beautify the place of Thy sanctuary; and
we pray Thee to accept *his* devotion, comfort *him*
with Thy favor, and reward *him* for the kindness
he has shown to Thy house and its worship.

Amen.

*When Memorials are to be dedicated, the following Prayer
may be added to the Prayer of Dedication:*

O THOU who art the Creator and Lover of
all men, by whom all souls do live: We
bless and praise Thee for all that was pure and
true, beautiful and good, in the *life* commemorated
this day; for the example *he has* left of faith and
hope and duty, and of love for Thy Church; and
for the hope we have, through Christ, that *he has*
entered into life eternal. *Amen.*

Our Father, . . .

*Ascription of Praise**

II

Prayer for the Dedication of a Pulpit or Lectern

ALMIGHTY God, who dost enlighten the minds
of Thy servants with the knowledge of Thy
truth: Cause Thy Church to arise and shine. Let
Thy blessing rest, O Lord, upon this Pulpit [*or*
Lectern] which we dedicate to Thee. Grant that
Thy truth here made known to Thy worshiping

**Proper Ascriptions of Praise, with which each Prayer of
Dedication is to be concluded, may be found on page 347.*

people may be effectual unto their faith and eternal life. May all who read be filled with the faith of the Gospel, and with thankfulness to Thee who dost in the Holy Scriptures reveal the Word of life. And grant that all who hear may receive that Word into honest and good hearts, and bring forth fruit with patience, to Thy glory; through Jesus Christ our Lord. *Amen.*

III

Prayer for the Dedication of a Communion Table

ETERNAL God, Father of our Lord Jesus Christ, of whom every family in heaven and earth is named: Accept us through Him, we beseech Thee, and hear us as we dedicate to Thy glory this Communion Table, and pray Thee, through the grace of Thy Holy Spirit, to hallow and consecrate it to the holy uses for which it is set apart.

Grant that whensoever Thy people come hither in obedience to their Saviour's command, they may, with humble penitence and in full assurance of Thy forgiveness, render unto Thee the sacrifice of thanksgiving, and, receiving the Sacrament of His body and blood, be filled with Thy grace and heavenly benediction, and made partakers of eternal life; in the name of Jesus Christ our Lord and Saviour. *Amen.*

IV

Prayer for the Dedication of Communion Vessels

ALMIGHTY God, who of old didst command Thy servant Moses to consecrate the vessels of the sanctuary, that thereafter they might be

used for Thy worship and service alone: Receive
at our hands, we beseech Thee, these vessels
which we set apart and separate from all unhallowed, ordinary, and common uses, and dedicate
entirely to the service of Thy house in the sacrament of the Holy Supper of our Lord. Accept,
consecrate, and bless them, we beseech Thee, that
ever hereafter men may know them to be holy
unto the Lord. We bless Thee that He who died
upon the cross for our salvation vouchsafes to give
Himself to be our spiritual life and food; and we
pray that whensoever Thy people, in faith, receive from these vessels the Communion of His
most precious body and blood, they may be made
glad by the Saviour's love, quickened by His life,
and filled with all heavenly grace and benediction;
through Jesus Christ our Lord. *Amen.*

V

Prayer for the Dedication of a Baptismal Font

ALMIGHTY God, our Heavenly Father, without whom no word or work of ours availeth,
but who dost accept the works of our hands for
the service of Thy Church: Have respect unto the
prayers of Thy servants, as we dedicate this Font
to Thine honor, and for the praise and glory of
Thy name.

Accept and consecrate it, O Lord, and grant
that whosoever shall come hither to be baptized
with water may receive also the baptism of Thy
Holy Spirit, and, being received into Thy Church,
may ever remain in the number of Thy faithful
children.

Let this Font ever witness to the hearts of all
who worship here of the covenant into which,

through baptism, they have entered with Thee, that they may renew their vows as they worship, and ever seek faithfully to fulfill them, until that day when, sign and symbol having passed away, they shall see Thee face to face, and glorify Thee in Thine everlasting kingdom; through Jesus Christ our Lord. *Amen.*

VI

Prayer for the Dedication of Other Church Furnishings

ALMIGHTY God, our Heavenly Father, without whom no word or work of ours availeth, but who dost accept the gifts of our hands for the beautifying of Thy sanctuary: Bestow Thy blessing upon us now as we dedicate *this Gift* to Thy glory, for the use and adornment of this holy place (and in memory of Thy servant).   Accept *it*, we pray Thee, as we set *it* apart from all common and unhallowed uses, ever to be devoted to the service of Thy Church and the honor of Thy holy name; through Jesus Christ our Lord.   *Amen.*

IV. THE TREASURY
OF PRAYERS

PRAYERS
FOR THE CHRISTIAN YEAR

ADVENT

PREPARE ye the way of the Lord, make straight in the desert a highway for our God.

Blessed is He that cometh in the name of the Lord. Hosanna in the highest.

First Sunday

ALMIGHTY God, give us grace that we may cast away the works of darkness, and put upon us the armor of light, now in the time of this mortal life, in which Thy Son Jesus Christ came to visit us in great humility; that in the last day, when He shall come again in His glorious majesty to judge both the quick and dead, we may rise to the life immortal; through Him who liveth and reigneth with Thee and the Holy Spirit, now and ever. *Amen.*

Second Sunday—Bible Sunday

Blessed Lord, who hast caused all holy Scriptures to be written for our learning: Grant that we may in such wise hear them, read, mark, learn, and inwardly digest them, that by patience, and comfort of Thy holy Word, we may embrace and ever hold fast the blessed hope of everlasting life, which Thou hast given us in our Saviour Jesus Christ. *Amen.*

Third Sunday

O Lord Jesus Christ, who at Thy coming into

the world didst send Thy messenger to prepare Thy way before Thee: Grant that the ministers and stewards of Thy mysteries may likewise so prepare and make ready Thy way, by turning the hearts of the disobedient to the wisdom of the just, that at Thy coming to judge the world we may be found an acceptable people in Thy sight, who livest and reignest with the Father and the Holy Spirit, ever one God, world without end. *Amen.*

Fourth Sunday

Almighty God, whose blessed Son Jesus Christ promised to come again to receive His people unto Himself: Keep us ever watchful for His glorious appearing. Help us to set our affection on things above, and to live as those who wait for their Lord; that when He shall appear we may be made like unto Him, and see Him as He is; through the same Jesus Christ our Lord. *Amen.*

Almighty and everlasting God, who orderest all things in heaven and in earth, and who didst make all ages a preparation for the coming of Thy Son: Prepare us by Thy Holy Spirit for the coming of Him whom Thou dost send, that we may behold His glory and receive the fullness of Thy blessing; through Jesus Christ our Lord. *Amen.*

CHRISTMAS DAY

The service is to follow the same Order as that of Morning Worship.

Call to Worship

LET us go even unto Bethlehem and see this thing which is come to pass, which the Lord hath made known unto us.

For unto us a Child is born, unto us a Son is given: and the government shall be upon His shoulder: and His name shall be called Wonderful, Counselor, the Mighty God, the Everlasting Father, the Prince of Peace.

Glory to God in the highest, and on earth peace, good will toward men.

Adoration

GLORY be to Thee, O Father Almighty, who hast given us Thine only-begotten Son, that we might live through Him. Glory be to Thee, O Lord Jesus Christ, who became man that we might become sons of God. Glory be to Thee, O Holy Spirit, who dost direct and rule our hearts. All glory be to Thee, Father, Son, and Holy Spirit, one God, world without end. *Amen.*

Confession   *Minister and People*

ALMIGHTY and all-holy Father; We confess ourselves unworthy of Thine unspeakable Gift. We have not loved Thee as we ought; Nor have we always been loving to one another; Kindhearted, forgiving one another; Even as Thou, for Christ's sake, hast forgiven us. We have lived in selfishness and worldly pride; And the good gifts Thou hast bestowed upon us; We have not used to relieve the burdens of others. Pardon and blot out our offenses, we beseech Thee; Through the incarnate life and willing sacrifice of Thy holy Son, even Jesus Christ our Lord. Amen.

Assurance of Pardon

ALMIGHTY God, our Heavenly Father, who of His great mercy hath promised forgiveness of sins to all those who with hearty repentance and true faith turn to Him, have mercy upon you; pardon and deliver you from all your sins; confirm and strengthen you in all goodness; and bring you to everlasting life; through Jesus Christ our Lord. *Amen.*

Thanksgiving   *Minister and People*

GLORY be to God on high; And on earth peace, good will toward men. We praise Thee; We bless Thee; We worship Thee; We glorify Thee; We give thanks to Thee for Thy great glory; O Lord God, Heavenly King, God the Father Almighty.

O Lord, the only-begotten Son, Jesus Christ; O Lord God, Lamb of God, Son of the Father; That takest away the sins of the world; Have mercy upon us. Thou that takest away the sins of the world; Receive our prayer. Thou that sittest at the right hand of God the Father; Have mercy upon us.

For Thou only art holy; Thou only art the Lord; Thou only, O Christ, with the Holy Spirit, art most high in the glory of God the Father. Amen.

Supplication

O ALMIGHTY God, who by the birth of Thy Holy One into the world didst give Thy true light to dawn upon our darkness: Grant that as Thou hast given us to believe in the mystery of His Incarnation, and hast made us partakers of the divine nature, so in the time to come we may ever abide with Him, in the glory of His kingdom; through Jesus Christ our Lord. *Amen.*

Intercession

O LORD our God, who didst send Thy Son to be the Saviour of the world: Make Thy salvation known to the ends of the earth, that in every place Thy name shall be worshiped and glorified. We beseech Thee, by the light of Thine Incarnate Word, to illumine and make glad the hearts of all who serve Thee in Thy Church. Give them the spirit of power, and of love, and of a sound mind; comfort them by His presence who is Immanuel, God with us, that in the faith they may endure unto the end.

O God our Father, who didst send Thy Son to be King of Kings and Prince of Peace: Grant that all the kingdoms of this world may become the kingdom of our Lord, and learn of Him the way of peace. Inspire all men continually with the spirit of unity and concord. Let those who are offended forgive, and those who have offended repent, so that Thy children may live as one family, through Jesus Christ our Lord.

We beseech Thee to be favorable unto our land; and to the President of the United States and all others in authority, that it may please Thee so to rule their hearts that they may rightly use the trust committed to them for the good of all the people.

O Thou, who by giving Thy Son to be born of Mary didst sanctify motherhood and exalt the families of earth: Bless, we pray Thee, our homes, kindred, and friends. Grant that in the reunions of this season all hearts may be glad and all pleasures pure. Let children be dear to us for the sake of the holy Child Jesus. Make them glad in His love as they keep the festival; give to all a childlike heart to share the children's joy. Take into Thy keeping our loved ones from whom we are now separated, and grant that both they and we, by drawing near to Thee, may be drawn closer to one another in Jesus Christ our Saviour.

Father of mercies, we commend to Thee the poor, the cold, the hungry, the lonely, and those who have no helper. So move the hearts of those to whom Thou hast freely given all things, that they also may freely give; through Jesus Christ our Lord. *Amen.*

Communion of Saints

ALMIGHTY God, who redeemest the souls of Thy servants: We praise Thee for the multitude which no man can number, and especially do we thank Thee for those dear to us who have once shared our Christmas joy, and now rejoice with Thy saints in light. Keep us evermore in this communion and fellowship, until we also receive the end of our faith, even life eternal. And unto Thee, Father, Son, and Holy Spirit, one God, be all honor and glory, world without end. *Amen.*

And now, as our Saviour Christ hath taught us, we humbly pray:
Our Father, . . .

ADDITIONAL CHRISTMAS PRAYERS

MOST merciful God, who hast so loved the world as to give Thine only-begotten Son, that whosoever believeth in Him should not perish but have everlasting life: Vouchsafe unto us, we humbly pray Thee, the precious gift of faith, whereby we may know that the Son of God is come; and, being always rooted and grounded in the mystery of the Word made flesh, may have power to overcome the world, and gain the blessing of immortality; through the merits of the same incarnate Christ, who liveth and reigneth with Thee in the unity of the Holy Spirit, ever one God, world without end. *Amen.*

O God, who makest us glad with the yearly remembrance of the birth of Thine only Son Jesus Christ: Grant that as we joyfully receive Him for our Redeemer, so we may with sure confidence behold Him when He shall come to be our Judge, who liveth and reigneth with Thee and the Holy Ghost, one God, world without end. *Amen.*

Almighty God, who hast given us Thine only-begotten Son to take our nature upon Him, and to be born of a pure virgin: Grant that we, being regenerate and made Thy children by adoption and grace, may daily be renewed by Thy Holy Spirit; through the same our Lord Jesus Christ, who liveth and reigneth with Thee and the Spirit, ever one God, world without end. *Amen.*

EPIPHANY

ARISE, shine; for thy light is come, and the glory of the Lord is risen upon thee.

O GOD, who by the shining of a star didst guide the Wise Men to behold Thy Son our Lord: Show us Thy heavenly light, and give us grace to follow until we find Him, and, finding Him, rejoice. And grant that as they presented gold, frankincense, and myrrh, we now may bring Him the offering of a loving heart, an adoring spirit, and an obedient will, for His honor, and for Thy glory, O God Most High. *Amen.*

O God, who by the leading of a star didst manifest to the Gentiles the glory of Thine only-begotten Son: Grant us that, being led by the light of Thy Holy Spirit, we may, in adoring love and lowliest reverence, yield ourselves to Thy service; that Thy kingdom of righteousness and peace may be advanced among all nations, to the glory of Thy name; through Jesus Christ our Lord. *Amen.*

Everlasting Father, the Radiance of faithful souls, who didst bring the nations to Thy light and kings to the brightness of Thy rising: Fill, we beseech Thee, the world with Thy glory, and show Thyself unto all the nations; through Him who is the true Light and the bright Morning Star, Jesus Christ Thy Son our Lord. *Amen.*

Almighty and everlasting God, who hast made known the Incarnation of Thy Son by the bright shining of a star, which, when the Wise Men beheld, they presented costly gifts and adored Thy majesty: Grant that the star of Thy righteousness may always shine into our hearts; and that, as our treasure, we may give ourselves and all we possess to Thy service; through Jesus Christ our Lord. *Amen.*

LENT

REND your heart, and not your garments, and turn unto the Lord your God; for He is gracious and merciful, slow to anger, and of great kindness, and repenteth Him of the evil.

O LORD, who for our sake didst fast forty days and forty nights: Give us grace to use such abstinence, that, our flesh being subdued to the spirit, we may ever obey Thy godly motions in righteousness and true holiness, to Thine honor and glory; who livest and reignest, with the Father and the Holy Spirit, one God, world without end. *Amen.*

Almighty God, who seest that we have no power of ourselves to help ourselves: Keep us both outwardly in our bodies, and inwardly in our souls; that we may be defended from all adversities which may happen to the body, and from all evil thoughts which may assault and hurt the soul; through Jesus Christ our Lord. *Amen.*

Almighty and everlasting God, who, of Thy tender love toward mankind, hast sent Thy Son our Saviour Jesus Christ, to take upon Him our flesh, and to suffer death upon the cross, that all mankind should follow the example of His great humility: Mercifully grant that we may both follow the example of His patience, and also be made partakers of His Resurrection; through the same Jesus Christ our Lord. *Amen.*

O merciful Father, who in compassion for Thy sinful children didst send Thy Son Jesus Christ to be the Saviour of the world: Grant us grace to feel and to lament our share in the evil which made it needful for Him to suffer and to die for our salvation. Help us by self-denial, prayer, and meditation to prepare our hearts for deeper penitence and a better life. And give us a true longing to be free from sin, through the deliverance wrought by Jesus Christ our only Redeemer. *Amen.*

O God, who by the example of Thy Son our Saviour Jesus Christ hast taught us the greatness of true humility, and dost call us to watch with Him in His Passion: Give us grace to serve one another in all lowliness, and to enter into the fellowship of His sufferings; who liveth and reigneth with Thee and the Holy Spirit, one God, world without end. *Amen.*

PALM SUNDAY

THE grace of God that bringeth salvation hath appeared to all men. Blessed is He that cometh in the name of the Lord. Hosanna in the highest.

HEAVENLY Father, who hast so loved the world as to send Thy dear Son Jesus Christ to seek and save the lost: We give thanks for the grace by which He laid aside celestial glory, and came among us as a servant, meek and lowly, the Friend of sinners, and the Companion of the poor. We remember with joy that the common people heard Him gladly, and the multi ude welcomed Him with palm branches and songs of praise. Grant us grace, O God, to join with all our hearts in the spiritual triumph of the Prince of Peace. *Amen.*

O Lord Jesus Christ, who as on this day didst enter the rebellious city where Thou wast to die: Enter into our hearts, we beseech Thee, and subdue them wholly to Thyself. And as Thy faithful disciples blessed Thy coming, and spread their garments in the way, covering it with palm branches, make us ready to lay at Thy feet all that we have and are, and to bless Thee, O Thou who comest in the name of the Lord. And grant that after having confessed and worshiped Thee upon earth, we may be among the number of those who shall hail Thine eternal triumph, and bear in their hands the palms of victory, when every knee shall bow before Thee, and every tongue confess that Thou art Lord, to the glory of God the Father. *Amen.*

O Lord Jesus Christ, who didst set Thy face steadfastly to go unto Jerusalem: Deliver us from the faithless mind that shrinks from the harder paths of dutiful life. Make us ready to meet all the counsels of Thy will, who, with the Father and the Holy Spirit, livest and reignest, world without end. *Amen.*

THURSDAY BEFORE EASTER

THE bread of God is He which cometh down from heaven, and giveth life unto the world.

O LORD JESUS CHRIST, who in the Holy Sacrament didst leave Thy Church a memorial of Thyself and a pledge and seal of Thy redeeming love: Grant that when, in obedience to Thy command, we keep the feast, we may approach Thy Table with love and humble hope; that discerning its sacred mystery, we may feed by faith on Thy holy body and blood, and be made partakers of Thy heavenly grace. Let the remembrance of Thy Passion and triumph ever abide within our hearts, that we may be fortified against the assaults of our enemies and strengthened to keep Thy commandments all the days of our life. *Amen.*

GOOD FRIDAY

G OD commendeth His love toward us, in that, while we were yet sinners, Christ died for us.

Worthy is the Lamb that was slain to receive power, and riches, and wisdom, and strength, and honor, and glory, and blessing.

O SAVIOUR of the world, who by Thy cross and precious blood hast redeemed us: Save us, and help us, we humbly beseech Thee, O Lord. *Amen.*

O Lord Jesus Christ, who for our sakes didst suffer death upon the cross: Help us to bear about with us Thy dying, and, in our living, to show forth Thy life. Looking on Thee whom we have pierced, we would mourn for our sins with unfeigned sorrow; we would learn of Thee to forgive, with Thee to suffer, and in Thee to overcome.

Lamb of God, who takest away the sins of the world, have mercy upon us. Lamb of God, who takest away the sins of the world, grant us Thy peace. Lord, we pray Thee, in Thy great mercy, remember us when Thou comest into Thy kingdom. *Amen.*

Most merciful Father, who of Thy great compassion toward us sinners didst give Thine only-begotten Son to be an offering for our sins: Grant us grace, we humbly beseech Thee, that being united unto Him by Thy Spirit, and made partakers of His sufferings and His death, we may die daily unto the world and lead holy and unblamable lives. Cleaving unto His cross in all the temptations of life, may we hold fast the profession of our faith without wavering, and finally attain unto the resurrection of the just; through the merits of the same once crucified but now risen and exalted Saviour. *Amen.*

Forbid, O God, that we should forget, amid our earthly comforts, the pains and mortal anguish that our Lord Jesus endured for our salvation. Grant us this day a true vision of all that He suffered, in His betrayal, His lonely agony, His false trial, His mocking and scourging, and the torture of death upon the cross. As Thou hast given Thyself utterly for us, may we give ourselves entirely to Thee, O Jesus Christ, our only Lord and Saviour. *Amen.*

O God, whose only-begotten Son followed the way of faith and duty even to the crown of thorns and the cross: Give us grace that we may learn the harder lessons of our faith. And so endue

us with power from on high that, taking up our
cross, and following our Saviour in His patience
and humility, we may enter into the fellowship
of His sufferings, and come at last to dwell with
Him in His eternal kingdom; through Jesus Christ
our Lord. *Amen.*

EASTER DAY

*The service is to follow the same Order as that of Morning
Worship.*

Call to Worship

THE Lord is risen indeed: Hallelujah. I am
He that liveth, and was dead, saith the Lord;
and behold, I am alive for evermore. Hallelujah.

Adoration

GLORY be to Thee, O Father Almighty, who
as on this day didst raise up Thy Son from
the dead and makest us partakers of His victory
over sin and death.

Glory be to Thee, O Christ, who for us men
and for our salvation hast overcome death, and
opened unto us the gate of everlasting life.

Glory be to Thee, O Holy Spirit, who dost lead
us into all truth as it is in the risen Christ.

Blessed be Thou, Father, Son, and Holy Spirit,
one God, who bringest life and immortality to
light through Thy Gospel, and blessed be Thy
glorious name for ever and ever. *Amen.*

Confession   *Minister and People*

O ALMIGHTY God, who broughtest again
from the dead our Lord Jesus; We acknowledge that we are unworthy of Thy redeeming

grace. We have not believed Thy promises; Nor trusted in our living Lord. Through worldliness of spirit; Our eyes have been holden that we have not discerned His presence with us. Through disappointment of mind and dejection of spirit; Our hearts have not burned within us as we have heard His Word. We have not trusted in His redeeming power; And have been overcome of evil. We have forgotten the glad tidings of His victory over death; And have not known the things that belong to our peace.

But now in penitence we come to Thee; Beseeching Thy forgiveness. Mercifully grant us absolution from all our sins; And restore unto us the joy of Thy salvation; For Jesus Christ's sake, our only Mediator and Advocate. Amen.

Assurance of Pardon

ALMIGHTY God, who of His great mercy hath promised forgiveness of sins to all those who with hearty repentance and true faith turn unto Him, have mercy upon you; pardon and deliver you from all your sins; confirm and strengthen you in all goodness; and bring you to everlasting life; through Jesus Christ our Lord. *Amen.*

Thanksgiving   Minister and People

O GOD most high; All praise and thanksgiving be unto Thee; For the multitude of Thy loving-kindness and tender mercies unto us; And to all men. It is meet and right that we should at all times give thanks unto Thee; But chiefly, this day, are we bound to praise Thee; For the glorious resurrection of Thy Son Jesus Christ our Lord; Who hath taken away the sins of the world;

Who by His death hath destroyed death; And by
His rising again hath brought us to everlasting
life.

We give Thee thanks; That, having overcome
the sharpness of death; He opened the kingdom
of heaven to all believers; And that because He
lives, we too shall live. Even now, having peace
with Thee through Him; We rejoice in the hope
of Thy great glory. Thanks be to Thee, O God;
Who givest us the victory; Through our Lord
Jesus Christ; To whom, with Thee the Father
and the Holy Ghost, be all honor and glory;
World without end. Amen.

Supplication

O GOD, who through the mighty resurrection
of Thy Son Jesus Christ from the dead hast
delivered us from the power of darkness into the
kingdom of Thy love: Grant, we beseech Thee,
that as by His death He has recalled us into life,
so by His presence ever abiding in us He may
raise us to joys eternal; through Him who for our
sakes died and rose again, and is ever with us in
power and great glory, even the same Jesus Christ
our Lord. *Amen.*

Intercession

ALMIGHTY God, whose blessed Son Christ
Jesus sent forth His apostles to make disciples of all nations: Fill Thy Church throughout
the world with His risen power. Pour out Thy
Spirit on those who are called to minister in His
name, at home and abroad. As they break the
bread of life to others, let their own souls be
nourished and sustained. Grant to Thy people

here and everywhere, that, abiding in Christ their Life, they may bear fruit abundantly to Thy glory.

O God, who hast promised Thy Son the uttermost parts of the earth for His possession: Take away the veil from all hearts that they may behold the Messiah promised of old, and hasten the day when all peoples shall know Him as Saviour and worship Him as Lord.

Let Thy mercy, we beseech Thee, rest upon our land and nation, upon all in authority, that there may be justice and peace at home and that we may show forth Thy praise among the nations of the earth. Break the power of unbelief and superstition, and preserve to us Thy pure Word, in its liberty and glory, to the end of our days.

O Heavenly Father, we commend to Thy merciful care all who are in any wise afflicted. Relieve those who suffer; restore health and strength, as Thou dost will, to those who are sick. In Christ, who is the Resurrection and the Life, let the heavy-laden find strength to endure and those who are in the valley of the shadow see the light of life eternal. Give to those in sorrow or loneliness the assurance that nothing can ever separate them from Thy love, which is in Christ Jesus our Lord. *Amen.*

Communion of Saints

ALMIGHTY God, who hast knit together Thine elect in one communion and fellowship, in the mystical Body of Thy Son Christ our Lord: Grant us grace so as to follow Thy blessed saints in all virtuous and godly living, that we may come to those unspeakable joys which Thou hast pre-

pared for those who unfeignedly love Thee;
through the same Thy Son Jesus Christ our Lord,
to whom, with Thee the Father and the Holy
Ghost, be all honor and glory, world without
end. *Amen.*

And now, as our Saviour Christ hath taught us,
we humbly pray:
Our Father, . . .

ADDITIONAL EASTER PRAYERS

ALMIGHTY God, who through Thine only-
begotten Son Jesus Christ hast overcome
death, and opened unto us the gate of everlasting
life: We humbly beseech Thee that, as by Thy
special grace directing us Thou dost put into our
minds good desires, so by Thy continual help we
may bring the same to good effect; through Jesus
Christ our Lord, who liveth and reigneth with
Thee and the Holy Ghost, ever one God, world
without end. *Amen.*

Almighty God, Father of our Lord Jesus Christ,
who didst raise up Thy Son and give Him glory,
that our faith and hope might be in Thee: Quicken
us also, we beseech Thee, by Thy mighty power,
from the death of sin to the life of righteousness, and cause us to set our affection on things
above; so that we may, at the last, have part in
the resurrection of the just, and in the glory of
Thy heavenly kingdom, whither Jesus the Fore-
runner is for us entered; where also He liveth
and reigneth with Thee and the Holy Spirit, God
blessed for ever. *Amen.*

Thou Brightness of God's glory and Express Image of His person, whom death could not conquer nor the tomb imprison: As Thou hast shared our mortal frailty in the flesh, help us to share Thine immortal triumph in the spirit. Let no shadow of the grave affright us and no fear of darkness turn our hearts from Thee. Reveal Thyself to us this day and all our days, as the first and the last, the Living One, our immortal Saviour and Lord. *Amen.*

O Thou who makest the stars, and turnest the shadow of death into the morning: On this day of days we meet to render Thee, our Lord and King, the tribute of our praise; for the new life of the springtime, for the everlasting hopes that rise within the human heart, and for the Gospel which hath brought life and immortality to light. Receive our thanksgiving, reveal Thy presence, and send into our hearts the Spirit of the risen Christ. *Amen.*

ASCENSION DAY

LIFT up your heads, O ye gates: even lift them up, ye everlasting doors: and the King of glory shall come in.
Who is this King of glory? The Lord of Hosts; He is the King of glory.

ALMIGHTY God, whose blessed Son our Saviour Jesus Christ ascended far above all heavens that He might fill all things: Mercifully give us faith to perceive that according to His promise He abideth with His Church on earth, even to the end of the world; through the same Jesus Christ our Lord. *Amen.*

PENTECOST *or* WHITSUNDAY

IT SHALL come to pass, saith the Lord, that I will pour out My Spirit upon all flesh.

Jesus saith to His disciples, I will pray the Father, and He shall give you another Comforter, that He may abide with you for ever: even the Spirit of truth, whom the world cannot receive because it seeth Him not, neither knoweth Him; but ye know Him, for He dwelleth with you and shall be in you.

SEND, we beseech Thee, Almighty God, Thy Holy Spirit into our hearts, that He may rule and direct us according to Thy will, comfort us in all our temptations and afflictions, defend us from all error, and lead us into all truth; that we, being steadfast in the faith, may increase in love and in all good works, and in the end obtain everlasting life; through Jesus Christ Thy Son our Lord. *Amen.*

O God, who dost sanctify Thy Universal Church in every race and nation: Shed abroad throughout the whole world the gift of the Holy Spirit, that the work wrought by His power at the first preaching of the Gospel may now be shed abroad among all believing hearts; through Jesus Christ our Lord. *Amen.*

O Lord, who didst come to seek and to save the lost and to whom all power is given in heaven and in earth: Hear the prayers of Thy Church for those who, at Thy command, go forth to preach the Gospel to every creature. Preserve them from all dangers; from perils by land and sea; from the deadly pestilence; from the violence of the persecutor; from doubt and impatience; from discouragement and discord; and from all the devices of the powers of darkness. While Thy servants plant and water, O Lord, send Thou the increase; gather in the multitude of the people; and convert in all lands such as neglect Thy great salvation; that Thy name may be glorified, and Thy kingdom come, O Saviour of the world; to whom, with the Father and the Holy Spirit, be honor and glory, world without end. *Amen.*

TRINITY SUNDAY

HOLY, holy, holy is the Lord God Almighty, which was, and is, and is to come.

O BLESSED Trinity, in whom we know the Maker of all things visible and invisible, the Saviour of all men near and far: By Thy Spirit enable us, we pray Thee, so to worship Thy divine majesty that with all the company of heaven we may magnify Thy glorious name, saying, Holy, holy, holy. Glory be to Thee, O Lord most high. *Amen.*

SUNDAYS AFTER TRINITY

Prayers for Grace

ALMIGHTY God, whom by searching we cannot find out unto perfection, but who in Jesus Christ hast revealed Thyself as Father, and who by Thy Spirit hast borne witness that we are joint heirs with Christ: Help us to confess our faith in Thee our Father by living as Thy children, our faith in Thy Son by following in His steps, and our faith in Thy Holy Spirit by our obedience to His light within our souls; through Jesus Christ our Lord. *Amen.*

O Lord, who never failest to help and govern those whom Thou dost bring up in Thy steadfast fear and love: Keep us, we beseech Thee, under the protection of Thy good providence, and make us to have a perpetual fear and love of Thy holy name; through Jesus Christ our Lord. *Amen.*

O Lord, we beseech Thee mercifully to hear us; and grant that we, to whom Thou hast given a hearty desire to pray, may, by Thy mighty aid, be defended and comforted in all dangers and adversities; through Jesus Christ our Lord. *Amen.*

O God, the Protector of all that trust in Thee, without whom nothing is strong, nothing is holy: Increase and multiply upon us Thy mercy; that, Thou being our Ruler and Guide, we may so pass through things temporal that we finally lose not the things eternal. Grant this, O Heavenly Father, for the sake of Jesus Christ our Lord. *Amen.*

Almighty and everlasting God, who art always more ready to hear than we to pray, and art wont to give more than we either desire or deserve: Pour down upon us the abundance of Thy mercy; forgiving us those things whereof our conscience is afraid, and giving us those good things which we are not worthy to ask, but through the merits and mediation of Jesus Christ Thy Son our Lord. *Amen.*

O God, who hast prepared for those who love Thee such good things as pass man's understanding: Pour into our hearts such love toward Thee that we, loving Thee above all things, may obtain Thy promises, which exceed all that we can desire; through Jesus Christ our Lord. *Amen.*

Lord of all power and might, who art the Author and Giver of all good things: Graft in our hearts the love of Thy name, increase in us true religion, nourish us with all goodness, and of Thy great mercy keep us in the same; through Jesus Christ our Lord. *Amen.*

Lord, we beseech Thee, grant Thy people grace to withstand the temptations of the world, the flesh, and the devil; and with pure hearts and minds to follow Thee, the only God; through Jesus Christ our Lord. *Amen.*

Grant to us, Lord, we beseech Thee, the spirit to think and do always such things as are right; that we, who cannot do anything that is good without Thee, may by Thee be enabled to live according to Thy will; through Jesus Christ our Lord. *Amen.*

O God, forasmuch as without Thee we are not able to please Thee: Mercifully grant that Thy Holy Spirit may in all things direct and rule our hearts; through Jesus Christ our Lord. *Amen.*

O God, who declarest Thine almighty power chiefly in showing mercy and pity: Mercifully grant unto us such a measure of Thy grace that we, running the way of Thy commandments, may obtain Thy gracious promises, and be made partakers of Thy heavenly treasure; through Jesus Christ our Lord. *Amen.*

Almighty and everlasting God, give unto us the increase of faith, hope, and charity. And, that we may obtain that which Thou dost promise, make us to love that which Thou hast commanded; through Jesus Christ our Lord. *Amen.*

Almighty and merciful God, of whose only gift it cometh that Thy faithful people do unto Thee true and acceptable service: Grant, we beseech Thee, that we may so faithfully serve Thee in this life that we fail not finally to attain the heavenly promises; through the merits of Jesus Christ our Lord. *Amen.*

ALL SAINTS' DAY
AND COMMEMORATION OF THE FAITHFUL DEPARTED

PRECIOUS in the sight of the Lord is the death of His saints.

One generation shall praise Thy works to another, and shall declare Thy mighty acts.

O ALMIGHTY God, who hast knit together Thine elect in one communion and fellowship in the mystical Body of Thy Son Christ our Lord: Grant us grace so as to follow Thy blessed saints in all virtuous and godly living that we may come to those unspeakable joys which Thou hast prepared for those who unfeignedly love Thee; through Jesus Christ our Saviour. *Amen.*

We give thanks to Thee, O Lord, for all saints and servants of Thine, who have done justly, loved mercy, and walked humbly with their God. For all the high and holy ones, who have wrought wonders and been shining lights in the world, we thank Thee. For all the meek and lowly ones, who have earnestly sought Thee in darkness, and held fast their faith in trial, and done good unto all men as they had opportunity, we thank Thee. Especially for those men and women whom we have known and loved, who by their patient obedience and self-denial, steadfast hope and helpfulness in trouble, have shown the same mind that was in Christ Jesus, we bless Thy holy name. As they have comforted and upheld our souls, grant us grace to follow in their steps, and at last to share with them in the inheritance of the saints in light; through Jesus Christ our Saviour. *Amen.*

PRAYERS FOR THE CIVIL YEAR

NEW YEAR'S DAY

ETERNAL God, who makest all things new, and abidest for ever the same: Grant us to begin this year in Thy faith, and to continue it in Thy favor; that, being guided in all our doings, and guarded in all our days, we may spend our lives in Thy service, and finally, by Thy grace, attain the glory of everlasting life; through Jesus Christ our Lord. *Amen.*

O God, who art, and wast, and art to come, before whose face the generations rise and pass away: Age after age the living seek Thee and find that of Thy faithfulness there is no end. Our fathers in their pilgrimage walked by Thy guidance, and rested on Thy compassion; still to their children be Thou the cloud by day and the fire by night. Where but in Thee have we a covert from the storm, or shadow from the heat of life? In our manifold temptations, Thou alone knowest and art ever nigh; in sorrow, Thy pity revives the fainting soul; in our prosperity and ease, it is Thy Spirit only that can keep us from pride and keep us humble. O Thou sole Source of peace and righteousness, take now the veil from every heart, and join us in one communion with Thy prophets and saints, who have trusted in Thee and were not ashamed. Not of our worthiness, but of Thy tender mercy, hear our prayer; for the sake of Jesus Christ Thy Son our Lord. *Amen.*

MEMORIAL DAY

ETERNAL God, Father of our spirits: We rejoice in all who have faithfully lived and
triumphantly died. We give Thee thanks for all
blessed memories and all enduring hopes; for the
ties that bind us to the unseen world; for all the
heroic dead who encompass us like a cloud of
witnesses. We pray that we who have entered
into the heritage of their heroism and self-sacrifice
may so honor their memory and so preserve and
further their high purposes that the nation which
they defended may stand in all coming years for
righteousness and peace; through Jesus Christ,
their Lord and ours. *Amen.*

Lord God of Hosts, in whom our fathers trusted:
We give Thee thanks for all Thy servants who
have laid down their lives in the service of our
country. Unite all the people of this nation in a
holy purpose to defend the freedom and brotherhood for which they lived and died. Grant, we
beseech Thee, that the liberty they bequeathed
unto us may be continued to our children and
our children's children, and that the power of
the Gospel may here abound, to the blessing of
all the nations of the earth, and to Thine eternal glory; through Jesus Christ Thy Son our
Lord. *Amen.*

INDEPENDENCE DAY

ALMIGHTY God, who hast given us this good
land for our heritage: We humbly beseech
Thee that we may always prove ourselves a people
mindful of Thy favor and glad to do Thy will.

Bless our land with honorable industry, sound learning, and pure manners. Save us from violence, discord, and confusion; from pride and arrogancy; and from every evil way. Defend our liberties, and fashion into one happy people the multitudes brought hither out of many kindreds and tongues. Endue with the spirit of wisdom those to whom in Thy name we entrust the authority of government, that there may be justice and peace at home, and that, through obedience to Thy law, we may show forth Thy praise among the nations of the earth. In the time of prosperity fill our hearts with thankfulness, and in the day of trouble suffer not our trust in Thee to fail; all which we ask through Jesus Christ our Lord. *Amen.*

Lord God of our fathers, who hast granted unto our country freedom, and established sovereignty by the people's will: We thank Thee for those whom Thou hast raised up for our ·nation, to defend our liberty, preserve our union, and maintain law and order within our borders. Ever give unto the republic wise and fearless leaders and commanders in every time of need. Enlighten and direct the multitudes whom Thou hast ordained in power, that their counsels may be filled with knowledge and equity, and the whole commonwealth be preserved in peace, unity, strength, and honor. Take under Thy governance and protection Thy servants, the President, the governors of the states, the lawgivers, the judges, and all who are entrusted with authority; so defending them from all evil and enriching them with all good that the people may prosper in freedom be-

neath an equal law, and our nation may magnify
Thy name in all the earth; through Jesus Christ
our Lord. *Amen.*

LABOR DAY

ALMIGHTY Father, who by Thy Son Jesus
Christ hast sanctified labor to the welfare of
mankind: Prosper, we pray Thee, the industries
of this land, and all those who are engaged therein;
that, shielded in all their temptations and dangers,
and receiving a due reward of their labors, they
may praise Thee by living according to Thy will;
through Jesus Christ our Lord. *Amen.*

O God, who in Thy providence hast appointed
to every man his work: We humbly beseech Thee
to put away all strife and contention between
those who are engaged in the labors of industry
and those who employ their labor. Deliver them
from all greed and covetousness, and grant that
they, seeking only that which is just and equal,
may live and work in brotherly union and concord, to Thy glory, their own well-being, and the
prosperity of their country; through Jesus Christ
our Lord. *Amen.*

O God, Thou mightiest Worker of the universe,
Source of all strength, and Author of all unity:
We pray Thee for our brothers the industrial
workers of the nation. As their work binds them
together in toil and danger, may their hearts be
knit together in a strong sense of their common
interests and so fulfill the law of Christ by bear-
ing the common burdens. Grant the organiza-
tions of labor quiet patience and prudence in all

disputes. Raise up leaders of able mind and large heart, and give them grace to follow wise counsel. Bless all classes of our nation and build up a great body of workers strong of limb, clear of mind, glad to labor, striving together for the final brotherhood of all men; through Jesus Christ our Lord. *Amen.*

ELECTION DAY

ALMIGHTY God, who dost hold us to account for the use of all our powers and privileges: Guide, we pray Thee, the people of these United States in the election of their rulers and representatives; that by wise legislation and faithful administration the rights of all may be protected, and our nation be enabled to fulfill Thy purposes; through Jesus Christ our Lord. *Amen.*

THANKSGIVING DAY

O ALMIGHTY God and Heavenly Father, we glorify Thee that Thou hast again fulfilled to us Thy gracious promise that while the earth remaineth seedtime and harvest shall not fail. We bless Thee for the kindly fruits of the earth, which Thou hast given to our use. Teach us, we beseech Thee, to remember that it is not by bread alone that man doth live, and grant us evermore to feed on Him who is the true Bread from heaven, even Jesus Christ our Lord, to whom, with Thee, and the Holy Spirit, be all honor and glory, world without end. *Amen.*

The eyes of all things do look up and trust in Thee, O Lord. Thou givest them their meat in due season; Thou dost open Thy hand and fillest with Thy blessing everything living. Good Lord, bless us and all Thy gifts, which we receive of Thy bounteous liberality; through Jesus Christ our Lord. *Amen.*

Most high and mighty Ruler of the universe, by whom our nation hath been established in freedom and preserved in union: In this feast of harvest we thank Thee for the fruits of the earth. We thank Thee also for Thy favor shown unto our fathers, and Thy faithfulness continued unto their children; for the rich land given us for an inheritance, and the great power entrusted to the people; for the fidelity of men set in authority, and the peace maintained by righteous laws; for protection from outward dangers, and deliverance from inward strife; for an honorable place among the nations, and the opportunity of increasing service to the world. Keep Thou the commonwealth beneath Thy care, and guide the State according to Thy will; and Thine shall be the glory and the praise and the thanksgiving, from generation to generation. *Amen.*

PEACE SUNDAY

ALMIGHTY God, from whom all thoughts of truth and peace proceed: Kindle, we pray Thee, in the hearts of all men the true love of peace, and guide with Thy pure and peaceable wisdom those who take counsel for the nations of the earth; that in tranquillity Thy kingdom may go forward, till the earth be filled with the knowledge of Thy love; through Jesus Christ our Lord. *Amen.*

O God, who hast made of one blood all nations to dwell on the face of the earth, and who hast revealed Thy will for men by Thy Son, the Prince of Peace: Give us charity, we pray Thee, to regard all men as our brethren, and to share with them the heritage we have received from Thee. Deliver us from pride, prejudice, and arrogancy. Put far from us all selfishness and malice, suspicion, envy, and anger, and the unrighteous passions which make men to be enemies one of another. Turn all peoples unto Thee, that, following Thy holy example and united in Thy service, they may become one brotherhood in Thee, and that Thy peace may possess every heart and rule in all the nations of the world; through Jesus Christ Thy Son our Lord. *Amen.*

PRAYERS FOR SPECIAL USE

FOR THE CHURCH

ALMIGHTY and everlasting God, who hast revealed Thy glory by Christ among all nations: Preserve the works of Thy mercy; that Thy Church, which is spread throughout the world, may persevere with steadfast faith in the confession of Thy name; through Jesus Christ our Lord. *Amen.*

O Almighty God, who hast built Thy Church upon the foundation of the apostles and prophets, Jesus Christ Himself being the head cornerstone: Grant, we beseech Thee, that being gathered together in unity by Thy Holy Spirit, Thy Church may manifest Thy power among all peoples to the glory of Thy name; through Jesus Christ our Lord, who liveth and reigneth with Thee and the same Spirit, one God, world without end. *Amen.*

FOR CHURCH UNITY

O GOD, the Father of our Lord Jesus Christ, our only Saviour, the Prince of Peace: Give us grace seriously to lay to heart the great dangers we are in by our unhappy divisions. Take away all pride and prejudice, and whatsoever else may hinder us from godly union and concord; that as there is but one Body and one Spirit, and one hope of our calling, one Lord, one faith, one baptism, one God and Father of us all, so we may be all of one heart and of one soul, united in one holy bond of truth and peace, of faith and charity, and may with one mind and one mouth glorify Thee; through Jesus Christ our Lord. *Amen.*

FOR CHRISTIAN MISSIONS

O GOD, who didst send the Holy Spirit upon the apostles, to teach them and lead them into all truth, that they might go into all the world and preach the Gospel to every creature: Pour out, we beseech Thee, the same Holy Spirit upon Thy Church, that it may send forth the good tidings of great joy unto all people. Revive Thy work, O Lord; raise up laborers, and strengthen their hands that they may tell of salvation unto the ends of the world. Bless with the mighty aid of the Holy Spirit those who now work to the glory of Thy name in distant lands. Give them faithfulness and courage, and take out of their way all hindrances. Hasten the time, O Lord, for the coming of Thy kingdom, and for the gathering in of all nations unto Thee. And we pray both for the outward growth of Thy kingdom in the world and for its inward growth in the hearts of men; and especially for our own Church and country, that true religion may abound unto all righteousness and peace; through Thine only Son our Saviour Jesus Christ. *Amen.*

FOR THE COMING OF GOD'S KINGDOM

O THOU King eternal, immortal, invisible, Thou only wise God our Saviour: Hasten, we beseech Thee, the coming of Thy kingdom upon earth, and draw the whole world of mankind into willing obedience to Thy blessed reign. Overcome all the enemies of Christ, and bring low every power that is exalted against Him. Cast out all the evil things which cause wars and fightings among us, and let Thy Spirit rule the hearts of men in righteousness and love. Build Thou the old wastes, and repair the desolations of many generations, that the wilderness may rejoice, and the city be made glad with Thy law. Establish every work that is founded on truth and equity, and fulfill all the hopes and desires of Thy people, through the victory of Christ our Lord. *Amen.*

FOR THE GENERAL ASSEMBLY

ALMIGHTY and everlasting God, who by Thy Holy Spirit didst preside in the first assembly of the apostles and elders at Jerusalem, and hast promised to be with Thy Church alway unto the end of the world: Vouchsafe, we pray Thee, unto Thy servants met in General Assembly Thy gracious presence and blessing. Deliver them from all error, pride, and prejudice; enlighten them with wisdom from above; and so order all their doings that Thy kingdom may be advanced, and all Thy ministers and congregations established in their most holy faith; until at length all Thy people shall be gathered into one fold of the great Shepherd, Jesus Christ our Lord; to whom be glory for ever. *Amen.*

Almighty God, who by Thy Holy Spirit dost inhabit the whole company of the faithful: Graciously regard, we beseech Thee, Thy servants gathered before Thee at this time, in the General Assembly and chief council of this Church. Shed down upon them heavenly wisdom and grace; enlighten them with true knowledge of Thy Word; inspire them with a pure zeal for Thy glory; and

so order all their doings through Thy good Spirit
that unity and peace may prevail among them;
that truth and righteousness may flow forth from
them; and that, by their endeavors, all Thy
ministers and congregations may be established
and comforted, Thy Gospel everywhere purely
preached and truly followed, Thy kingdom among
men extended and strengthened, and the whole
body of Thy people grow up into Him who is
Head over all things to the Church, Jesus Christ
our Lord. *Amen.*

FOR THE SYNOD OR PRESBYTERY

ALMIGHTY God, who through the apostles
of Thy Son Jesus Christ didst order the
governance of Thy flock: Send now Thy blessing
upon (*the Synod or Presbytery of* . . . .)
assembled in Thy name. Grant unto Thy servants the spirit of power, and of love, and of a
sound mind, that they may be wise in counsel and
diligent in service, faithful stewards of the things
belonging to Thy kingdom, and worthy successors
of the apostles whom our Lord sent forth to testify
of Him. Direct and govern them by Thy Holy
Spirit, preserving them from hasty judgment and
vain dispute, inspiring them with hearty love and
true devotion, and guiding them both to devise
and to do those things which shall be for the
glory of Christ's name, for the welfare of His
Church, for the peace of all believers, for the
spread of the Gospel, and for the good of the
whole world; through the Head of the Church,
Jesus Christ Thy Son, to whom, with Thee, O
Father, and the Holy Spirit, be all honor and
glory, world without end. *Amen.*

FOR CHURCH SCHOOLS

O HOLY Lord and Saviour, who didst call little children unto Thee and bless them: Guide, we pray Thee, Thy Church in the teaching of the young, that it may wisely order the work of our schools, and strive earnestly to feed the lambs of Thy flock. Grant alike to pastors and people to see and know the greatness of this work, and give us grace to fulfill it. Make us ever mindful of Thy presence in our homes, that our children may be brought up in Thy nurture and admonition. Give to our teachers aptness to teach, and to our scholars willingness to learn Thy blessed will. All this we ask in Thy name, O merciful Saviour, whom, with the Father and the Holy Spirit, we worship as one God, blessed for ever. *Amen.*

FOR SCHOOLS, COLLEGES, AND UNIVERSITIES

ALMIGHTY God, we beseech Thee with Thy gracious favor to behold our universities, colleges, and schools, that knowledge may be increased among us, and all good learning flourish and abound. Bless all who teach and all who learn, and grant that in humility of heart they may ever look unto Thee, who art the Fountain of all wisdom; through Jesus Christ our Lord. *Amen.*

FOR THEOLOGICAL SEMINARIES

O GOD, who through Thy Holy Spirit dost illuminate the minds and sanctify the lives of those whom Thou dost call to the work of pastors and teachers: Look with Thy favor upon all schools for the instruction and discipline of those who are to serve in the sacred ministry of

Thy Church. Bless those who teach and those
who learn, that they may apply themselves with
such diligence to the knowledge which is able to
make men wise unto salvation, and submit themselves with such ready obedience to the law of
Thy Son our Saviour that they may fulfill their
ministry with joy; through the same Jesus Christ
our Lord. *Amen.*

FOR THE MINISTRY

O LORD, we beseech Thee to raise up for the
work of the ministry faithful and able men
who will count it all joy to spend and be spent
for the sake of Thy dear Son, and for the souls
for which He shed His most precious blood upon
the cross, and we pray Thee to fit them for their
holy office by Thy bountiful grace and heavenly
benediction; through Jesus Christ our Lord, who
liveth and reigneth with Thee and the Holy
Spirit, one God, world without end. *Amen.*

FOR OUR COUNTRY

O GOD, who by Thy providence didst lead
our forefathers to this good land wherein
they found liberty and freedom to worship Thee:
We beseech Thee ever to guide our nation in the
way of Thy truth and peace, so that we may never
fail in the blessing which Thou hast promised to
that people whose God is the Lord; through
Jesus Christ Thy Son our Lord. *Amen.*

FOR DELIVERANCE FROM NATIONAL SINS

WE BESEECH Thee, O God, to forgive those
national sins which do so easily beset us:
our wanton waste of the wealth of soil and sea; our

desecration of natural beauty; our heedlessness of those who come after us, if only we be served; our love of money, our contempt for small things and our worship of big things; our neglect of backward peoples; our complacency; and our pride of life. For these wrongs done to our land and our heritage, as for right things left undone, forgive us, O Lord. *Amen.*

FOR BETTER RACE RELATIONS

O GOD, who art the Hope of all the ends of the earth, the God of the spirits of all flesh: We beseech Thee to hear our humble intercessions for all races and kindreds of men, that Thou wilt turn all hearts unto Thyself. Remove from our minds hatred, prejudice, and contempt for those who are not of our own race or color, class or creed; that, departing from everything that estranges and divides, we may by Thee be brought into unity of spirit, in the bond of peace. *Amen.*

FOR THE PERSECUTED

MOST merciful Father, we humbly beseech Thee for all who suffer persecution for the sake of the Gospel, that the comfort of Thy Holy Spirit may never depart from them; so that by their witness the kingdom of Thy Son may increase and shine throughout all the world, to the glory of Thy holy name. *Amen.*

FOR OUR ENEMIES

WE PRAY, O Lord, as Christ hath taught us, for our enemies, that their hearts and ours may be drawn to God the Father of all, and filled with a desire to serve Him, that peace may be re-established on the foundation of justice, truth, and good will; through Jesus Christ our Lord. *Amen.*

FOR WORLD PEACE

O GOD, who hast made of one blood all the nations of the earth: Mercifully hear our supplications, and remove from the world for ever the dreadful menace of war. Guide the rulers with Thy counsel and restrain the passions of the people, so that bloodshed may be averted and peace be preserved. By the pouring out of Thy Spirit upon all flesh, quicken the sense of our common brotherhood, bring the nations into a new bond of fellowship, and hasten the time when the kingdoms of this world shall become the kingdom of our Lord and Saviour Jesus Christ. *Amen.*

Almighty God, from whom all thoughts of truth and peace proceed: Kindle, we pray Thee, in the hearts of all men, the true love of peace, and guide with Thy pure and peaceable wisdom those who take counsel for the nations of the earth; that in tranquillity Thy kingdom may go forward, till the earth be filled with the knowledge of Thy love; through Jesus Christ our Lord. *Amen.*

Eternal God, in whose perfect kingdom no sword is drawn but the sword of righteousness, and no strength known but the strength of love: So guide and inspire, we pray Thee, the work of all who seek Thy kingdom at home and abroad, that all peoples may seek and find their security, not in force of arms, but in the perfect love that casteth out fear, and in the fellowship revealed to us by Thy Son Jesus Christ our Lord. *Amen.*

FOR THE CONGRESS

MOST gracious God, we humbly beseech Thee, as for the people of this nation in general, so especially for the Senate and Representatives in Congress assembled; that Thou wouldst be pleased to direct and prosper all their consultations, to the advancement of Thy glory, the good of Thy Church, the safety, honor, and welfare of the people; that all things may be so ordered and settled by their endeavors, upon the best and surest foundations, that peace and happiness, truth and justice, virtue and piety, may be established among us. These and all other necessaries, for them, for us, and for Thy whole Church, we humbly beg in the name of Jesus Christ, our most blessed Lord and Saviour. *Amen.*

FOR THOSE IN THE SERVICE

O GOD our Father, we commend to Thy keeping all the men and women serving our country by sea, land, and air, that we may win for the whole world the fruits of our sacrifice and a just peace; through the grace of Jesus Christ our Lord. *Amen.*

FOR THE ARMY

O LORD God of Hosts, stretch forth, we pray Thee, Thine almighty arm to strengthen and protect the soldiers of our country in every peril; shelter them in the day of battle, and in time of peace keep them safe from all evil; endue them ever with loyalty and courage, and grant that in all things they may serve as seeing Thee who art invisible; through Jesus Christ our Lord. *Amen.*

FOR THE NAVY

O GOD, who art the confidence of all who dwell upon the earth and of them that are afar off upon the sea: Hear our prayer for Thy servants who defend their country on the oceans and maintain the justice and freedom of nations. Safeguard their lives amid the perils of the deep and the violence of foes. Keep them strong in faith, in courage, and in self-control. Let Thy presence calm their minds in the hour of danger and hold them fast from temptation in times of ease. Enable them to fulfill their duty with fidelity throughout the voyage of life and bring them at length to their desired haven; through Jesus Christ, their Captain and Lord. *Amen.*

FOR THE AIR FORCES

ALMIGHTY God, who makest the clouds Thy chariot and walkest upon the wings of the wind: Have mercy, we beseech Thee, on our airmen, and when they are amidst the clouds and wonders of the sky, give unto them the assurance of Thy protection, that they may do their duty with clear minds and fearless hearts, confident that in life or in death Thou, the eternal God, art their Refuge and underneath are Thine everlasting arms; through Jesus Christ our Lord. *Amen.*

FOR THE MERCHANT MARINE

O ETERNAL Lord God, who alone spreadest out the heavens and rulest the raging of the sea: Be pleased to receive into Thy protection the men of the Merchant Marine and all those who go down to the sea in ships and do business in great waters.   Make them to see Thy wonders in the deep.   Grant them safe voyages, and give good success to their journeys.   Make them faithful to the trusts imposed in them, that in time of war they may serve their nation with honor, and at all times look in faith and loyalty to Thee, who rulest over lands and seas; through Jesus Christ our Lord.   *Amen.*

FOR PHYSICIANS, NURSES, AND HOSPITALS

ALMIGHTY God, whose blessed Son Jesus Christ went about continually doing good, and healing all manner of sickness and all manner of disease among the people: Continue, we beseech Thee, this His gracious work among us; cheer, heal, and sanctify the sick and the wounded; grant to the physicians, surgeons, and nurses wisdom and skill, sympathy and patience; and send down Thy blessing on all who labor to prevent suffering and to forward Thy purposes of love; through Jesus Christ our Lord.   *Amen.*

FOR ALL WHO DO GOOD TO THEIR FELLOW MEN

O GOD, who hast given unto Thy servants diversities of gifts by the same Spirit, and hast taught us by Thy holy apostle that all our doings without charity are nothing worth: Be pleased to bless and prosper all who love and serve their fellow men with a pure heart fervently, remembering the poor, healing the sick, comforting the sorrowful, teaching the ignorant, and lifting up the afflicted; let their prayers and alms come up for a memorial before Thee; and reward them plentifully with peace; through the merits of Jesus Christ our only Saviour.   *Amen.*

FOR PEACE RESTORED

ALMIGHTY and everlasting God, who makest wars to cease unto the ends of the earth: We praise and magnify that great mercy whereby Thou hast given us rest and quietness, and out of Thine abundant goodness art shedding down the same blessed tranquillity upon the nations round about us; and we humbly beseech Thee, that, being subdued by Thy truth, we and they may evermore dwell together in peace, as one family of mankind; through Jesus Christ our Lord. *Amen.*

FOR THE BLESSING OF A NEW HOME

O LORD our God, Giver of life and love: We beseech Thee to bestow Thy blessing upon Thy servants whom Thou hast appointed to dwell together under the shelter of this roof. May they ever seek Thy presence, that their home may be an abode of peace and holy love. Bless their going out and their coming in, from this time forth; graciously shield and protect them from all evil; prosper them in all rightful undertakings; and whether in prosperity or in adversity, in health or in sickness, let them know that Thy Fatherly hand is upon them for good. Knit them closely together in worship of Thee and love for Thy house; and grant that, united by the loyalties of this earthly home, and by fidelity to Thee, they may be one in that heavenly home which Thou preparest for them that love Thee; through Jesus Christ our Lord. *Amen.*

FOR HOME AND KINDRED

O GOD, our Heavenly Father, who hast set the solitary in families: Look in favor, we beseech Thee, upon the homes of Thy people. Defend them against all evil, and supply all their needs according to the riches of Thy grace. Make them sanctuaries of purity and peace, love and joy. Bless all dear to us wheresoever they are, and grant that they and we may follow Thee at every step of our daily life, that, though our paths may lead us far from one another, we may all abide within the safe shelter of Thy love; through Jesus Christ our Lord. *Amen.*

FOR CHILDREN

O HEAVENLY Father, who long ago didst watch Thy Son on earth grow as in stature so in wisdom and in perfect love of Thee: Teach by the wondrous life of Jesus and His Church the children whom Thou watchest now; that they may grow into His likeness, loving Thee, obedient to Thy will, and happy in Thy house; through the same Jesus Christ our Lord. *Amen.*

FOR YOUNG PEOPLE

O GOD, from whom cometh every good and perfect gift: Grant unto all young men and women that they may be worthy of their heritage. Quicken their minds in the desire for knowledge, and their hearts in the love of virtue. Deliver them from fear of that which is new, and from scorn of that which is old. Lead them forward in the spirit of understanding, and confirm them in the confidence that all truth is for their good

and to Thy glory. Out of weakness give them
strength; support them in the time of temptation;
help them to do Thy work with good courage
and continue Thy faithful soldiers and servants
until their life's end; through Jesus Christ our
Lord. *Amen.*

FOR TRAVELERS

ALMIGHTY God, who art the sure Guide and
strong Refuge of all who put their trust in
Thee: We beseech Thee to watch over all travelers
by land or sea or air, and to vouchsafe to them
Thy favor and protection; preserve them from all
evils and dangers on their way; and of Thy mercy
bring them again to their homes and friends in
peace; through Jesus Christ our Lord. *Amen.*

FOR THE BLIND AND THE DEAF

ALMIGHTY Father, whose blessed Son Jesus
Christ went about doing good, opening the
eyes of the blind, loosing the tongue of the dumb,
and unstopping the ears of the deaf: We bring
to Thee all those who are likewise afflicted. Let
Thy voice be heard in the hearts of those who
cannot hear; let the beauty of Thy presence be
visible to the souls of those who cannot see; let
Thy word be spoken through the lives of those
who cannot speak; through Jesus Christ our
Lord. *Amen.*

FOR THE SICK

O LORD JESUS CHRIST, Thou great Physician: Look with Thy gracious favor upon
this Thy servant; give wisdom and discretion to
those who minister to *him* in *his* sickness; bless all

the means used for *his* recovery; stretch forth Thy hand, and, according to Thy will, restore *him* to health and strength, that *he* may live to praise Thee for Thy goodness and Thy grace; to the glory of Thy holy name. *Amen.*

Almighty and immortal God, Giver of life and health: We beseech Thee to hear our prayers for this Thy servant, that, by Thy blessing upon *him* and upon those who minister to *him, he* may be restored to health of body and mind, and give thanks to Thee in Thy holy Church; through Jesus Christ our Lord. *Amen.*

FOR THE MENTALLY SICK

FATHER of mercies and God of all comfort, we commend to Thy Fatherly goodness all those who are in any way afflicted or distressed in mind. Cheer the melancholy; restore hope to the hopeless; protect the unconscious; calm the violent: suffer them not to do harm to themselves or others, and let no one do injury to them. Lay not to their charge whatever evil they may say or do in time of their affliction. Confirm the health of those who are recovering. Bless the endeavors of all who labor and pray on their behalf, and bring us all to Thine everlasting kingdom; through Jesus Christ our Lord. *Amen.*

FOR A SICK CHILD

O LORD JESUS CHRIST, Good Shepherd of the sheep, who dost gather the lambs with Thine arms, and carry them in Thy bosom: We commit into Thy loving hands this child. Relieve *his* pain, guard *him* in all danger; restore unto *him* Thy gifts of gladness and strength, and raise *him* up to a life of service to Thee. Hear us, we beseech Thee, for Thy dear name's sake. *Amen.*

FOR THE DYING

O GOD, our Heavenly Father, in whom we live and move and have our being: Grant to this Thy servant grace to desire only Thy most holy will; that, whether living or dying, *he* may be Thine; for His sake who loved us and gave Himself for us, Jesus Christ our Lord. *Amen.*

BEFORE AN OPERATION

ALMIGHTY God, who didst send Thy Son Jesus Christ to be the Great Physician of our souls and bodies: Grant us Thy peace. Thou who givest rest to those who wait upon Thee, grant us Thy courage. In quietness and confidence may we find strength. Give wisdom and skill to those who operate and to those who serve as nurses. We give ourselves into Thy sustaining presence, knowing that in Thee is our peace; through Jesus Christ our Lord. *Amen.*

FOR THE ABSENT

O GOD, who art present in every place: Mercifully hear our prayers for those whom we love, now absent from us; watch over them, we beseech Thee, and protect them in all anxiety, danger, and temptation; teach us and them to know that Thou art always near, and that we are one in Thee for ever; through Jesus Christ our Lord. *Amen.*

FOR THOSE IN THE SERVICE OF OUR COUNTRY

O GOD, whose Fatherly care reacheth to the uttermost parts of the earth: We humbly beseech Thee graciously to behold and bless those whom we love, now absent from us, especially those of our families, friends, and neighbors who are away in the service of our country. Defend them in all dangers of soul and body; and grant that both they and we, drawing nearer to Thee, may be bound together by Thy love in the communion of Thy Holy Spirit, and in the fellowship of Thy saints; through Jesus Christ our Lord. *Amen.*

PRAYERS FOR SPECIAL GRACES

FOR A SPIRITUAL MIND

ALMIGHTY God, who alone canst order the unruly wills and affections of sinful men: Grant unto Thy people that they may love the thing which Thou commandest, and desire that which Thou dost promise; that so, among the sundry and manifold changes of the world, our hearts may surely there be fixed, where true joys are to be found; through Jesus Christ our Lord. *Amen.*

FOR FAITH

O HEAVENLY Father, who in Thy Son Jesus Christ hast given us a true faith and a sure hope: Help us, we pray Thee, to live as those who believe and trust in the communion of saints, the forgiveness of sins, and the resurrection to life everlasting; and strengthen this faith and hope in us all the days of our life; through the love of Thy Son Jesus Christ our Saviour. *Amen.*

FOR HOPE

O GOD of hope, fill Thy children with all joy and peace in believing, that in this world of mystery we be not cast down nor dismayed, but may abound in hope in the power of the Holy Spirit; and grant that, laying hold of the hope set before us, it may be to us an anchor of the soul, both sure and steadfast, entering into that which is within the veil; through Jesus Christ our Lord. *Amen.*

FOR LOVE

O LORD, who hast taught us that all our doings without love are nothing worth: Send Thy Holy Spirit, and pour into our hearts that most excellent gift of love, the very bond of peace and of all virtues; grant this for Thine only Son Jesus Christ's sake. *Amen.*

FOR JOY

O GOD, who hast made the heaven and the earth and all that is good and lovely therein, and hast shown us through Jesus our Lord that the secret of joy is a heart set free from selfish desires: Help us to find delight in simple things and ever to rejoice in the richness of Thy bounty; through the same Jesus Christ our Lord. *Amen.*

FOR JOY IN OTHERS' HAPPINESS

O GOD, the wind of whose Spirit bloweth where it listeth, and whose rain falleth where it will: Quicken our ears to hear and our eyes to see the signs of Thy presence, not only where our habits and conventions expect them, but wherever Thy bounty bestows them. So shall our lives be gladdened by every miracle of grace, and our wills be alert to praise Thy goodness to every creature; for His name's sake who was born of the Spirit, the only Saviour of the world. *Amen.*

FOR JOY IN GOD'S CREATION

O HEAVENLY Father, who hast filled the world with beauty: Open, we beseech Thee, our eyes to behold Thy gracious hand in all Thy works; that, rejoicing in Thy whole creation, we

may learn to serve Thee with gladness; for the
sake of Him by whom all things were made, Thy
Son Jesus Christ our Lord. *Amen.*

FOR COURAGE

ALMIGHTY God, give us grace to contend
always for what is true and right, and to be
ready if need be to suffer for it. Give us not
over to fearfulness of soul, but lift us into that
love which casteth out fear, so that we may glorify
and enjoy Thee now and for ever; through Jesus
Christ our Lord. *Amen.*

FOR GUIDANCE

O GOD, by whom the meek are guided in
judgment, and light riseth up in darkness
for the godly: Grant us, in our doubts and uncertainties, the grace to ask what Thou wouldst
have us to do; that the Spirit of wisdom may save
us from all false choices, and that in Thy light we
may see light, and in Thy straight path may not
stumble; through Jesus Christ our Lord. *Amen.*

Direct us, O Lord, in all our doings, with Thy
most gracious favor, and further us with Thy
continual help; that in all our works begun, continued, and ended in Thee, we may glorify Thy
holy name, and finally, by Thy mercy, obtain everlasting life; through Jesus Christ our Lord. *Amen.*

FOR PURITY

O GOD, whose blessed Son was manifested
that He might destroy the works of the devil,
and make us the sons of God and heirs of eternal
life: Grant us, we beseech Thee, that having this

hope we may purify ourselves, even as He is pure,
that when He shall appear again with power and
great glory, we may be made like unto Him in
His eternal and glorious kingdom. *Amen.*

FOR TRUTH AND BEAUTY

O GOD, who by Thy Spirit dost lead men to
desire Thy perfection, to seek for truth and
to rejoice in beauty: Illuminate and inspire, we
beseech Thee, all thinkers, artists, craftsmen; that,
in whatsoever is true and pure and lovely, Thy
name may be hallowed and Thy kingdom come
on earth; through Jesus Christ our Lord. *Amen.*

FOR TEMPERANCE

ALMIGHTY God, gracious Father of men, who
openest Thine hand and fillest all things with
plenty: Teach us to use the gifts of Thy providence soberly and temperately. Grant, O Lord,
that the blessings which Thou givest us may
minister neither to sin nor to sickness, but to
health and holiness and thanksgiving; that in the
strength of Thy provision we may faithfully and
diligently serve Thee here, and be accounted
worthy to be made partakers of Thine eternal
kingdom; through Jesus Christ our Lord. *Amen.*

FOR ZEAL

O GOD, the sovereign Good of the soul, who
requirest the hearts of all Thy children:
Deliver us from all sloth in Thy work, all coldness
in Thy cause; and grant us by looking unto Thee
to rekindle our love, and by waiting upon Thee
to renew our strength; through Jesus Christ our
Lord. *Amen.*

FOR PEACE OF HEART

O GOD, who art the Author of peace and Lover of concord, in knowledge of whom standeth our eternal life, whose service is perfect freedom: Defend us Thy humble servants in all assaults of our enemies; that we, surely trusting in Thy defense, may not fear the power of any adversaries; through the might of Jesus Christ our Lord. *Amen.*

FOR KNOWLEDGE OF GOD

O THOU who art the Light of the minds that know Thee, the Life of the souls that love Thee, and the Strength of the wills that serve Thee: Help us so to know Thee that we may truly love Thee, so to love Thee that we may fully serve Thee, whom to serve is perfect freedom; through Jesus Christ our Lord. *Amen.*

DEDICATION OF OFFERINGS

O GOD, of whose bounty we have all received: Accept this offering of Thy people; and so follow it with Thy blessing that it may promote peace and good will among men, and advance the kingdom of our Lord and Saviour Jesus Christ. *Amen.*

O God, the Fountain of all good: We bring to Thee our gifts, according as Thou hast prospered us. Enable us, with our earthly things, to give Thee the love of our hearts and the service of our lives. Let Thy favor, which is life, and Thy loving-kindness, which is better than life, be upon us now and always; through Jesus Christ our Lord. *Amen.*

Almighty God, our Heavenly Father, who hast not spared Thine own Son, but delivered Him up for us all, and who, with Him, hast freely given us all things: Receive these offerings which we bring and dedicate to Thee; and enable us, with all our gifts, so to yield ourselves to Thee that with body, soul, and spirit we may truly and freely serve Thee, and in Thy service find our deepest joy; through Jesus Christ our Lord. *Amen.*

O Lord our God, the Giver of all good: We beseech Thee to behold in these our gifts the earnest of our consecration to Thy service; and grant that now and at all times our gratitude to Thee may be as great as our need of Thy mercy; through Jesus Christ our Lord. *Amen.*

O Lord our God, Thou King of all the earth: Accept, of Thine infinite goodness, the offerings of Thy people, which, in obedience to Thy commandment and in honor of Thy name, we give and dedicate to Thee; and grant unto us that the same, being devoted to Thy service, may be used for Thy glory; through Jesus Christ our Lord. *Amen.*

O God, who needest not to be enriched with any gifts that we may bring, yet who lovest the cheerful giver: Receive these our offerings which we present before Thee, and with them ourselves, our souls and our bodies, a living sacrifice, holy and acceptable to Thee; through Jesus Christ our Lord. *Amen.*

O Lord our God, who givest liberally and upbraidest not: Teach us to give cheerfully of our substance for Thy cause and kingdom. Let Thy blessing be upon our offerings, and grant us to know the joy of those who give with their whole heart; through Jesus Christ our Lord. *Amen.*

ASCRIPTIONS

NOW unto Him that is able to do exceeding abundantly above all that we ask or think, according to the power that worketh in us; unto Him be glory in the Church by Christ Jesus, throughout all ages, world without end. *Amen.*

Now unto Him that is able to keep you from falling, and to present you faultless before the presence of His glory with exceeding joy; to the only wise God our Saviour, be glory and majesty, dominion and power, both now and ever. *Amen.*

Unto Him that loved us, and washed us from our sins in His own blood, and hath made us kings and priests unto His God and Father; to Him be glory and dominion for ever and ever. *Amen.*

Now unto the blessed and only Potentate, the King of kings, and Lord of lords; who only hath immortality, dwelling in the light which no man can approach unto; whom no man hath seen nor can see: to whom be honor and power everlasting. *Amen.*

Now unto the God of all grace, who hath called us unto His eternal glory by Christ Jesus, be glory and dominion for ever and ever. *Amen.*

And now to the Father, Son, and Holy Spirit, three Persons and one God, be ascribed by us, and by the whole Church, as is most due, the kingdom, the power, and the glory, for ever and ever. *Amen.*

Unto the Father, and unto the Son, and unto the Holy Spirit, be ascribed in the Church all honor and glory, might, majesty, dominion, and blessing, now, henceforth, and for ever. *Amen.*

Blessing, and honor, and glory, and power, be unto Him that sitteth upon the throne, and unto the Lamb, for ever and ever. *Amen.*

Now unto the King eternal, immortal, invisible, the only wise God, be honor and glory for ever and ever. *Amen.*

Blessing, and glory, and wisdom, and thanksgiving, and honor, and power, and might, be unto our God for ever and ever. *Amen.*

BENEDICTIONS

THE grace of the Lord Jesus Christ, and the love of God, and the communion of the Holy Spirit, be with you all. *Amen.*

The very God of peace sanctify you wholly, and preserve you blameless unto the coming of our Lord Jesus Christ. *Amen.*

The Lord bless you, and keep you: the Lord make His face to shine upon you, and be gracious unto you: the Lord lift up His countenance upon you, and give you peace; through Jesus Christ our Lord. *Amen.*

The peace of God, which passeth all understanding, keep your hearts and minds in the knowledge and love of God, and of His Son Jesus Christ our Lord; and the blessing of God Almighty, the Father, the Son, and the Holy Spirit, be upon you, and remain with you always. *Amen.*

The God of peace, that brought again from the dead our Lord Jesus, that great Shepherd of the sheep, through the blood of the everlasting covenant, make you perfect in every good work to do His will, working in you that which is well-pleasing in His sight; through Jesus Christ, to whom be glory for ever and ever. *Amen.*

Grace, mercy, and peace from God the Father, Son, and Holy Spirit, be with you henceforth and for ever. *Amen.*

Unto God's gracious mercy and protection we commit you.

And the blessing of God Almighty, the Father, the Son, and the Holy Spirit, be upon you and remain with you for ever. *Amen.*

Go in peace; God the Father, Son, and Holy Spirit, preserve and keep you this *day* and for evermore. *Amen.*

ASSURANCES OF PARDON

ALMIGHTY God, who doth freely pardon all who repent and turn to Him, now fulfill in every contrite heart the promise of redeeming grace; remitting all our sins, and cleansing us from an evil conscience; through the perfect sacrifice of Christ Jesus our Lord. *Amen.*

Wash you, make you clean; put away the evil of your doings before Mine eyes; cease to do evil; learn to do well. Let the wicked forsake his way and the unrighteous man his thoughts, and let him return unto the Lord, for He will have mercy upon him; and to our God, for He will abundantly pardon. *Amen.*

Be comforted and hear the good tidings of the Gospel: If any man hath sinned, we have an Advocate with the Father, Jesus Christ the righteous; and He is the propitiation for our sins, and not for ours only, but also for the sins of the whole world. Believe the Gospel and live in peace. *Amen.*

Almighty God have mercy upon you, forgive you all your sins, and deliver you from all evil, comfort and strengthen you in all goodness, and bring you to life everlasting. *Amen.*

Hearken now unto the comforting assurance of the grace of God, promised in the Gospel to all who repent and believe: If we confess our sins, He is faithful and just to forgive us our sins and to cleanse us from all unrighteousness. *Amen.*

May the almighty and merciful Lord grant unto you pardon and remission of all your sins, true repentance, amendment of life, and the grace and comfort of the Holy Spirit. *Amen.*

The Lord is merciful and gracious, slow to anger, and plenteous in mercy. He hath not dealt with us after our sins, nor rewarded us according to our iniquities. As the heaven is high above the earth, so great is His mercy toward them that fear Him. As far as the east is from the west, so far hath He removed our transgressions from us. *Amen.*

Hear the gracious words of our Lord Jesus Christ unto all that truly repent and turn to Him: Come unto Me, all ye that labor and are heavy-laden, and I will give you rest. Him that cometh to Me I will in no wise cast out.

The grace of our Lord Jesus Christ be with you all. *Amen.*

The Lord is gracious and full of compassion; slow to anger, and of great mercy. The Lord is good to all; and His tender mercies are over all His works. The Lord is nigh unto all them that call upon Him, to all that call upon Him in truth. He will fulfill the desire of them that fear Him: He also will hear their cry, and will save them. *Amen.*

FAMILY PRAYERS

A special Prayer or brief Petition, suited to the need of the household, to any particular occasion, or at the special season of the year, may be added; and let all join in the Lord's Prayer.

Sunday Morning

O LORD, our Heavenly Father, at the beginning of another week we come to Thee for help and light. Grant, we beseech Thee, that we may hallow this day of rest to Thy service, and find in Thee all peace and strength. Quicken our devotion, that we may serve Thee in spirit and in truth, and lay a good foundation for our coming work. Be with us in all the public services of Thy day, that we may join in them with heart and soul, and receive the blessing which Thou hast promised to all who sincerely pray to Thee and faithfully hear Thy Word. This we ask for the sake of Jesus Christ our Lord. *Amen.*

WE PRAISE Thee, O Lord our God, for this Thy holy day. Grant that it may be to us a day of rest from worldly toil and care. Refresh our souls with Thy heavenly gifts. Enable us to worship Thee in Thy house of prayer, in spirit and in truth. Bless the ministers of Thy Church, especially those who labor in this place; make Thy Word in their mouth powerful to the conversion of sinners and to the building up of Thy people in the faith of Thy blessed Son. Grant that all who confess Thy holy name may be of one heart and of one soul, united in one holy bond of truth and peace, of faith and love, and may with one

mind and one mouth glorify Thee; through Jesus
Christ our Lord. *Amen.*

ALMIGHTY God, we praise Thee for the mercies which Thou hast bestowed upon us as
a household, and we beseech Thee to bless all the
families of earth with a Father's blessing. Look
mercifully upon the solitary and the lonely, the
weary and the heavy-laden, and grant them rest unto their souls. Pity and relieve the sorrows of all
mankind. Shed abroad the holy influence of the
Lord's Day throughout our land, and keep our
whole country, with those who are chosen to govern it, in the way of righteousness and peace.
Finally, we commend to Thy Fatherly goodness
all who are near and dear to us, wherever they
may be today, praying Thee to watch over them,
to provide for them, to bless them in body and
soul, and at last to bring them and us into the
perfect and eternal joy of heaven; through Jesus
Christ our Lord. *Amen.*

Monday Morning

O GOD, our Father, of whom the whole family
in heaven and on earth is named: Bestow
upon our household, at the beginning of this day,
that grace which shall keep us in the fellowship
of the Christian way; and grant unto each one of
us that heavenly guidance and control, in all our
labors, pleasures, and trials, which shall maintain
our hearts in peace with one another and with
Thee. Graciously help and prosper us in the
doing of our various duties with a willing and
cheerful mind; and defend us all, by Thine almighty power, both from inward evil and from

outward harm; so that when the day is ended it may not leave us in sorrow, strife, or shame, but in true unity and thankful rest, through Thy merciful favor and Thy forgiving love; in Christ Jesus our Lord. *Amen.*

O GOD, who art, and wast, and art to come, before whose face the generations rise and pass away: Age after age the living seek Thee and find that of Thy faithfulness there is no end. Our fathers in their pilgrimage walked by Thy guidance, and rested on Thy compassion; still to their children be Thou the cloud by day and the fire by night. Where but in Thee have we a covert from the storm, or shadow from the heat of life? In our manifold temptations, Thou alone knowest and art ever nigh; in sorrow, Thy pity revives the fainting soul; in our prosperity and ease, it is Thy Spirit only that can keep us from pride and keep us humble. O Thou sole Source of peace and righteousness, take now the veil from every heart, and join us in one communion with Thy prophets and saints who have trusted in Thee and were not ashamed. Not of our worthiness, but of Thy tender mercy, hear our prayer; for the sake of Jesus Christ Thy Son our Lord. *Amen.*

O LORD, our Heavenly Father, almighty and everlasting God, who hast safely brought us to the beginning of this day: Defend us in the same with Thy mighty power; and grant that this day we fall into no sin, neither run into any kind of danger; but that all our doings, being ordered by Thy governance, may be righteous in Thy sight; through Jesus Christ our Lord. *Amen.*

Tuesday Morning

O THOU, who art the true Sun of the world, evermore rising, and never going down; who by Thy most wholesome appearing and light dost nourish and make joyful all things both in heaven and on earth: We beseech Thee mercifully and favorably to shine into our hearts, that the night and darkness of sin, and the mists of error on every side, being driven away, we may all our life long go without any stumbling or offense, and may walk as in the daytime, being pure and clean from the works of darkness, and abounding in all good works which Thou hast prepared for us to walk in; through Jesus Christ our Lord. *Amen.*

O THOU in whose hand are the hearts of Thy children: Shed abroad Thy peace upon the world. By the might of Thy Holy Spirit quench the pride and anger and greediness which cause man to strive against man, and people against people. Lead all nations in the ways of mutual help and good will, and hasten the time when the earth shall confess Thee indeed for its Saviour and King, and no evil deeds of man shall defile Thy glorious creation; through Jesus Christ our Lord. *Amen.*

O GOD, Lord of all power and might, Preserver of all Thy creatures: Keep us this day in health of body and soundness of mind, in purity of heart and cheerfulness of spirit, in contentment with our lot and charity with our neighbor; and further all our lawful undertakings with Thy blessing. In our labor strengthen us; in our

pleasure purify us; in our difficulties direct us; in
our perils defend us; in our troubles comfort us;
and supply all our needs, according to the riches
of Thy grace in Christ Jesus our Lord. *Amen.*

Wednesday Morning

ALMIGHTY and most merciful Father, in
whom we live and move and have our being,
to whose tender compassion we owe our safety in
days past, together with all the comforts of this
present life, and the hopes of that which is to
come: We praise Thee, O God, our exceeding joy,
who daily pourest Thy benefits upon us. Grant,
we beseech Thee, that Jesus our Lord, the Hope
of glory, may be formed in us, in all humility,
patience, and absolute surrender of our souls and
bodies to Thy holy will and pleasure. Leave us
not, nor forsake us, O Father, but conduct us safe
through all changes of our condition here, in an
unchangeable love to Thee, and in holy tranquillity of mind in Thy love to us, till we come to dwell
with Thee and rejoice in Thee for ever. *Amen.*

GRANT, O Lord, that this day which Thou
hast given unto us in mercy may be returned
unto Thee in service. As Thou hast guarded us
during the hours of sleep, so do Thou guide us
during the appointed hours of labor; that all our
tasks may be gladly and faithfully performed, as in
Thy sight; that our burdens may not be too heavy
for us, because Thine aid and comfort are with us
continually; and that in nothing may we displease
Thee or injure one another. But if in anything
we fail or come short, through ignorance or weakness, O God, let Thy Fatherly wisdom correct us,

and Thine infinite mercy forgive us, and Thy
divine love amend our fault; through Jesus Christ
our Saviour. *Amen.*

O THOU who hast ordered this wondrous
world and who knowest all things in earth
and heaven: So fill our hearts with trust in Thee
that by night and by day, at all times and in all
seasons, we may without fear commit ourselves
and those who are dear to us to Thy never-failing
love, for this life and the life to come. *Amen.*

Thursday Morning

O LORD, lift up the light of Thy countenance
upon us; let Thy peace rule in our hearts,
and may it be our strength and our song. We
commit ourselves to Thy care and keeping this
day; let Thy grace be mighty in us and sufficient
for us. Keep us from sin; give us the rule over
our own spirits; and prevent us from speaking
unadvisedly with our lips. May we live together
in peace and holy love, and do Thou command
Thy blessing upon us, even life for evermore.
Prepare us for all the events of the day; for its
joys as well as for its trials. Give us grace to
deny ourselves, to take up our cross daily, and to
follow in the steps of our Lord and Master. *Amen.*

ETERNAL God, who committest to us the
swift and solemn trust of life: Since we know
not what a day may bring forth but only that the
hour for serving Thee is always present, may we
wake to the instant claims of Thy holy will, not
waiting for tomorrow, but yielding today. Consecrate with Thy presence the way our feet may

go, and the humblest work will shine, and the
roughest place be made plain. Lift us above unrighteous anger and mistrust, into faith, and
hope, and charity, by a simple and steadfast reliance on Thy sure will. In all things draw us
to the mind of Christ, that Thy lost image may
be traced again, and Thou mayest own us as at
one with Thee, to the glory of Thy great name.
Amen.

O LORD of all good life, we pray Thee to
purify our lives. Help us each day to know
more of Thee, and by the power of Thy Spirit
use us to show forth Thyself to others. Make
us humble, brave, and loving; make us ready for
adventure. We do not ask that Thou wilt keep
us safe, but that Thou wilt keep us ever loyal to
the example of our Lord and Saviour Jesus Christ.
Amen.

Friday Morning

WE PRAISE Thee, O God, with the morning light, and in the brightness of a new
day we bless Thy holy name. For all Thou hast
bestowed upon us with the gift of life, making us
in Thine own image and granting us to share as
children in Thy knowledge and Thy love, in Thy
work and Thy joy, we thank Thee, Heavenly
Father. For all good things in the world, for food
and raiment, for home and friendship, for useful
tasks and pure pleasures, we thank Thee, Heavenly
Father. For all spiritual blessings, for Thy holy
Word, for the Christian fellowship, for the good
example and blessed memory of Thy saints, for
the secret influence of Thy Spirit, we thank Thee,

Heavenly Father. And above all we bless Thee
for the redeeming life and death of Thy dear Son
our Saviour Jesus Christ. *Amen.*

O LORD, give Thy blessing, we pray Thee,
to our daily work, that we may do it in
faith and heartily, as to the Lord and not unto
men. All our powers of body and mind are
Thine, and we would fain devote them to Thy
service. Sanctify them, and the work in which
they are engaged; let us not be slothful, but fer-
vent in spirit, and do Thou, O Lord, so bless
our efforts that they may bring forth in us the
fruits of true wisdom. Teach us to seek after
truth and enable us to gain it; but grant that we
may ever speak the truth in love; that, while we
know earthly things, we may know Thee, and be
known by Thee, through and in Thy Son Jesus
Christ. Give us this day Thy Holy Spirit, that
we may be Thine in body and spirit; through
Jesus Christ Thy Son our Lord. *Amen.*

ALMIGHTY God, who seest that we have no
power of ourselves to help ourselves: Keep
us both outwardly in our bodies and inwardly
in our souls, that we may be defended from all
adversities which may happen to our body, and
from all evil thoughts which may assault and hurt
the soul; through Jesus Christ our Lord. *Amen.*

Saturday Morning

ALMIGHTY God, our Father and Preserver:
We give Thee thanks that of Thy goodness
Thou hast watched over us the past night and
brought us to a new day; and we beseech Thee

to strengthen and guard us by Thy Spirit, that we may spend it wholly in Thy service and to Thy glory, looking for all prosperity to Thy blessing, and seeking only those things which are well-pleasing in Thy sight. Enable us, O Lord, while we labor for the life that now is, ever to have regard unto that heavenly life which Thou hast promised Thy children. Defend us in soul and body from all harm. Show Thy loving-kindness unto all men and women and little children, according to the need of every living soul, especially unto those whom we love, and those who are in any kind of trouble or distress, whom we now remember silently before Thee (*here let there be a moment of prayer in silence*); protect our country, and prosper Thy Church; bless all who do good in the world, and restrain and convert all who do evil. And finally, be pleased to cast out of Thy remembrance all our past offenses, forgiving them in Thy boundless mercy and purifying our hearts, that we may lead a better life; through Jesus Christ our Lord. *Amen.*

O GOD, the Protector of all that trust in Thee, without whom nothing is strong, nothing is holy: Increase and multiply upon us Thy mercy, that, Thou being our Ruler and Guide, we may so pass through things temporal that we may finally lose not the things eternal. Grant this, O Lord most merciful, for the sake of Thy dear Son our Saviour. *Amen.*

O GOD, the Holy Spirit, Sanctifier of the faithful: Visit us, we pray Thee, with Thy love and favor; enlighten our minds more and more

with the everlasting Gospel; graft in our hearts
a love of the truth; increase in us true religion;
nourish us with all goodness, and of Thy great
mercy keep us in the same, O blessed Spirit,
whom with the Father and Son together we worship and glorify as one God, world without end.
Amen.

EVENING PRAYERS

O GOD, who hast appointed the day for labor
and the night for rest: Grant, we beseech
Thee, that we may so rest in peace and quietness
during the coming night that afterward we may
go forth to our appointed labors. Take us into
Thy holy keeping, so that no evil may befall us
nor any ill come nigh our dwelling. And when
at length our days are ended and our work is finished in this world, grant that we may depart in
Thy peace and in the sure hope of that glorious
kingdom where there is day without night, and
light without darkness, and life without the
shadow of death for ever; through Jesus Christ
our Lord. *Amen.*

WE BESEECH Thee, Lord, to behold us
with favor, gathered together in the peace
of this roof, weak men and women subsisting under
the covert of Thy patience. Be patient still; suffer
us yet awhile longer—with our broken purposes of
good, with our idle endeavors against evil—suffer us
awhile longer to endure and, if it may be, help
us to do better. Bless our extraordinary mercies;
if the day come when these must be taken, brace
us to play the man under affliction. Be with our
friends; be with ourselves. Go with each of us

to rest; if any awake, temper to them the dark hours of watching; and when the day returns, return to us, our Sun and Comforter, and call us up with morning faces and with morning hearts, eager to labor, eager to be happy, if happiness shall be our portion, and, if the day be marked for sorrow, strong to endure it. *Amen.*

ALMIGHTY Father, who slumberest not nor sleepest: We humbly pray Thee to watch over us this night with the eyes of Thy mercy. Grant us quiet and refreshing sleep, such as may fit us for the duties of the morrow. Put far from us all worldly cares and earthly fears, and give us holy thoughts of Thee, that we may repose in peace, and, whether we wake or sleep, may live together with Him who died and was buried and rose again for us, Thy Son Jesus Christ our Lord. *Amen.*

WE BESEECH Thee to continue Thy gracious protection to us this night. Defend us from all dangers, and from the fear of them, that we may enjoy such refreshing sleep as may fit us for the duties of the coming day. And grant us grace always to live in such a state that we may never be afraid to die, so that, living and dying, we may be Thine; through the merits and satisfaction of Thy Son Jesus Christ our Lord. *Amen.*

INTO Thy hands we now commend ourselves this night. We will lay us down in peace, if Thou speak peace to us through Jesus Christ. May our last thoughts be of Thee. And when we awake may Thy Spirit bring heavenly things to our mind. Pardon the imperfections of our prayers.

Supply what we have omitted to ask for, and do for us exceeding abundantly above all that we ask or think; for the merits of Jesus Christ our Lord. *Amen.*

ALMIGHTY God, the Father of our spirits: Meet with us at close of day, and grant unto us Thy children the peace which the world cannot give. May no unhallowed thoughts or cares disturb the quiet of this evening hour. Deliver us from the vain things which have such power over us. May we learn wisdom, receive strength, gain hope, feel the influence of things unseen, and find rest in God. *Amen.*

O LORD, support us all the day long, until the shadows lengthen and the evening comes, and the busy world is hushed, and the fever of life is over, and our work is done. Then in Thy mercy grant us a safe lodging, and a holy rest, and peace at the last; through Jesus Christ our Lord. *Amen.*

SEND Thy peace into our hearts, O Lord, at the evening hour, that we may be contented with Thy mercies of this day, and confident of Thy protection for this night; and now, having forgiven others, even as Thou dost forgive us, may we have a pure comfort and a healthful rest within the shelter of this home; through Jesus Christ our Saviour. *Amen.*

LIGHTEN our darkness, we beseech Thee, O Lord, and by Thy great mercy defend us from all perils and dangers of this night; for the love of Thine only Son our Saviour Jesus Christ. *Amen.*

O GOD, who art the Life of mortal men, the Light of the faithful, the Strength of those who labor, and the Repose of the dead: We thank Thee for the timely blessings of the day, and humbly supplicate Thy merciful protection all this night. Bring us, we beseech Thee, in safety to the morning hours; through Him who died for us and rose again, Thy Son our Saviour Jesus Christ. *Amen.*

BE PRESENT, O merciful God, and protect us through the silent hours of this night, so that we, who are wearied by the changes and chances of this fleeting world, may repose upon Thine eternal changelessness; through Jesus Christ our Lord. *Amen.*

O GOD, with whom there is no darkness, but the night shineth as the day: Keep and defend us and all Thy children, in soul and body, during the coming night. Make us to rest in the peace of a good conscience, in the hope of a better life, in the faith of Thy providence, and in the comfort of Thy love; through Jesus Christ our Lord. *Amen.*

O LORD our God, we pray Thee at this evening hour to take us, and all whom we love, into Thy holy keeping, that no evil may befall us nor any plague come nigh our dwelling.

Be pleased to cover our sins with Thy mercy, as Thou dost cover the earth with Thy darkness; and grant that as our bodies are refreshed with quiet sleep so our souls may rest in the sense of Thy forgiving mercy; through Jesus Christ our Lord. *Amen.*

ALMIGHTY God, with whom do rest the spirits of just men made perfect: We bless and praise Thy holy name for all Thy servants departed this life in Thy faith and fear; and especially for those most dear to us who have fallen asleep in Jesus. And we beseech Thee to give us grace so to follow their good example that we may continue united to them in fellowship of spirit, and that finally we may be gathered together in Thy heavenly kingdom; through Jesus Christ our Lord. *Amen.*

SPECIAL INTERCESSIONS

For the Sick

O THOU who art the great Physician: Come and lay Thy hand upon Thy servant. Renew *his* strength and restore *him* to health, if it be Thy gracious will. Give *him* in the time of bodily weakness the renewal of Thy Spirit, and the upholding power of Thy love; and as all things work together for good to them that love Thee, so do Thou shed abroad in *his* heart Thy love, that out of this weakness *he* may grow strong in Thee and in Thy love; for the sake of Jesus Christ our Lord. *Amen.*

For the Absent

O LORD of love, who art not far from any of Thy children: Watch with Thy care those who are away from us; be Thou about their path; be Thou within their hearts; be Thou their defense upon their right hand; give them unfailing trust in Thee; grant them power against temptation; qualify them for whatever task Thou givest them to do; deliver them from the snares of setting duty aside; make it their joy to do Thy will. Let not distance break the bonds of love which bind them to us and to Thee, but knit us closer in Thy love; for the sake of Jesus Christ our Lord. *Amen.*

For the Traveler

MOST merciful Father, we beseech Thee to protect and prosper Thy servant on *his* journey. May the angel of Thy presence be with *him* wherever *he* may go, and may all *his* steps be ordered of Thee in wisdom and love, so that *he* shall travel with Thee as *his* Guardian and *his* Guide, and arrive in safety at *his* desired haven. O Lord, bless *his* going out and *his* coming in, from this time forth and even for evermore; through Jesus Christ our Lord. *Amen.*

For Holidays

O GOD the Father, who alone satisfiest the desire of every living thing, who ordainest our strength for Thy service and grantest us intervals of rest for the renewal of our strength: Sanctify, we beseech Thee, to Thy glory our labor and our rest, our seriousness and our mirth, our sorrow and our joy; and send us forth with Thy blessing, that we may go on our way rejoicing; through Jesus Christ our Lord. *Amen.*

In a Time of Trouble

O GOD, most wise and faithful Redeemer, who hast permitted us to come into this present trial: Grant that we may learn obedience by the things that we suffer, and turn to Thee, our Helper in the time of trouble. May there be

no bitterness in our sorrow, no despair in our
submission, and no doubt of Thee in our perplexity. Teach us to face our trial bravely; make
even the dark things of life to work together for
our good; and bring us speedily out of our distress, that we may praise Thee with a joyful
heart; in Christ Jesus our Lord. *Amen.*

Gratitude for Recovery

O FATHER of mercies, we thank Thee in
behalf of Thy servant whom Thou hast
restored to health. We cried unto Thee, and
Thou hast healed *him.* We trusted in Thee, and
Thou hast helped us. Therefore will we praise
Thy name together. Grant, O Lord, that the life
which Thou hast saved may be more entirely
devoted to Thy service, and that we may learn to
love Thee, and trust in Thee more and more;
through Jesus Christ our Lord. *Amen.*

A Death in the Home

O GOD, our Heavenly Father, who art leading
us through the changes of time to the rest
and blessedness of eternity: Be Thou near to us
now, to comfort and to uphold. Make us to know
that Thy children are precious in Thy sight, that
they live evermore with Thee and that Thy mercy
endureth for ever. Thankful for the life that
Thou didst give us for a season, may we be trustful
in Thee now that it has been taken away. Give
us Thy strength, that we may seek to be more
faithful, more loving, more helpful to others, for
the sake of *him* who is no longer with us. And
may our Lord Jesus Christ Himself and God, even
our Father which hath loved us and hath given

us everlasting consolation and good hope through grace, comfort our hearts and establish us in every good word and work; through Jesus Christ our Lord. *Amen.*

For Guidance

O GOD, by whom the meek are guided in judgment and light riseth up in darkness for the godly: Grant us, in all our doubts and uncertainties, the grace to ask what Thou wouldst have us to do, that the Spirit of wisdom may save us from all false choices, and that in Thy light we may see light, and in Thy straight path may not stumble; through Jesus Christ our Lord. *Amen.*

For Peace

ALMIGHTY God, from whom all thoughts of truth and peace proceed: Kindle, we pray Thee, in the hearts of all men, the true love of peace, and guide with Thy pure and peaceable wisdom those who take counsel for the nations of the earth; that in tranquillity Thy kingdom may go forward, till the earth be filled with the knowledge of Thy love; through Jesus Christ our Lord. *Amen.*

For Our Country

ALMIGHTY God, who hast given us this good land for our heritage: We humbly beseech Thee that we may always prove ourselves a people mindful of Thy favor and glad to do Thy will. Bless our land with honorable industry, sound learning, and pure manners. Save us from violence, discord, and confusion; from pride and arrogancy; and from every evil way. Defend our liberties, and fashion into one happy people the multitudes brought hither out of many kindreds and tongues. Endue with the spirit of wisdom those to whom in Thy name we entrust the authority of government, that there may be justice and peace at home, and that, through obedience to Thy law, we may show forth Thy praise among the nations of the earth. In the time of prosperity fill our hearts with thankfulness, and in the day of trouble suffer not our trust in Thee to fail; all which we ask through Jesus Christ our Lord. *Amen.*

For the Church

O GRACIOUS Father, we humbly beseech Thee for Thy Holy Catholic Church, that Thou wouldst be pleased to fill it with all truth in all peace. Where it is corrupt, purify it; where it is in error, direct it; where in any thing it is amiss, reform it. Where it is right, establish it; where it is in want, provide for it; where it is divided, reunite it; for the sake of Him who died and rose again and ever liveth to make intercession for us, Jesus Christ Thy Son our Lord. *Amen.*

For Missions

O ALMIGHTY God, whose dearly beloved Son after His resurrection sent His apostles into all the world, and on the Day of Pentecost endued them with special gifts of the Holy Spirit, that they might gather in the spiritual harvest: We beseech Thee to look down from heaven upon the fields now white unto the harvest, and to send forth more laborers to gather fruit unto eternal life. And grant us grace so to help them with our

prayers and offerings that, when the harvest of
the earth is ripe and the time for reaping is come,
we, together with them, may rejoice before Thee
according to the joy in harvest; through Jesus
Christ our Lord. *Amen.*

For Those Who Toil by Night

OUR Father, as we turn to the comfort of our
rest, we remember those who must wake
that we may sleep. Bless the guardians of peace
who protect us against men of evil will, the
watchers who save us from the terrors of fire, and
all the many who carry on through the hours of
the night the restless commerce of men on sea and
land. We thank Thee for their faithfulness and
sense of duty. We pray for Thy pardon if our
covetousness or luxury makes their nightly toil
necessary. Grant that we may realize how de-
pendent the safety of our loved ones and the comforts of our life are on these our brothers, that
so we may think of them with love and gratitude
and help to make their burden lighter. *Amen.*

BRIEF PETITIONS

O GOD, who hast taught us to keep all Thy
heavenly commandments by loving Thee
and our neighbor: Grant us the spirit of peace
and grace, that we may be both devoted to Thee
with our whole heart and united to each other with
a pure will; through Jesus Christ our Lord. *Amen.*

O God, who hast commanded us to be perfect,
as Thou our Father in heaven art perfect: Put into
our hearts, we pray Thee, a continual desire to
obey Thy holy will. Teach us day by day what

Thou wouldst have us do, and give us grace and power to fulfill the same. May we never from love of ease decline the path which Thou pointest out, nor for fear of shame turn away from it; through Jesus Christ our Lord. *Amen.*

O Almighty Lord and everlasting God, vouchsafe, we beseech Thee, to direct, sanctify, and govern both our hearts and our bodies in the ways of Thy laws, and in the works of Thy commandments; that, through Thy most mighty protection both here and ever, we may be preserved in body and soul; through our Lord and Saviour Jesus Christ. *Amen.*

O Heavenly Father, who hast filled the world with beauty: Open, we beseech Thee, our eyes to behold Thy gracious hand in all Thy works; that, rejoicing in Thy whole creation, we may learn to serve Thee with gladness; for the sake of Him by whom all things were made, Thy Son Jesus Christ our Lord. *Amen.*

O God, who art the Author of peace and Lover of concord, in knowledge of whom standeth our eternal life, whose service is perfect freedom: Defend us Thy humble servants in all assaults of our enemies; that we, surely trusting in Thy defense, may not fear the power of any adversaries; through the might of Jesus Christ our Lord. *Amen.*

O God, from whom all holy desires, all good counsels, and all just works do proceed: Give unto Thy servants that peace which the world cannot give; that our hearts may be set to obey Thy commandments, and also that by Thee, we, being defended from the fear of our enemies, may pass our time in rest and quietness; through the merits of Jesus Christ our Saviour. *Amen.*

O God of peace, who hast taught us that in returning and rest we shall be saved, in quietness and in confidence shall be our strength: By the might of Thy Spirit lift us, we pray Thee, to Thy presence, where we may be still and know that Thou art God; through Jesus Christ our Lord. *Amen.*

O most loving Father, who willest us to give thanks for all things, to dread nothing but the loss of Thee, and to cast all our care on Thee, who carest for us: Preserve us from faithless fears and worldly anxieties, and grant that no clouds of this mortal life may hide from us the light of that love which is immortal, and which Thou hast manifested unto us in Thy Son Jesus Christ our Lord. *Amen.*

GRACE BEFORE MEAT

THE Lord make us grateful for all His mercies, and add His blessing, for Christ's sake. *Amen.*

Almighty God, who providest for us, nourish our souls with the Bread of Life in Jesus Christ. *Amen.*

Bless us, O Lord, in blessing Thee, as we receive Thy gift of daily bread. *Amen.*

The Lord bless this food to our use, and us to His service. *Amen.*

Lord, help us to receive all good things from Thy hand and use them to Thy praise. *Amen.*

Heavenly Father, make us thankful to Thee, and mindful of others, as we receive these blessings; in Jesus' name. *Amen.*

Father in heaven, sustain our bodies with this food, our hearts with true friendship, and our souls with Thy truth; for Christ's sake. *Amen.*

Refresh us, O Lord, with Thy gifts, and sustain us with the bounty of Thy riches; through Jesus Christ our Lord. *Amen.*

Blessed be Thou, O God, who givest us day by day our daily bread; in the name of Jesus Christ our Lord. *Amen.*

Lord Jesus, be our holy Guest,
Our morning Joy, our evening Rest;
And with our daily bread impart
Thy love and peace to every heart. *Amen.*

V. LECTIONARY

TABLE OF LESSONS
FROM HOLY SCRIPTURE
FOR TWO YEARS

This Lectionary follows the course of the Christian Year. For the morning services three lessons are provided, one from the Old and two from the New Testament, one of the latter being taken from the Gospels. The evening services have an Old and a New Testament lesson, the latter taken in alternate years from the Gospels and from The Acts and the Epistles. A psalm (or psalms) is also given for each service.

FIRST YEAR : MORNING

Sundays, &c.	Psalm	Old Testament	Epistle	Gospel
1st in Advent	50	Isa. 1: 1–20	Rom. 13: 8–14	Mark 13: 1–13
2d ,,	9	,, 5: 1–16	,, 15: 4–13	,, 13: 24–37
3d ,,	67; 75	,, ch. 25	I Cor. 3: 16 to 4: 5	Matt. 11: 2–11
4th ,,	97	,, ch. 32	Phil. 4: 4–9	{ John 1: 19–28 or Matt. 3: 1–12
Christmas Day	85	,, 9: 2–7	Titus 2: 11 to 3: 7	Luke 2: 1–20
1st After Christmas	45	,, 40: 1–11	Heb. 1: 1–12	John 1: 1–18
2d ,,	91	Deut. 11: 1–17	I John 4: 9–16	Luke 1: 46–55
Epiphany	72	Isa., ch. 60	Eph. 2: 11–18	Matt. 2: 1–12
1st After Epiphany	47	,, ch. 55	Rom. 12: 1–9	Luke 2: 39–52
2d ,,	27	,, 41: 1–20	,, 12: 10–21	John 2: 1–11
3d ,,	33	Prov., ch. 2	I John 3: 1–8	Matt. 8: 1–13
4th ,,	63	,, ch. 3	Rom. 3: 21–26; 5: 18–21	Mark 4: 35–41
5th ,,	119: 17–32	,, ch. 4	Col. 3: 12–17	Matt. 13: 24–30
6th ,,	119: 49–64	,, 8: 12–36	I John 1: 1–9	,, 24: 23–31
3d Before Lent	86	Gen. 1: 1–19	I Cor. 9: 24 to 10: 6	,, 11: 28–30
2d Before Lent	139	,, 2: 4–17	II Cor. 11: 19–31	Luke 8: 4–15
1st Before Lent	15; 16	,, 4: 1–16	I Cor., ch. 13	,, 18: 18–31
1st in Lent	51	Isa., ch. 58	I John 2: 7–17	Matt. 4: 1–11
2d ,,	143	Gen., ch. 8	I Thess. 4: 1–8	,, 15: 21–28
3d ,,	56	,, 11: 1–9	Eph. 5: 1–14	{ Luke 11: 14–28 or Matt. 20: 17–28
4th ,,	130; 131	,, ch. 13	Heb. 12: 22–29	{ John 6: 1–14 or Matt. 18: 15–22
5th ,,	42; 43	Ex. 2: 1–22	,, 9: 11–22	{ John 6: 27–35 or 10: 7–18
Palm Sunday	23; 24	Zech. 9: 9–14	Phil. 2: 5–11	{ John 12: 1–16 or Matt. 27: 1–54
Monday Before Easter	27	Isa. 42: 1–16	I Cor. 1: 18–25	{ Matt. 21: 12–17 or Mark, ch. 14
Tuesday ,,	31	Zech., ch. 13	Eph. 2: 13–22	{ Matt. 21: 23–32 or Mark 15: 1–39

FIRST YEAR : EVENING

Psalm	Old Testament	New Testament	Sundays, &c.
46	Isa. 2: 1–17	Luke 1: 1–17	1st in Advent
96	,, ch. 12	,, 1: 18–35	2d ,,
98	,, 26: 1–15	,, 1: 39–56	3d ,,
24	,, ch. 35	,, 1: 59–80	4th ,,
132	,, 11: 1–13	Matt. 1: 18–25	Christmas Day
2	,, 40: 12–31	Luke 2: 1–20	1st After Christmas
85	Deut., ch. 30	,, 2: 21–38	2d ,,
145	Isa. 49: 5–23	Matt. 2: 13–23	Epiphany
72	,, ch. 60	Mark 1: 1–11	1st After Epiphany
36	,, 42: 1–12	Luke 3: 1–22	2d ,,
34	Job, ch. 1	Mark 1: 14–28	3d ,,
119: 1–16	,, ch. 2	,, 1: 29–45	4th ,,
119: 33–48	,, ch. 14	Luke 4: 16–32	5th ,,
119: 65–80	,, ch. 28	,, 5: 1–15	6th ,,
148	Gen. 1: 20 to 2: 3	Mark 2: 1–17	3d Before Lent
92; 93	,, ch. 3	Luke 6: 27–49	2d ,,
23	,, ch. 6	,, 7: 1–16	1st ,,
130	Jonah, ch. 3	,, 4: 1–13	1st in Lent
32	Gen. 9: 1–17	,, 15: 1–10	2d ,,
6	,, 11: 31 to 12: 9	,, 15: 11–32	3d ,,
39	,, 18: 16–33	,, 18: 1–17	4th ,,
51	Ex. 6: 1–13	,, 13: 22–35	5th ,,
8; 62	Mal. 3: 1–12	Mark 11: 1–11	Palm Sunday
6	Lam. 1: 1–14	,, 11: 12–24	Monday Before Easter
32	,, 3: 1–7, 18–33	Matt. 22: 1–14	Tuesday ,,

FIRST YEAR : MORNING

Sundays, &c.	Psalm	Old Testament	Epistle	Gospel
Wednesday Before Easter	55	Isa. 63: 7–19	I John 4: 7–11	{ Mark 14: 1–11 or Luke, ch. 22
Thursday ,,	56	,, 50: 4–11	I Cor. 11: 17–34	John 13: 1–17 or Luke 23: 1–49
Good Friday	22	,, 52: 13 to 53: 5	Heb. 10: 1–25	Matt. 27: 33–50 or John 19: 1–37
Saturday Before Easter	30	Hos. 6: 1–6	I Peter 3: 17–22	John 19: 38–42 or Matt. 27: 57–66
Easter Day	115	Ex. 12: 1–14	Col. 3: 1–11	John 20: 1–10
1st After Easter	103	,, 14: 1–22	Rom. 6: 1–14	,, 20: 19–31
2d ,,	147	Lev. 6: 1–13	I Peter 2: 11–25	,, 10: 1–10
3d ,,	120; 121	,, 19: 1–18	Rev. 22: 1–5	,, 16: 16–22
4th ,,	124; 125	,, 23: 1–14	James 1: 17–27	,, 16: 2–15
5th ,,	135	,, 26: 1–17	,, 3: 2–13	,, 16: 23–33
Ascension Day	68: 1–20	II Kings 2: 1–15	Acts 1: 1–11	Luke 24: 44–53
Sunday After Ascension	68: 1–20	Dan. 7: 9–14	Heb., ch. 4	Matt. 28: 16–20
Whitsunday	145	Isa. 11: 1–10	Acts 2: 1–11	John 3: 16–21
Trinity Sunday	139	,, 6: 1–8	Rev., ch. 4	,, 3: 1–15
1st After Trinity	1; 3	Josh., ch. 1	Eph. 4: 1–16	Matt. 16: 13–19
2d ,,	11; 12	,, 4: 1–14	I John 3: 13–18	Luke 14: 16–24
3d ,,	18: 1–27	,, 6: 1–20	{ Acts 3: 1–10 or 2: 37–47	,, 15: 1–10
4th ,,	20; 21	,, 8: 1–20	{ Acts 3: 11–21 or 4: 5–13	,, 15: 11–32
5th ,,	25	,, ch. 20	Acts 5: 17–32	,, 5: 1–11
6th ,,	28	,, 24: 1–15	,, 7: 51–60	Matt. 5: 1–16
7th ,,	30	,, 24: 16–28	,, 8: 1–13	,, 5: 17–26
8th ,,	37	Judg., ch. 5	,, 8: 14–24	,, 5: 27–37
9th ,,	44	,, 7: 1–21	,, 8: 26–40	,, 5: 38–48
10th ,,	57	,, 11: 1–11, 29–40	,, 9: 1–9	,, 6: 1–15
11th ,,	62	Ruth 1: 1–17	,, 9: 10–22	,, 6: 19–34
12th ,,	66	,, 2: 1–17	,, 9: 36–43	,, 7: 1–6
13th ,,	73	I Sam., ch. 3	,, 10: 9–16	,, 7: 7–14
14th ,,	76	,, 4: 1–18	,, 13: 14–52	,, 7: 15–23
15th ,,	77	,, 9: 1–20	,, 14: 8–18	,, 7: 24–29
16th ,,	95	,, 10: 1–9, 17–27	{ ,, 16: 11–18 or 16: 25–34	Luke 7: 11–17
17th ,,	99; 100	I Sam. 16: 1–13	Acts 17: 22–33	,, 14: 1–11

FIRST YEAR : EVENING

Psalm	Old Testament	New Testament	Sundays, &c.
143	Gen. 37: 13–28	Matt. 26: 1–16	Wednesday Before Easter
64	Ex. 24: 1–11	„ 26: 36–46	Thursday „
69	Gen. 22: 1–19	Mark 15: 15–39	Good Friday
23	Job 33: 22–30	„ 15: 42–47	Saturday Before Easter
118	Ex. 12: 21–28, 40–42	Luke 24: 13–49	Easter Day
145	„ 16: 1–15	John 21: 1–14	1st After Easter
148	Deut. 6: 1–15	„ 21: 15–25	2d „
122; 123	„ ch. 8	„ 11: 1–29	3d „
126; 127	„ 26: 1–11, 16–19	„ 11: 30–54	4th „
133; 134	„ 28: 1–14	„ 12: 1–11	5th „
24	„ ch. 34	Heb., ch. 4	Ascension Day
24	Ex., ch. 24	Acts 1: 1–11	Sunday After Ascension
48	Joel 2: 21–32	Rom. 8: 1–18	Whitsunday
149; 150	Ex. 3: 1–15	Matt. 28: 16–20	Trinity Sunday
4; 5	Jer., ch. 1	Luke 7: 19–35	1st After Trinity
13; 14	„ 2: 1–13	„ 7: 36–50	2d „
19	„ 10: 1–16	Mark 4: 1–20	3d „
23; 24	„ 17: 1–14	„ 4: 21–41	4th „
26	„ 31: 1–14, 31–34	Luke 8: 41–56	5th „
29	„ ch. 35	Mark 6: 31–44	6th „
31	Lam. 3: 22–41	„ 6: 45–56	7th „
40	Ezek. 2: 1 to 3: 11	„ 7: 24–37	8th „
49	„ 14: 1–11	„ 8: 1–13	9th „
60; 61	„ 18: 1–4, 19–32	Luke 9: 18–27	10th „
65	„ 33: 1–16	„ 9: 28–45	11th „
71	„ 34: 1–24	„ 10: 1–22	12th „
74	„ 36: 21–38	„ 10: 25–42	13th „
80	Dan., ch. 1	„ 11: 1–20	14th „
84	„ 2: 1–3, 27–45	„ 12: 16–40	15th „
94	„ 3: 1–6, 16–30	„ 13: 1–17	16th „
101	„ 4: 1–9, 19–27	„ 14: 15–33	17th „

FIRST YEAR : MORNING

Sundays, &c.	Psalm	Old Testament	Epistle	Gospel
18th After Trinity	111; 112	I Sam. 17: 1–11, 32–49	{ Acts 18: 1–11 *or* 20: 17–35	Matt. 22: 34–46
19th ,,	120; 121	I Sam. 18: 1–16	{ Acts 22: 1–21 *or* 26: 1–20	,, 9: 1–8
20th ,,	124; 125	,, ch. 24	Acts 28: 16–31	,, 22: 15–22
21st ,,	128; 129	II Sam. 1: 1–12, 17–27	Eph. 6: 10–20	Luke 21: 1–9
22d ,,	143	II Sam. 7: 1–17	Phil. 1: 3–11	Matt. 18: 21–35
23d ,,	146	,, 12: 1–10, 15–23	,, 3: 17–21	Luke 12: 49–59
24th ,,	119: 81–96	II Sam. 15: 1–15	Col. 1: 3–18	,, 11: 14–28
25th ,,	119: 113–128	,, 15: 17–29	I Cor. 12: 12–31	,, 19: 11–26
26th ,,	119: 145–160	II Sam. 18: 5–33	Eph. 2: 1–10	Matt. 12: 38–50
Next Before Advent	148	Eccl. 11: 9 to 12: 14	I Cor. 1: 26–31	Luke 4: 16–24

FIRST YEAR : EVENING

Psalm	Old Testament	New Testament	Sundays, &c.
113; 114	Dan. 5: 1–8, 17–30	Luke 18: 18–34	18th After Trinity
122; 123	„ 6: 1–23	„ 18: 35 to 19: 10	19th „
126; 127	„ 7: 1–14	Mark 12: 1–17	20th „
138; 142	„ 9: 1–19	„ 12: 28–44	21st „
144	Hos., ch. 6	„ 14: 1–17	22d „
147	„ 10: 12 to 11: 12	Luke 22: 14–30	23d „
119: 97–112	„ ch. 14	Mark 14: 26–46	24th „
119: 129–144	Job, ch. 14	„ 14: 53–72	25th „
119: 161–176	„ ch. 28	„ 15: 1–21	26th „
149; 150	Hag. 2: 1–9	Luke 23: 27–47	Next Before Advent

SECOND YEAR : MORNING

Sundays, &c.	Psalm	Old Testament	Epistle	Gospel
1st in Advent	50	Isa. 43: 1–13	Rom. 13: 8–14	Matt. 21: 1–9
2d ,,	9	,, 45: 1–19	,, 15: 4–13	,, 25: 1–13
3d ,,	67; 75	,, 51: 1–16	I Cor. 3: 16 to 4: 5	,, 13: 14–52
4th ,,	97	ch. 54	Phil. 4: 4–9	{ Luke 1: 68–79 *or* Luke 3: 1–14
Christmas Day	89: 1–37	,, 9: 2–7	Gal. 4: 1–7	Matt. 1: 18–25
1st After Christmas	45	,, 40: 1–11	I John 4: 9–16	John 1: 1–18
2d ,,	91	Josh. 1: 1–9	I Thess., ch. 5	Luke 2: 21–32
Epiphany	72	I Kings 10: 1–13	Eph. 2: 11–18	Matt. 2: 1–12
1st After Epiphany	47	Isa., ch. 60	Rom. 12: 1–9	Luke 2: 40–52
2d ,,	27	,, ch. 62	,, 12: 10–21	{ Mark 1: 14–28 *or* Matt. 3: 13–17
3d ,,	33	Job 37: 1–19	,, 8: 1–9, 12–17	Matt. 9: 9–17
4th ,,	63	,, 38: 1–21	Rom. 8: 18–25	Luke 14: 25–35
5th ,,	119: 17–32	,, 38: 22–41	Col. 3: 12–17	Matt. 13: 24–30
6th ,,	119: 49–64	,, ch. 42	I John 1: 1–9	,, 24: 23–31
3d Before Lent	86	Gen. 22: 1–18	I Cor. 9: 24 to 10: 6	,, 20: 1–16
2d ,,	139	,, 28: 10–22	II Cor. 11: 19–31	John 12: 20–32
1st ,,	15; 16	,, 37: 1–22	I Cor., ch. 13	Luke 18: 18–31
1st in Lent	51	Isa. 1: 1–20	II Tim. 3: 14 to 4: 8	,, 4: 1–13
2d ,,	143	Gen., ch. 40	Rom. 2: 1–10	{ Matt. 16: 21–28 *or* Matt. 17: 1–9
3d ,,	56	,, 42: 1–21	Acts 12: 1–11	{ Matt. 21: 33–46 *or* Luke 13: 31–35
4th ,,	130; 131	,, ch. 45	Phil. 3: 7–15	{ John 8: 1–11 *or* ,, 2: 13–22
5th ,,	42; 43	Ex. 19: 1–13	Heb. 9: 11–22	{ John 8: 46–59 *or* Matt. 12: 14–21
Palm Sunday	23; 24	Jer. 7: 1–11	Phil. 2: 5–11	{ Matt. 21: 1–11 *or* Matt. 27: 1–54

SECOND YEAR : EVENING

Psalm	Old Testament	New Testament	Sundays, &c.
46	Isa. 44: 6-23	Rev. 14: 13 to 15: 4	1st in Advent
96	,, ch. 46	,, 19: 1-16	2d ,,
98	,, 52: 1-12	,, ch. 21	3d ,,
24	,, ch. 64	,, ch. 22	4th ,,
132	Micah 4: 1-7	I John 4: 7-21	Christmas Day
2	Isa. 40: 12-31	Heb., ch. 1	1st After Christmas
85	Eccl. 3: 1-15	Phil. 2: 1-11	2d ,,
145	I Chron. 29: 10-19	Eph., ch. 3	Epiphany
72	Isa. 49: 5-23	Col. 1: 21 to 2: 7	1st After Epiphany
36	,, 63: 7-19	I Cor. 1: 1-17	2d ,,
34	Prov., ch. 9	,, ch. 3	3d ,,
119: 1-16	,, ch. 22	,, 4: 1-16	4th ,,
119: 33-48	,, 25: 1-22	,, ch. 9	5th ,,
119: 65-80	,, 31: 10-31	,, 10: 1-14	6th ,,
148	Gen. 27: 6-40	,, 11: 17-34	3d Before Lent
92; 93	,, 32: 1-12, 24-31	,, 12: 1-11	2d ,,
23	,, 37: 23-36	,, 12: 12-31	1st ,,
130	Ezek. 33: 1-16	II Cor. 1: 1-20	1st in Lent
32	Gen. 41: 15-36	,, ch. 3	2d ,,
6	,, 43: 1-14	,, ch. 4	3d ,,
39	,, ch. 48	,, 5: 14 to 6: 10	4th ,,
51	Ex. 20: 1-17	,, 11: 22 to 12: 11	5th ,,
8; 62	Isa. 59: 1, 2, 12-21	Luke 19: 29-44	Palm Sunday

SECOND YEAR : MORNING

Sundays, &c.	Psalm	Old Testament	Epistle	Gospel
Monday Before Easter	27	Isa. 42: 1–16	I Cor. 1: 18–25	{ Matt. 21: 12–17 or Mark, ch. 14
Tuesday „	31	Zech., ch. 13	Eph. 2: 13–22	Mark 12: 1–12 or Mark 15: 1–39
Wednesday „	55	Isa. 63: 7–19	I John 4: 7–11	Mark 14: 1–11 or Luke, ch. 22
Thursday „	56	„ 50: 4–11	I Cor. 11: 17–34	Matt. 26: 17–30 or Luke 23: 1–49
Good Friday	22	„ 52: 13–53	Heb. 10: 1–25	Matt. 27: 33–50 or John 19: 1–37
Saturday Before Easter	30	Hos. 6: 1–6	I Peter 3: 17–22	John 19: 38–42 or Matt. 27: 57–66
Easter Day	118	Isa. 25: 1–9	Rev. 1: 10–18	Luke 24: 1–12
1st After Easter	103	Ex. 32: 1–20	Acts 13: 26–33a	„ 24: 36–49
2d „	147	Num. 13: 1–3, 17–33	Rev. 21: 10–14, 21–27	John 10: 11–16
3d „	120; 121	Num. 21: 1–9	I Cor. 15: 20–28	„ 14: 1–13
4th „	124; 125	„ 23: 1–12	II Cor. 5: 17–21	„ 16: 2–15
5th „	135	„ 24: 10–25	I John 2: 7–17	„ 16: 23–33
Ascension Day	68: 1–20	Dan. 7: 9–14	Eph. 4: 1–16	Luke 24: 44–53
Sunday After Ascension	68: 1–20	II Kings 2: 1–15	Acts 1: 1–11	Matt. 28: 16–20
Whitsunday	145	Isa., ch. 61	Acts 10: 34–48a	John 14: 15–31
Trinity Sunday	139	„ 63: 7–19	Rev., ch. 4	„ 4: 1–26
1st After Trinity	1; 3	Joel 2: 12–32	I John 4: 7–21	Luke 16: 19–31
2d „	11; 12	„ 3: 9–21	{ Gal. 5: 16–25 or Rev. 19: 4–9	Matt. 11: 28–30
3d „	18: 1–27	Amos 5: 4–24	I Peter 1: 1–11	Luke 15: 1–10
4th „	20; 21	„ ch. 6	Heb. 11: 1–6, 8–10	„ 15: 11–32
5th „	25	„ ch. 7	I Cor. 6: 9–11	{ Luke 6: 36–42 or John 5: 17–27
6th „	28	„ ch. 8	„ 10: 14–24	Luke 12: 13–21
7th „	30	Obadiah	Rom. 6: 19–23	Mark 6: 35–46
8th „	37	Jonah 1: 1–16	II Cor. 4: 1–10	John 10: 1–10
9th „	44	„ ch. 3	Gal. 6: 1–10	Luke 16: 1–13
10th „	57	„ ch. 4	I Cor. 12: 1–11	„ 19: 41–48
11th „	62	Micah 4: 1–8	„ 15: 1–11	„ 18: 9–14

SECOND YEAR : EVENING

Psalm	Old Testament	New Testament	Sundays, &c.
6	Lam. 1: 1–14	John, ch. 14	Monday Before Easter
32	,, 3: 1–7, 18–33	,, ch. 15	Tuesday ,,
143	Gen. 37: 13–28	,, ch. 16	Wednesday ,,
64	Ex. 24: 1–11	,, ch. 17	Thursday ,,
69	Gen. 22: 1–19	Luke 23: 33–46	Good Friday
23	Job 33: 22–30	,, 23: 50–56	Saturday Before Easter
115	Ex. 15: 1–18	,, 24: 13–35	Easter Day
145	,, ch. 33	Rev., ch. 1	1st After Easter
148	Num. 14: 1–24	I Cor. 15: 1–22	2d ,,
122; 123	,, 22: 1–21	,, 15: 42–58	3d ,,
126; 127	,, 23: 13–26	II Cor. 5: 1–15	4th ,,
133; 134	,, 27: 12–23	James 1: 22–27	5th ,,
24	Ex., ch. 24	Heb., ch. 4	Ascension Day
24	Deut., ch. 34	Phil. 2: 1–11	Sunday After Ascension
48	Ezek. 37: 1–14	John 14: 15–31	Whitsunday
149; 150	Job 23: 3–10	I Peter 1: 1–12	Trinity Sunday
4; 5	I Kings 3: 1–15	Acts, ch. 3	1st After Trinity
13; 14	,, 8: 22–36	,, 4: 8–37	2d ,,
19	,, 8: 54–66	,, 5: 11–42	3d ,,
23; 24	,, 12: 1–20	,, chs. 6; 7: 54–60	4th ,,
26	,, 17: 1–16	, 8: 26–40	5th ,,
29	,, 18: 1–20	,, 9: 1–22	6th ,,
31	,, 18: 21–39	,, 9: 23–43	7th ,,
40	,, ch. 19	,, 10: 1–22	8th ,,
49	,, 20: 1–21	,, 10: 24–48	9th ,,
60; 61	,, 20: 28–43	,, 11: 1–18	10th ,,
65	,, 21: 1–22	,, 12: 1–19	11th ,,

SECOND YEAR : MORNING

Sundays, &c.	Psalm	Old Testament	Epistle	Gospel
12th After Trinity	66	Micah, ch. 6	II Cor. 4: 16 to 5: 1	Mark 7: 31–37
13th ,,	73	,, ch. 7	Heb. 13: 1–6	{ Luke 10: 23–37 or Matt. 18: 1–9
14th ,,	76	Nahum, ch. 1	II Cor. 6: 1–10	Luke 17: 11–19
15th ,,	77	Hab. 2: 1–14, 18–20	Gal. 6: 11–18	Matt. 8: 5–13
16th ,,	95	Hab., ch. 3	Eph. 3: 13–21	,, 10: 1–15
17th ,,	99; 100	Zeph. 3: 8–20	I Cor. 9: 6–15	,, 10: 16–23
18th ,,	107	Hag., ch. 1	II Peter 3: 8–14	,, 10: 24–33
19th ,,	120; 121	,, ch. 2	Eph. 4: 17–32	,, 10: 34–42
20th ,,	124; 125	Zech., ch. 2	{ ,, 5: 1–14 or 5: 6–21	,, 11: 16–27
21st ,,	128; 129	,, ch. 7	Eph. 6: 10–20	Luke 20: 19–26
22d ,,	143	,, ch. 8	I Peter 5: 1–11	,, 20: 27–38
23d ,,	146	,, ch. 11	I Cor. 1: 18–31	Matt. 25: 14–30
24th ,,	119: 81–96	,, ch. 13	Col. 1: 3–18	,, 9: 18–26
25th ,,	119: 113–128	Mal., ch. 1	I Cor. 12: 12–31	,, 9: 27–38
26th ,,	119: 145–160	,, ch. 3	Eph. 2: 1–10	,, 12: 38–50
Next Before Advent	148	,, ch. 4	I Cor. 2: 1–10	{ ,, 4: 12–17 or John, ch. 17

HOLY COMMUNION

	Psalm	Old Testament	Epistle	Gospel
	23; 24	Ex. 12: 1–14	Heb. 12: 18–24	John 6: 27–35
	34	,, 20: 1–17	Gal. 5: 22–26	Matt. 5: 1–16
	65	Isa., ch. 53	Heb. 10: 19–25	Luke 23: 33–46
	116	,, ch. 55	Eph. 3: 14–21	John 6: 47–58

SECOND YEAR : EVENING

Psalm	Old Testament	New Testament	Sundays, &c.
71	II Kings 4: 1–17	Acts 13: 1–33	12th After Trinity
74	„ 4: 18–37	„ 14: 1–18	13th „
80	„ 5: 1–14	„ 16: 1–18	14th „
84	„ 6: 8–23	„ 16: 19–40	15th „
94	„ 12: 1–16	„ 17: 16–34	16th „
102	„ 17: 24–41	„ 19: 21–41	17th „
104	„ 18: 1–18, 28–37	„ 20: 17–38	18th „
122; 123	II Kings 19: 8–37	„ 21: 39 to 22: 21	19th „
126; 127	„ 20: 1–11	„ ch. 26	20th „
138; 142	II Chron. 30: 1–21	Rom. 1: 1–17	21st „
144	II Kings 22: 1 to 23: 3	„ ch. 5	22d „
147	II Chron. 36: 1–21	„ 8: 1–18	23d „
119: 97–112	Ezra, ch. 3	„ 8: 24–39	24th „
119: 129–144	Neh., ch. 2	„ ch. 10	25th „
119: 161–176	„ 8: 1–12	„ ch. 12	26th „
149; 150	Jer. 23: 1–8	„ ch. 13	Next Before Advent

PREPARATORY SERVICES

Psalm	Old Testament	New Testament
26	II Chron. 30: 13–21	I Cor. 10: 1–17
51	Isa., ch. 58	Phil. 2: 5–13
15	„ ch. 53	Luke 24: 13–32
63	„ 51: 9–16	John 6: 41–59
103	Deut. 6: 1–12	Matt. 26: 17–30

SPECIAL SERVICES : MORNING

Day	Psalm	Old Testament	Epistle	Gospel
New Year's	91	Deut. 11: 1–17	Phil. 3: 7–14	Matt. 6: 19–34
Missionary Service	67; 72	Isa., ch. 60 or Jer. 33: 10–16	Eph. 2: 13–22 or Rom., ch. 10	Luke 10: 1–20 or John, ch. 17
General Assembly	48	Isa., ch. 61	Heb. 12: 14–25	John 21: 15–17
Memorial	46	Isa. 52: 3–12	Rev. 7: 9–17	John 14: 1–15
Children's	148	Prov. 3: 13–26	Phil. 4: 4–13	Luke 2: 40–51
All Saints'	1; 149	Isa. 51: 1–11	Rev. 7: 9–17	Matt. 5: 1–12
Armistice	121	Micah 4: 1–5	Eph. 6: 10–20	John 14: 18–31
Thanksgiving	65	Deut. 26: 1–11	Gal. 6: 6–10	Luke 12: 13–34
End of Year	103	Deut., ch. 8	II Peter 3: 8–14	Luke 12: 32–48

20-0501-07

THE NICENE CREED

I BELIEVE in one God the Father Almighty, Maker of heaven and earth, and of all things visible and invisible;

And in one Lord Jesus Christ, the only-begotten Son of God, begotten of His Father before all worlds; God of God; Light of Light; Very God of Very God; Begotten, not made; Being of one substance with the Father, by whom all things were made; Who for us men, and for our salvation, came down from heaven; And was incarnate by the Holy Ghost of the Virgin Mary, and was made man; And was crucified also for us under Pontius Pilate. He suffered and was buried; And the third day He rose again according to the Scriptures; And ascended into heaven; And sitteth on the right hand of the Father. And He shall come again with glory to judge both the quick and the dead; Whose kingdom shall have no end.

And I believe in the Holy Ghost; The Lord and Giver of Life; Who proceedeth from the Father and the Son; Who with the Father and the Son together is worshiped and glorified; Who spake by the prophets. And I believe one Holy Catholic and Apostolic Church. I acknowledge one Baptism for the remission of sins. And I look for the Resurrection of the dead; And the Life of the world to come. Amen.

CPSIA information can be obtained
at www.ICGtesting.com
Printed in the USA
BVHW032359220719
554106BV00001B/2/P